# PRAISE FOR *PROVISIONS*

"An elegant balance of heritage and health. This comprehensive book celebrates the plant-based flavors of the pan-Caribbean basin and the spectacular ways in which the intellect and aesthetic of the Islands impacts one of its most enduring legacies . . . its plates. The authors have produced an heirloom volume."

—MICHAEL W. TWITTY, James Beard award–winning author of *The Cooking Gene* and creator of Afroculinaria

"Sustaining legacy is the highest power of any cookbook. *Provisions* stands on the shoulders of all of the women who came before Suzanne and Michelle Rousseau. This is not only an important book, it's also a beautiful and useful one. You'll find yourself making a grocery list in no time."

—JULIA TURSHEN, author of *Now & Again*, *Feed the Resistance*, and *Small Victories*

"Our female forbearers traveled to extraordinary lengths to nourish others with ordinary, often overlooked ingredients, in the most challenging circumstances. To grow, cook, and sell the food of the earth is the very definition of necessity breeding invention. In the tradition of generations of strong woman cooks, Michelle and Suzanne continue to innovate with these modern and craveably delicious recipes."

—LUCINDA SCALA QUINN, chef, author, and host of *Mad Hungry: Bringing Back the Family Meal*

"If you love cookbooks with a strong dash of storytelling, you'll love *Provisions* from sisters Michelle and Suzanne Rousseau. They pay tribute to their family matriarchs and explain the history behind their favorite classic and contemporary Caribbean recipes."

—KERRY DIAMOND, editor-in-chief of *Cherry Bombe*

"Engaging, informative, and as witty as the play on words hidden in its full title, *Provisions: The Roots of Caribbean Cooking* takes the reader on a tour of the region's food. Packed with recipes that made me want to head to the nearest market, taste memories that made me dream of the islands, a brief history of their family and of Caribbean food, and a glossary of local ingredients, it is simply a Caribbean vacation between two covers."

—JESSICA B. HARRIS, PhD, author, food historian, lecturer, professor (retired)

"This book is truly special. At a time when women aren't celebrated enough in the culinary world, *Provisions* shows that women have always been the backbone of every facet of food. The recipes paint a picture of the flavors in 'mi grand mudda's kitchen' but with a modern and refreshing approach."

—JEROME GRANT, executive chef, Sweet Home Café

"*Provisions* is so much more than a collection of recipes. This rich and fulfilling work of art takes us deep into the minds and kitchens of the resilient, brave and genius women of the Caribbean. Michelle and Suzanne creatively pay homage to the past while bringing the recipes and ingredients back to life with their modern interpretations."

—ROCK HARPER, founder and president, RockSolid Creative Food Group

# PRAISE FOR *CARIBBEAN POTLUCK*

"Anyone who has eaten many plates of blackened, mangy-looking jerk chicken might get the impression that Caribbean cooking is fairly limited. The cuisine of most of the English-speaking islands is often lumped under the umbrella of stews, dumplings and pineapple-strewn desserts. But Suzanne and Michelle Rousseau say there's much more to island cooking."

—NPR

"With their new book, *Caribbean Potluck*, the Kingston, Jamaica-based sisters present a new face for island cuisine: young, sophisticated, and in tune with the region's complex history and culinary traditions."

—*BOSTON GLOBE*

# PROVISIONS

ALSO BY
MICHELLE ROUSSEAU & SUZANNE ROUSSEAU

*Caribbean Potluck:*
*Modern Recipes from Our Family Kitchen*

# PROVISIONS

*The Roots of Caribbean Cooking—*
*150 Vegetarian Recipes*

### MICHELLE ROUSSEAU
### &
### SUZANNE ROUSSEAU

Da Capo
LIFE
LONG

Photographs by Ellen Silverman, except as noted on page 285

Da Capo Press
Hachette Book Group
1290 Avenue of the Americas, New York, NY 10104
www.dacapopress.com
@DaCapoPress

Printed in the United States of America

First Edition: October 2018

Published by Da Capo Press, an imprint of Perseus Books, LLC, a subsidiary of Hachette Book Group, Inc.

The publisher is not responsible for websites (or their content) that are not owned by the publisher.

Additional photography credits information is on page 285.

Book design by Shubhani Sarkar, sarkardesignstudio.com

Library of Congress Cataloging-in-Publication Data
Names: Rousseau, Michelle, author. | Rousseau, Suzanne, author.
Title: Provisions: the roots of Caribbean cooking / Michelle Rousseau and Suzanne Rousseau.
Description: First edition. | New York, NY: Da Capo Press, 2018. | Includes  bibliographical references and index.
Identifiers: LCCN 2018014939| ISBN 9780738234670 (hardcover) | ISBN 9780738234663 (e-book)
Subjects: LCSH: Cooking, Caribbean. | LCGFT: Cookbooks.
Classification: LCC TX716.C27 R68 2018 | DDC 641.59729—dc23
LC record available at https://lccn.loc.gov/2018014939

ISBNs: 978-0-7382-3467-0 (hardcover),
978-0-7382-3466-3 (ebook)

LSC-C

10 9 8 7 6 5 4 3 2 1

This book is dedicated both to the women of our past whose stories have disappeared from the family tree because they were deemed unimportant, irrelevant, or unnecessary, and to the women of our future who will carry on this beautiful lineage and create new stories and recipes to share with their daughters.

*Sit here...*
*Feast on your life.*

—SIR DEREK WALCOTT

# CONTENTS

*Chapter 3*

# SPROUTS & STARCHY FRUITS

*Hearts of Palm, Artichoke Hearts,
Pumpkin, Banana, Plantain
& Breadfruit*

*Chapter 4*

# GREENS, LEAVES & SHOOTS

*Callaloo, Pak Choi,
Lettuce, Arugula, Cabbage,
Broccoli & Cauliflower*

*Chapter 5*

## BEANS, PULSES & LEGUMES

*Black Beans, Gungo Peas,
Chickpeas, Lentils, Red Peas
& Black-Eyed Peas*

*Chapter 6*

## GRAINS

*Rice, Quinoa, Wheat & Corn*

# PROVISIONS

# A SISTERLY WELCOME

THE STORY OF CARIBBEAN FOOD CANNOT BE told without telling the story of Caribbean women. The women of our region—the mothers, grandmothers, sisters and aunts, the caregivers, the homemakers, the housekeepers and the cooks—are the wheels on which our society turns.

For centuries, our womenfolk have created delicious meals from sometimes meager fare to feed all those who gathered at their table. The food they cooked came from their own toil: from provision grounds and kitchen gardens they planted during slavery; from lands they farmed and produce they sold at market when free; from jobs they worked at all levels of society that allowed them to buy food to feed hungry children. From slavery through emancipation into the modern day, our feminine ancestors have sustained and nourished their own families and a multitude of others. They cooked everything from simple to more complex dishes over coal pots and open fires, in kitchens modest and grand, across the length and breadth of our islands' homes. Their meals are laced with the aroma of fortitude, the memory of pain, the spicy taste of resilience, and a legacy of love that continues to nurture us to this day. But for too long these women have been forgotten,

unacknowledged, and unseen. We have not told their stories.

In fact, it was only in the pursuit of our dream to write a cookbook that we discovered how important a role cooking had played in our female line, and by extension in the narrative of our own lives. Good cooks were a dime a dozen in our family, and our childhoods were filled with dazzling meals at the tables of our female relatives and caregivers: our mother, Beverly; our grandmothers, Enid and Mavis; our aunts, Doris, Viva, Kay, and Winsome. All of them served wonderful food, each in her own distinct way. But despite these vivid family memories, there were no detailed records about the women in our history. We saw how easy it was to find information about the men in our family line and how often we were told glorious and fantastic stories about our great-grandfathers, and even our great-great-grandfathers. Yet outside the random casual anecdote, passing comment, or distant memory told by an old aunt or family friend, we simply could not find much information about the four women who were our great-grandmothers: Martha Matilda Briggs, Henrietta Cleopatra Clark, Adeline Jemima Duckett, and Eulalie Eugenie Marche.

*(Above) Our maternal great grandmother Henrietta with son Hugh (our grandfather, far right) and siblings*

*(Right) Our paternal great grandmother Ma Briggs, creator of Briggs Patty, with daughter Enid (our grandmother)*

It was our research into the culinary habits of the British West Indies for our first cookbook that inadvertently introduced us to our great-grandmother Martha Matilda Briggs, a formidable woman whom we had known of only vaguely through family stories told by our father, Peter, his brother Pat, and our grandmother Enid (whom we called Manga). Born in Manchester, Jamaica, Martha was an independent entrepreneur in a time when societal standards for women dictated otherwise. She never married, but was a single mother to seven children, born of three different men. The youngest of her children were our grandmother Enid Augusta and her twin sister, Doris. Peter,

Pat, and Enid heralded Martha as the first and finest commercial patty maker in Jamaica. They referred to her as a "handsome and powerful woman" whose baking skills were as legendary as her Briggs Patty, which was the most expensive and most delicious patty in all of Kingston.

Ma Briggs, as she was called, moved up the ranks of society through a liberated and determined spirit, working at turns as a domestic and laundress before finding her calling as a business owner and restaurateur when she purchased the well-known Royal Café at 75A Barry Street, next to the legal offices of Myers Fletcher in downtown Kingston. There, she first sold her famous Briggs Patties and Baked

Black Crabs along with cakes and pastries. It is said that all the well-known barristers of the day dined at the Royal Café, among them the man who would become Jamaica's first premier, the Right Honorable Norman Washington Manley. He would later defend Ma Briggs in a court case over a denial of her tavern license when the business relocated to Mark Lane. From Mark Lane her business expanded, eventually morphing into her most famous legacy, the Briggs Restaurant, located on Retirement Road in the busy Cross Roads area of Kingston.

On March 20, 1936, Ma Briggs opened the Briggs Restaurant and Ice Cream Garden with much fanfare, hosting an all-night event that is documented in the local paper. Her menu promised, "Late Suppers, Cold Beers, Ice Cream, Teas & Cakes, Baked Black Crabs," and her famous "Briggs Crisp Crust Patties," which sold at six pence per patty.

Back then, patties for sale were displayed on a restaurant's countertop. We are told that Ma Briggs invented a "tin griddle" of sorts that sat atop a metal box filled with hot coals to keep the patties warm when they were brought out from the oven in the back. They were not the commercial, mass-produced, quick lunches we know of today. Briggs Patties would have been piping-hot, hearty, delicious meals that hungry consumers savored for their perfectly crisp crust and delectable savory filling. (In fact, our love of Jamaican "veggie patties" is partly what inspired our Plantain and Cheese Empanadillas, page 67, and our One-Pot Pie with Callaloo, Plantain, Goat Cheese, and Cornmeal Crust, page 111.)

That our great-grandmother, a woman who began her adult life as a domestic worker and who

*Grand Opening Announcement for the Briggs Restaurant and Ice Cream Garden,* The Gleaner, *1936*

was a single mother with seven mouths to feed, had the vision and drive to become an independent black female entrepreneur in the colonial Jamaica of the early 1900s—a time when women did not commonly work outside the home, let alone own and operate businesses—was an astounding discovery. Her name appears many times over in the archives of Jamaica's oldest newspaper, the *Daily Gleaner*, and it is evident from these articles and advertisements that she had a savvy head for business and was unafraid of a fight.

Martha Matilda Briggs was an innovator, the creator of her own destiny, a leader among women when there were few women leaders. In fact, it is through her involvement in food that we were able to find out anything more about her. And so we came to understand that the professional lives we thought we'd arrived at by chance were

MILKWOMAN.

Kingston-Jamaica

Drawn from Life and Lithog.d by I. M. Belisario

Printed by A. Duperly.

*Isaac Mendes Belisario's "Milkwoman" on indefinite loan to the National Gallery of Jamaica:*
*Collection of the Hon. Maurice W. Facey and Mrs. Valene Facey.*

much more about fulfilling our destiny. Having operated our own restaurant for many years, and having written two cookbooks, we now see that our work to create and cook and share delicious food continues the legacy Martha Briggs and so many other female relatives have left for us. In unearthing her story, we discovered our own.

The desire to know our family history from both sides led us to ask the question that turned out to be the catalyst for this book: what about all those women whose stories, for so many generations, have been undocumented, untold, silenced? It was daunting and sad to think about. To avoid being overly ambitious, we decided to confine our search to the late 1800s, which was as far back as we could trace our family tree.

## THE ROOTS OF
## WEST INDIAN COOKING

The roots of the ways we cook, eat, and produce food in the West Indies can be traced to an often overlooked aspect of our heritage as a plantation society: the women. More specifically the way women farmed, harvested, bartered, sold, prepared, manipulated, and, ultimately, redefined the ingredients that were available to them. The region's culinary history and the life stories of Afro-Caribbean women are intrinsically intertwined. They are parallel journeys that began under the blistering sun of a sugar plantation, meandered through the struggles of a burgeoning society striving for independence and a new identity, and culminate in the gritty urban streets, beautiful homes, and picturesque country markets of today's Caribbean.

In British West Indian plantation society,

slaves were fed in three main ways: purchased food distributed as rations; food cultivated on plantations using gang labor; and food grown and harvested by slaves themselves on small plots of land called "provision grounds" allocated to them by plantation owners. Subsisting on food from provision grounds demanded ingenuity, innovation, creativity, and practicality, particularly in the kitchen. Women had to use this ingenuity to feed themselves, their families, and their masters, and the culinary techniques and eating habits they developed form the root of what we know as the West Indian diet of today. The typical diet of a Caribbean slave was thus made up of a variety of roots, tubers, and vegetables that they farmed for themselves and supplemented with small amounts of protein, mostly in the form of salted fish or meat. This way of eating, with some modification, ultimately evolved to become the preferred diet for all residents on the islands, from master to slave and every social group in between.

In post-emancipation society, farming, producing, and selling food provided one of the easiest pathways to financial freedom and independence for people of color. It also created a unique opportunity for entrepreneurial women to support their families, find social advancement, and establish financial autonomy. (See the Afterword on page 253 for a more detailed overview of West Indian culinary history and the role women have played in the development of the cuisine.)

Caribbean cuisine also developed around the specific ingredients that were farmed and traded. The ways these ingredients were prepared were largely determined by the cooking facilities that were available to women. And so, to unearth the roots of our cooking, we must look to the matriarch. Women of color in the Caribbean are beacons of power who, throughout the generations, have used the superior skills of craftsmanship learned at the feet of their mothers and grandmothers to improve the quality of their lives. In West Indian food, we have a truly artisanal style of cooking in which most recipes, techniques, and specialty dishes were passed orally from generation to generation, usually through the female line. And, as in any great cuisine, the ingredients' freshness and sources are as central to their method of preparation as the stories behind the dishes and recipes.

The region as a whole is referred to as the "Caribbean" and encompasses British, French, Dutch, and Spanish islands. The British islands, which were once former colonies of Great Britain, are referred to as the West Indies, formerly known as the British West Indies. Within the English-speaking Caribbean region, people still refer to themselves as West Indians and consider their islands to be located in the West Indies. For example, the cricket team that represents the region is called the West Indies Cricket Team because it is made up of players from all islands. Mailing addresses from islands like Trinidad, Jamaica, Barbados, Grenada, and St. Lucia end with "W.I."

# THE WEST INDIAN TABLE: A SOPHISTICATED, ARTISANAL DINING EXPERIENCE

The aspect of West Indian food most often misrepresented is a belief that it is only a rustic, unrefined cuisine. Yes, there is a simple rusticity to how we eat (and live), but there is also a great deal of grace, elegance, and dignity; it's evident in how women dress, carry themselves, entertain, and dine. Jamaican newspaper columnist Louise, in an article from 1935 titled "Lady, Look at Your Husband!," explains why being well put together at all times is of critical importance, even for men:

> If you can persuade your menfolk to give more thought to what they wear, for your sake, they will soon be doing it for their own, for dress is only next to food as one of the deep primitive pleasures of life and they will soon discover that a whole new field of interest has opened up to them.[1]

West Indian women are masters at creating unassuming polished luxury. There is great pride in the homestead, in the table, in the meals, in the way we cook, and in how the food tastes. We love to entertain; our personal lives are filled with memories of elegant and gracious female hosts who enjoyed cooking and sharing their gifts. We see this in our own family. Our grandmother Ma Ma (or Mavis) adored having us over for lunch when we were girls and always took her time to prepare a wonderful feast of mince, rice, and peas, her signature macaroni and cheese,

1. *Daily Gleaner,* March 23, 1935.

*Our maternal grandmother, Mavis*

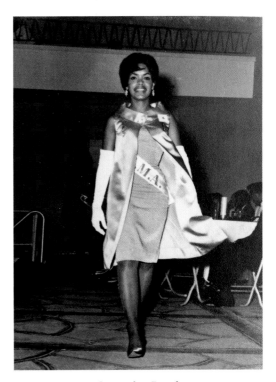

*Our mother, Beverly*

accompanied of course by typical ingredients like fried plantain, sliced avocado, and spicy shallot pickle, which she served with Jamaican brown sugar limeade and rum-and-raisin ice cream for dessert. Those lunches became our ritual with our Ma Ma and are cherished memories that we will never forget. On the other side of the family, our grandmother Enid's, or Manga's, Easter bun, made with stout, molasses, and dried fruits, and boasting a sticky, crispy, sugary top, was beyond memorable. Manga's bun was legendary. Every year, people would beg her to bake a bun for them to enjoy with their families on Good Friday. She would do so with relish, always baking enough to distribute among friends and family. Irrespective of skin tone, ethnicity, or social

status, our women always cook from source, cook from scratch, cook with love, and serve with style.

The objects we have in our kitchens and homes tell the story of the unique way that we in the West Indies have juxtaposed the refined with the rustic: imported fine china, silverware, and crystal from Europe are often paired with meals made using traditional cooking utensils like coal pots and yabbas. The furniture, fretwork, bedding, needlework, crochet, and batik in a West Indian home show mastery and a high level of craftsmanship dedicated to quality. Family heirlooms play an important role in the West Indian home, and many beautiful examples appear in photos throughout this book. The crochet and cotton-lace tablecloth pictured on the book's cover was graciously loaned to us by Mrs. Gwen Donaldson, whose recipe for Dover Seville Orange Marmalade appears on page 234. A gift from a family friend, the cloth has been in the Donaldson family for more than five decades and is still cherished and used on special occasions. Another valued family heirloom, the boxed collection of silver cutlery shown on page 10, belongs to our mother. Aside from housing beautiful flatware, the mahogany box is symbolic of the spirit of the generations of family members who have dined with these utensils, as well as the quality of the meals served and the gracious hospitality shared at a West Indian table.

Dining at any West Indian table puts on display the impressive artistry and skill of West Indians from all walks of life. Imagine the experience of being seated on hand-woven wicker chairs at a wonderful hand-carved mahogany table laid with a hand-crocheted tablecloth and fine china. The table groans with classic European recipes that have been adjusted to a local palate (such as the Stewed Guava with Red Wine, page 171, served with Coconut-Ginger Ice, page 196, in lieu of strawberries and cream); "slave foods" that have been rendered sophisticated for table service (Fire-Roasted Breadfruit with Flaked Sea Salt and Honey, page 78; Curried Green Banana with Pineapple and Raisins, page 65); and demonstrations of culinary techniques and flavor profiles from across the globe (Sevens Mango Chutney, page 240; Good Hope Gungo Pea Falafel, page 126). The result: a surprisingly sophisticated cuisine served everywhere from homes to street stalls, beach shacks, and small community restaurants called cook-shops that perfectly combines simplicity with layers of flavor, fresh local ingredients, and culinary innovation.

## INGREDIENT-FOCUSED VEGETARIAN

This is an ingredient-focused vegetarian book. The foods we present here—the roots and vegetables, abundant fruits and flowers, luxurious spices, coffee, cocoa, and (yes!) even rum—are both good for you and delicious. In the Caribbean, we have been eating them for over three hundred years. We showcase a wide variety of fresh fruits and vegetables, healthy, fibrous starches, and vegetarian proteins that make for filling and supremely satisfying meals that are accessible to all. Whether you grew up eating these ingredients or not, you will appreciate them; they are prepared in various ways all throughout the former British, French, Spanish, and Dutch colonies of the Caribbean, with each country putting a unique spin on a shared ingredient. We suspect it would surprise most people to know that a wide variety of nontropical fruits and vegetables, like strawberries, blackberries, peaches, asparagus, artichokes, eggplant, mint, and marjoram, were grown locally, in regular supply in nineteenth-century West Indian markets. They appear in cookbooks and journals of the era from Jamaica to St. Vincent and even Trinidad and Tobago. If the land could sustain it, the residents grew it. This knowledge reaffirmed our decision to explore a much wider range and more varied combinations of vegetarian ingredients, and validated the concept that "Caribbean" food need not be limited to specific preparations of particular ingredients for fear of being perceived as inauthentic. You'll find these ingredients in recipes such as Mango, Blackberry, and Peach Pie with Cornmeal Brown Sugar Crumble (page 181); Roasted Carrots, Beets, and Asparagus with Basil (page 29); and Roasted Tomatoes and Eggplant with Spiced Cilantro Yogurt and Feta (page 47).

We are inspired by the cooking of our island neighbors and our ancestors, who used what they had available to create imaginative dishes of all kinds that ranged from sophisticated and complex to humble. (If you eat meat, our recipes pair beautifully with animal proteins, which you easily can incorporate by adding small portions of well-seasoned grilled or roasted seafood, poultry, or meat.) Many of the local ingredients used in the recipes are described in the chapter toward the end of the book titled "Local Produce, Preparation Notes, and Ingredient Substitutions" (page 271). There, for those unfamiliar with the tropical produce of the islands, we explain how the ingredients are used, list possible substitutions, and describe how to prepare them. Our aim is to make these ingredients (and this book) accessible and easy to work with so that you can have some experimental fun in the kitchen.

## A CONTEMPORARY APPROACH

Despite our pleasure at discovering the unknown recipes of our heritage, we did not wish to focus on re-creating dishes of the past. We love the traditional recipes of our grandparents, but there needs to be a new presentation of our food that is both accessible to all and relevant to modern life. This cookbook draws on inspiration from our culinary heritage but offers a new spin on the typical ingredients so often featured in "old time" West Indian cooking. Cooks in the West Indies have a long tradition of absorbing and adapting new ingredients, methods, and dishes. We are reminded of how Asian, South Asian, and Middle Eastern foods and flavors became staples of the daily diets in Trinidad, Guyana, and Jamaica as far back as the nineteenth century, showing that this cuisine is dynamic and continually expanding. In the spirit of our ancestors' adaptations and ingenuity in the kitchen, the recipes here pay homage to traditional Caribbean ingredients and flavors, but update them for today's cooks. Our style of Caribbean food is easy and accessible, and takes you on a fun culinary journey that explores the connection between the region's history, food, culture, and identity. The recipes are vibrant and healthy, and bursting with color, flavor, vitality, and nutrients. In this work, we present our Caribbean food our way, and in our voice—a contemporary Caribbean voice that has been inspired by the voices of our collective past.

It is our greatest desire to take you back to simpler times and simpler meals—to a time when a single pot over an open flame was enough to bring a family together, to a time when despite brutal hardship and meager provisions, the day ended with a coming together over a hot coal fire to tell stories, share, laugh, dance, and celebrate the gift of life. We hope that the recipes herein will be cooked with abandon and shared

around a table crowded with family, friends, and an abundance of joy. To us, there is no greater blessing. We hope that this work will celebrate all the women who have gone before us, who have been forgotten, unseen, and unknown. We hope that through this book we can inspire you to explore your personal histories and pay homage to the legacy of generations of women. We believe that there is no better way to honor those who have fed, nurtured, and raised us than by cooking the foods that our grandmothers used to cook, but doing it in our way, with our interpretation of their recipes. We hope that we have done them justice.

# CHAPTER I

# PROVISIONS

*Roots & Tubers, Yam, Cassava, Dasheen,*
*Sweet Potato & Coco*

AN OLD JAMAICAN PROVERB SAYS, "ONE ONE COCO FULL BASKET," WHICH SIMPLY MEANS THAT EVERY LITTLE BIT ADDS UP TO FILL YOUR basket. We love this ancient wisdom not only because it is true, but also because its common use in the Jamaican dialect speaks to the relevance of the role that ground provisions (roots, tubers, and starchy fruits) play in the Caribbean diet. Starches like coco, yam, dasheen, sweet potato, and cassava appear daily in all kinds of ways at a Caribbean table, be it at breakfast, lunch, or dinner. "Food," as these starchy staples are often called at homes and restaurants across the islands, accompanies the main component of the meal—often meat or fish. Food can be boiled, baked, or roasted, but is most commonly boiled, and usually more than one type are boiled together.

Provisions were the main source of sustenance for slaves in the Caribbean. One planter's journal described how the slaves' "provision grounds furnish them with plantains, bananas, cocoa-nuts, and yams…but in this parish their most valuable and regular supply of food arises from the coco-finger, or coccos, a species of the yam. These vegetables form the basis of [the slaves'] sustenance."[2] These nutritious, dense, high-fiber carbohydrates filled the stomach with slow-burning, high-energy fuel that could support a long day of manual labor under the blisteringly hot sun. Because slaves farmed their own provisions in their allotted provision grounds and kitchen gardens, they were able to include some variety in their diet. Yam, which came from Africa, has always been available in many varieties and was by far the most popular starch among slaves for both its familiarity and its long shelf life.

Cassava was indigenous to the islands, and methods for its processing and consumption were taught to early slaves by the native Indian communities of the Caribbean islands. Sweet potato, malanga coco, and dasheen are also very popular starches. All of them were relished by our African ancestors for their similarity in texture and methods of preparation to the very familiar yam, and all are still voraciously consumed with great pleasure today by islanders from all walks of life.

2. Lewis, 106–107.

Coco, also referred to as taro, cocoyam, or malanga, is a tuber that is harder than the yam. It is typically boiled (served mashed and with butter) or roasted. According to *The Jamaica Cookery Book* (1893), the roasted coco skin is "very nice" when eaten with butter. Grated coco is also tasty and versatile; it makes good fritters.

# ROAST PROVISIONS
## *with Haitian Pikliz*

This is a simple and clean way to enjoy ground provisions, which, as noted above, in the West Indies refers to any starch or root vegetable that comes out of the ground, among them yam, sweet potato, potato, cassava, dasheen, yampi, and coco. In this recipe a selection of local starches is roasted, buttered, and topped with delicious pickled vegetables typical of Haiti.

*Serves 6 to 8*

6 medium yellow yams, sweet potatoes, and dasheen (any combination)

½ cup (1 stick) salted butter, softened

½ teaspoon chopped, seeded Scotch bonnet pepper

½ teaspoon ground allspice

1 teaspoon minced garlic

½ teaspoon minced ginger

2 tablespoons minced scallion

Haitian Pikliz (page 229)

salt and freshly cracked black pepper

Wash the provisions thoroughly. Roast them whole on a low open flame for 45 minutes to 1 hour, until they are cooked inside and the skin is charred. Alternately, preheat the oven to 375°F, place the cleaned provisions directly on the middle rack, and roast for 45 minutes to 1 hour until the insides are soft.

While the provisions are roasting, in a small bowl combine the softened butter, Scotch bonnet pepper, allspice, garlic, and ginger, and mix thoroughly. Set aside and leave at room temperature.

Peel the cooked provisions, slice them in half, and slather generously with the butter mixture. Sprinkle with salt and pepper, and top with the scallions and pikliz.

# SWEET POTATO GNOCCHI
## *with Smashed Grape Tomatoes and Country Pepper*

Throughout our years in the food business we have experimented with various versions of gnocchi that utilized local starchy vegetables in lieu of the classic potato. In our latest favorite manifestation, we combine sweet potato and pumpkin to create a delicate gnocchi that is full of flavor and texture. The addition of smashed cherry tomatoes and mixed herb pesto creates an unforgettable twist on a classic Italian recipe.

*Serves 8 to 10*

**2 cups peeled and cubed sweet potato**

**1 cup peeled and cubed pumpkin**

**1 8-ounce container ricotta cheese, drained**

**1 cup grated Parmesan cheese plus ½ cup shaved Parmesan cheese (about 3 ounces total)**

**2 tablespoons brown sugar**

**1 to 2 teaspoons salt**

**½ teaspoon ground nutmeg**

**2 cups all-purpose flour plus more for rolling**

**1 teaspoon butter**

**2 cloves garlic, thinly sliced**

**½ Scotch bonnet pepper, seeded and sliced**

**3 tablespoons Mixed Herb Pesto (page 17), divided**

**1 tablespoon olive oil**

**1 cup grape tomatoes**

**salt and freshly cracked black pepper**

Boil the sweet potato and pumpkin in a large pot of salted water until soft, about 15 minutes. Transfer to a bowl and mash until smooth. Add the ricotta, 1 cup grated Parmesan cheese, brown sugar, 1 to 2 teaspoons salt (to taste), and nutmeg, and stir until just combined. Mix in flour, about ½ cup at a time, until a soft dough forms.

On a floured surface, divide the dough into about six equal pieces, and roll each piece into a long rope, about 1 to 1½ inches wide. Sprinkle with flour as needed if the dough gets sticky. Cut each rope into about twenty 1-inch pieces. To create the distinctive ridges, gently roll the tines of a fork over each piece. Place the cut gnocchi on waxed paper or parchment paper until ready to cook.

Bring a large pot of salted water to boil. Working in batches, boil the gnocchi until tender, about 5 to 6 minutes per batch. Transfer the gnocchi to a clean plate or baking sheet lined with waxed or parchment paper. Cool completely.

Melt the butter in a sauté pan over medium heat. Add the garlic and Scotch bonnet pepper, and cook for about 1 minute until fragrant. Add 2 tablespoons pesto, the olive oil, and the grape tomatoes, tossing quickly while cooking. Allow the tomatoes to cook for about 5 minutes, then add a splash of water. After another 3 minutes, smash the tomatoes with the back of a spoon. Add the

gnocchi to the skillet to heat through, and season with salt and pepper.

To serve, swirl the remaining 1 tablespoon pesto on the base of a large serving plate. Add gnocchi and cherry tomatoes, mix to coat, and sprinkle liberally with the remaining shaved Parmesan.

# MIXED HERB PESTO

This versatile and simple pesto is a great condiment to keep on hand. It is delicious as a dip but also is particularly decadent when tossed with pasta or spread on sandwiches and flatbreads as a base.

*Makes 2 cups*

¾ cup plus 3 tablespoons olive oil

6 cloves garlic (3 cloves coarsely chopped, 3 cloves minced)

1 cup fresh parsley

1 cup fresh basil

1 cup fresh cilantro

1 cup fresh mint

½ cup walnuts

½ cup grated Parmesan cheese

salt

In a blender or food processor fitted with the metal blade, combine ¾ cup olive oil, 3 cloves rough-chopped garlic, the fresh herbs, and the walnuts. Process until nearly smooth. Add the Parmesan cheese and minced garlic, and pulse to combine. Season to taste with salt, pulsing to mix. Transfer to a storage container, top with the remaining 3 tablespoons olive oil, cover, and refrigerate.

# PROVISIONS BOWL

A piping-hot dish of mashed potatoes is considered one of the most satisfying comfort foods. In our healthy island version, we mash cassava, white potato, and sweet potato, layer them in a bowl, and serve the whole topped with delicious callaloo. Each ground provision has its own pure flavor, texture, and density. Layering them keeps them separate so that you can distinguish between each one. Substitute any provisions you want for the mash; green banana, yams, coco, or dasheen would all work equally well. For a fun serving idea, set up individual bowls with the mashed, layered provisions, and create a topping bar so that your family or party guests can assemble their own bowls. Besides callaloo, other possible toppings include wilted kale, grilled or sautéed mushrooms, caramelized red onions, grilled asparagus, roasted pumpkin, grated Parmesan, goat or blue cheese, and coconut flakes. For meat eaters, you could include crispy bacon, grilled lobster, chicken breast, or steak.

*Serves 4 to 6*

1½ cups peeled and cubed sweet potato

3 cups peeled and cubed white potato

1½ cups peeled and cubed cassava

2 tablespoons butter, divided into thirds

½ cup canned coconut milk, divided into thirds

pinch of ground nutmeg, divided into thirds

salt to taste

pinch of freshly cracked black pepper

### TO SERVE

Callaloo in Coconut Milk (page 104), or toppings of your choice

handful toasted unsweetened coconut flakes for garnish

Fill three medium pots with water, add a pinch of salt to each, and bring to a boil over high heat. Place each provision in its own pot of boiling, salted water. Boil until cooked through and soft, about 15 minutes. Drain, and transfer the provisions into three separate bowls. Mash until smooth, leaving a few lumps for texture.

Stir one-third each of the butter, coconut milk, and nutmeg into the mashed white potato; season to taste with salt and pepper. Divide the remaining butter, coconut milk, and nutmeg between the cassava and the sweet potato, stir to blend, and season with salt and pepper.

To serve, spoon one scoop each of the hot provisions into individual bowls, spreading each to make a layer before adding the next one. Alternatively, for a different presentation, arrange the scoops side by side. Top the bowl with a heaping serving of callaloo in coconut milk and a sprinkling of toasted coconut flakes, or whatever toppings you like.

# CASSAVA PANCAKES
## *with Sorrel Syrup*

These pancakes, made with the traditional Caribbean ingredients cassava flour and coconut milk, are fantastic, especially when finished with fresh sorrel syrup. Cassava flour (or meal) is made by grating and drying fresh cassava. Not only is this dish 100 percent gluten free, but the fluffy pancakes are supremely satisfying because of their denser texture. The flavor combination is out of this world. Mango, guava, passionfruit, or tamarind syrup all work equally well in place of the sorrel syrup.

*Serves 2 to 4*

1¾ cups cassava flour

1 teaspoon baking powder

large pinch of salt

1 cup canned coconut milk

2 eggs

1½ teaspoons coconut oil for the pancake batter, plus 1 tablespoon for cooking

1 teaspoon honey

nutmeg to taste

cinnamon to taste

Sorrel Syrup (page 187)

Greek yogurt

Diced fresh fruit such as mango or grapes, or Candied Sorrel Buds (page 187, optional)

Combine cassava flour, baking powder, and salt in a mixing bowl and set aside. In a separate bowl, whisk together the coconut milk, eggs, coconut oil, and honey; season with nutmeg and cinnamon. Add the wet ingredients to the dry ingredients, and stir until just combined.

Heat 1 tablespoon coconut oil in a medium sauté pan over medium-high heat. Ladle the batter into the sauté pan, using about 3 tablespoons of batter for each pancake. Cook about 2 minutes until lightly browned on one side, and then flip carefully. Continue to cook until both sides are golden-brown. Serve hot, drizzled with fresh sorrel syrup and topped with Greek yogurt and fruit.

# CASSAVA FRIES
## *with Sous de Pinda*

L et's just say French fries with peanut sauce are to die for! We had this dish at a food truck in Curacao some years ago and fell immediately in love, so naturally we were inspired to create our own version. Here we use cassava as an alternative to potato for the French fries, and we fry them twice, first sautéing with garlic for added flavor, then deep frying just before serving. They have great texture and flavor and work beautifully with the zing of the peanut sauce.

*Serves 8*

### SOUS DE PINDA

½ cup peanut butter

¼ teaspoon ginger

¼ teaspoon cumin

¼ teaspoon garlic

¼ teaspoon curry powder

¼ teaspoon minced habanero or red chili

salt and freshly cracked black pepper to taste

Culantro Pepper Oil (page 250)

### CASSAVA FRIES

5 pounds cassava root

1 cup vinegar

3 tablespoons salt

3 tablespoons olive oil

3 cloves chopped garlic

2 cups coconut oil

Make the sous de pinda. In a small saucepan over gentle heat, stir together the peanut butter and ½ cup water until mixed. Add all the other ingredients, blending well. The sauce should be of a thick yet pourable consistency. Adjust seasonings if necessary.

Make the cassava fries. Peel the cassava, and cut each one into 4-inch lengths. Cut them again into quarter wedges, removing any fibrous centers. Submerge them in cold water to prevent discoloration until ready to cook.

Bring 2 quarts water, the vinegar, and the salt to a boil in a large pot over high heat. Add the cassava wedges, and boil for 10 to 12 minutes until cooked through and tender. Drain, and run them under cold water to halt the cooking process.

Warm the olive oil in a sauté pan over medium-high heat. Working in batches to avoid overcrowding, add the garlic and cassava, and pan fry for about 5 minutes. Remove the cassava wedges from the pan, and drain them on paper towels.

Heat the coconut oil to 350°F in a deep fryer or deep pot. Carefully drop the cassava wedges into the oil, working in batches to avoid overcrowding. Deep fry the cassava wedges until they're crispy and golden-brown on the outside, 4 to 5 minutes per batch.

Remove the cassava wedges from the oil, and drain them on paper towels. Sprinkle with salt and black pepper, and drizzle with culantro pepper oil and sous de pinda. Serve immediately.

# STEAMED BAMMY
## *with Coconut, Pumpkin, Ginger, and Tomato*

Bammy is a Jamaican flatbread made from grated cassava that has been soaked in water, transferred to a cloth, and pressed to extract as much liquid as possible. The cassava is then flattened into a thick, disc-shaped flatbread and cooked over dry heat. Fortunately, you don't have to make your own to enjoy this dish. Premade bammy is sold online and in Caribbean markets. It is delicious roasted or fried, but one of our favorite preparations is bammy steamed in coconut milk. Easy and quick to prepare, it makes a tasty gluten-free dish that is super filling, full of fiber, and really good for you.

### *Serves 2*

1 tablespoon olive oil

1 onion, chopped

1 clove garlic, chopped

2 teaspoons minced ginger

¼ cup chopped scallion

½ small yellow bell pepper, sliced

½ cup diced tomatoes

1 cup julienned pumpkin

salt and freshly cracked black pepper

1 teaspoon ground coriander

2 tablespoons chopped cilantro, plus more for garnish

⅓ to ½ cup canned coconut milk

1 whole Scotch bonnet pepper

1 bunch thyme

1 pack bammy (2 large premade cassava cakes)

unsweetened coconut flakes, for garnish (optional)

Heat the olive oil in a medium sauté pan over medium heat. Add the onion, garlic, ginger, scallion, and yellow bell pepper, and sauté for 2 to 3 minutes. Add the tomato and pumpkin, and sauté for 2 minutes. Season with salt, pepper, coriander, and cilantro, and stir.

Add just enough coconut milk to cover the vegetables, thinning with a little water if necessary. Add the whole Scotch bonnet pepper and the bunch of thyme. Reduce heat to low and cover. Allow to steam for 15 minutes until the pumpkin is cooked through.

Arrange the bammy in a single layer on top of the vegetables, cover, and let steam for another 5 to 7 minutes. Remove the thyme stems from the pot. To serve, place each cooked bammy in a bowl, top with delicious steamed vegetables, and finish by pouring liquid over everything.

Garnish with coconut flakes and cilantro.

# FRITTER PLATTER
## *Coconut Corn Fritters,*
## *Dasheen Balls, and Coco Fritters*

In the Caribbean we make fritters out of just about everything, and these three are so yummy you will want to serve this fritter platter for all kinds of occasions. Of course, you could make just one of the fritter recipes, but where's the fun in that? Curry, grated coconut, fresh corn kernels, and cilantro dance together in a most groovy way in our coconut corn fritters. The creamy goodness of dasheen perfectly complements a melty cheese center in our dasheen balls. And the freshly grated coco and aromatic turmeric give the coco fritters amazing texture and flavor that will keep you coming back for more.

Combine all that with the three dynamically different dipping sauces—Classic Pepper, Coconut-Lime, and Tamarind-Raisin Ketchup—and "the thing sell off," as we say in Jamaica, which loosely translated means it's wicked good.

*Serves 12 to 15*

## COCONUT CORN FRITTERS

¾ cup all-purpose flour

¼ cup cornmeal

1 teaspoon baking powder

½ teaspoon salt

1 teaspoon sugar

½ teaspoon curry powder

1 egg

1 cup coconut milk

1½ tablespoons butter, melted

1¼ cups fresh corn kernels
(from about 2 ears)

1 cup grated fresh coconut
(or substitute unsweetened
coconut flakes)

¼ cup thinly sliced scallion

1 Scotch bonnet pepper,
finely sliced (optional)

2 tablespoons finely chopped
yellow or red bell pepper

2 tablespoons chopped cilantro

1 tablespoon chopped
fresh thyme

vegetable oil, for frying
(about 2 cups)

salt and freshly cracked black
pepper to taste

Classic Pepper Sauce
(page 246) or sauce of choice

*(Continued)*

In a bowl, sift together the flour, cornmeal, baking powder, salt, sugar, and curry powder. In another bowl, beat together the egg, coconut milk, and butter. Add the wet ingredients to the dry ingredients, and mix just until the batter comes together. Don't overmix. Fold in the corn, coconut, scallion, Scotch bonnet pepper (if using), bell pepper, cilantro, and thyme, blending gently until evenly distributed.

In a large, heavy saucepan, heat about 2 inches of vegetable oil to 325°F. Working in batches, carefully drop the batter by the tablespoonful into the oil, and cook for about 5 minutes until golden-brown, turning halfway through. Remove to a paper towel–lined plate and sprinkle with salt and pepper. Serve with Classic Pepper Sauce or a dipping sauce of your choice.

# DASHEEN BALLS

**1 pound dasheen (about 5 to 6 cups, cubed)**

**2 tablespoons butter**

**¼ cup milk**

**1 egg, beaten**

**2 tablespoons scallion**

**2 teaspoons fresh thyme leaves**

**4 tablespoons unsweetened coconut flakes**

**2 tablespoons panko breadcrumbs**

**2 tablespoons cassava flour (or all-purpose wheat flour)**

**4 ounces cheddar cheese, cut into ½-inch cubes**

**vegetable oil, for frying (about 2 cups)**

**Coconut-Lime Dipping Sauce (page 244) or sauce of choice**

Wash and peel the dasheen, then cut into 1-inch cubes. Place in a large pot of boiling salted water (make sure you have enough water to cover the dasheen). Cook for about 15 minutes or until soft. Drain, and return the dasheen to the pot.

Crush the dasheen finely with a fork or potato masher. Add the butter, milk, egg, scallion, thyme, and coconut flakes, and stir to form a soft dough.

In a small bowl, stir together the panko breadcrumbs and cassava flour. Set aside.

With floured hands, roll the dasheen dough into balls, about 1 tablespoon each. Press a hole in the center of each ball and insert a cube of cheese. Form the ball around the cube of cheese. Roll the balls in the mixture of breadcrumbs and flour. Refrigerate until ready to fry.

In a heavy saucepan or sauté pan, heat about 2 inches of vegetable oil to 375°F. Working in batches, fry the dasheen balls to a golden color, about 4 minutes per batch, turning halfway through to brown them evenly. Remove to a paper towel–lined plate to drain. Serve with Coconut-Lime Dipping Sauce or any other sauce.

# COCO (MALANGA/TANNIA) FRITTERS

3 to 4 coco (tannia) roots

¼ cup chopped chives

1 bunch culantro or chadon beni,
chopped (see "Local Produce,"
in the back of the book)

1 teaspoon minced
Scotch bonnet pepper

1 teaspoon grated ginger

1 teaspoon turmeric

salt and freshly cracked
black pepper to taste

vegetable oil, for frying
(about 1 cup)

Tamarind-Raisin Ketchup
(page 243)

Wash and peel the coco roots under running water. Grate the coco. To prevent browning, submerge the grated coco in salted water until you're ready to use it.

To make the fritters, squeeze the excess liquid from the grated coco. In a mixing bowl, combine the coco with the chives, culantro, Scotch bonnet pepper, ginger, and turmeric. Season with salt and pepper to taste.

Cover the bottom of a heavy sauté pan with about 1 inch of vegetable oil, and heat over medium heat. Using your hands, form the coco mixture into mini-fritters, each about 1 tablespoon.

Once the oil is hot, drop the fritters into the oil, flattening each one with the back of spoon. Cook until brown and crispy, about 2 to 3 minutes per side. Remove from oil to a paper towel–lined plate. Serve warm with Tamarind-Raisin Ketchup or any other sauce.

# ROASTED CARROTS, BEETS, AND ASPARAGUS
## *with Basil*

S low-roasted carrots are one of life's most wonderful treats. In this vegetarian delight, the natural sweetness of the caramelized carrots pairs perfectly with beets and asparagus; the whole is wonderfully accentuated by the tart goat cheese. The added crunch of hazelnuts will make you want this side dish as a main course.

*Serves 4*

**6 to 8 medium-sized heirloom carrots**

**5 tablespoons olive oil, divided**

**¼ cup chopped fresh basil, divided**

**4 whole cloves garlic, peeled, plus 2 tablespoons chopped garlic**

**2 tablespoons fresh thyme leaves, divided**

**salt and freshly cracked black pepper to taste**

**6 red or yellow beets**

**1 pound asparagus stalks**

**zest of 1 orange**

**¼ cup chopped toasted hazelnuts**

**4 ounces soft goat cheese**

Preheat the oven to 350°F.

Peel the carrots, leaving the green tops on. Toss with 2 tablespoons olive oil, 1 tablespoon basil, 4 whole garlic cloves, and 2 teaspoons thyme. Season with salt and pepper, and arrange on a baking sheet.

Peel and quarter the beets. Toss them with 1 tablespoon olive oil, 1 tablespoon basil, 1 tablespoon chopped garlic, and 2 teaspoons thyme. Season with salt and pepper, and arrange on a separate baking sheet.

Roast the vegetables for about 45 minutes until carrots are caramelized and beets cooked through. Depending on the size and cut of your vegetables, the cooking time may vary, so test with a knife to be sure they're done.

Wash the asparagus, and trim off the tough ends.

After the carrots and beets have roasted about 40 minutes, heat 1 tablespoon olive oil in a medium saucepan over high heat. Add 1 tablespoon chopped garlic, the asparagus, and the orange zest. Season with salt and pepper, and toss, cooking quickly for about 2 minutes or until the asparagus stalks are bright green but still crispy. Remove from heat. Combine carrots, beets, and asparagus on a platter. Top with the remaining basil and the hazelnuts, and dot with the goat cheese. Drizzle with 1 tablespoon olive oil and serve.

# CHAPTER 2

# SAVORY FRUITS & VEGETABLES

*Ackee, Cho Cho, Peppers, Eggplant,
Avocado & Okra*

**T**HIS CHAPTER SHOWCASES ALL OUR TASTY ISLAND VEGETABLES AND SAVORY FRUITS—FROM ACKEE TO ZABOCA AND EVERYTHING IN between. To supplement the diet slaves would have farmed a great variety of savory fruits and vegetables in their kitchen gardens. These ingredients added flavor, nutrients, and variety to the slaves' diet, which would otherwise have been limited to salted fish and cornmeal. West Indian slave villages were often well fruited, with produce from a wide variety of plants and vines providing freshness, sustenance, and nutrition. One planter's wife described how the tomato "comes to great perfection" in the region, and other foods "grow luxuriantly."[3] As a result, "fruits" like ackee, tomato, cho cho, cucumber, okra, avocado, eggplant, and peppers featured prominently in many recipes from the colonial era, and they became staples of cooking in the region.

Ackee, for the uninitiated, is a savory fruit with a thick red skin that forms a pod. It is sealed closed when unripe. Once ripened, the pod opens to reveal a beautiful petal-like shape containing three or four yellow "pegs," each topped with a single black seed. Freshly cooked ackee is creamy and buttery with a mild nutty taste that is neutral enough to absorb the flavor of whatever it is cooked with; one nineteenth-century book on cooking in the West Indies described using ackee as a substitute for eggs in a bread pudding. Ackee is a great ingredient to

---

3. Carmichael, vol. 1, 162.

Every variety of capsicum is to be found upon a West Indian estate; indeed, they are almost a weed; but peppers, nevertheless, are purchased in town with avidity.

—Mrs. A. C. Carmichael, 1833

The cho cho is a very useful vegetable it can be cooked in various ways, and the natives are very partial to it, it being as they say "so cooling". They often put it in their soups as an addition. Plain, boiled with butter or some white sauce, it is excellent, mashed with butter and black pepper it is very nice. Put in stews it makes a pleasant variety, and made into boiled puddings with a judicious addition of sugar and lime juice, it so much resembles apple as to deceive one into believing one is eating apple pudding or apple tart.

—*The Jamaica Cookery Book,* 1893

have fun with in the kitchen as it can be prepared in a myriad of unexpected ways.

Cho cho, also known as chayote, mirleton, or christophene, is one of the most widely consumed vegetables in the Caribbean and Latin America. A type of squash, it is a pear-shaped "fruit" that is light green in color with a prickly skin.

There is, however, one fruit that stands above all others for most West Indians: the avocado. Avocado, known as pear in Jamaica and zaboca in Trinidad, is not available all year round, so when it comes into season and the trees are laden, we are overjoyed.

Although avocado may be our first love, we indulge in many other love affairs with the wide array of savory fruits the Caribbean region has to offer. Unlike avocado, most of these savories—like ackee, cho cho, eggplant, peppers, and okra—are in season and available year round in the West Indies. That is why they appear on our tables with great regularity, often acting as the accompaniment to a meal of protein and starch.

# ISLAND SQUASH SALAD
## with Arugula

Christophene, also known as chayote, mirleton, or, as we call it in Jamaica, cho cho, is a delicate pear-shaped squash with a neutral flavor that is usually stewed in hot dishes or baked. Here, it is blanched before being added to a simple, delightful salad. Its subtle flavor combines very well with the peppery kick of arugula and the creaminess of yellow squash. A light champagne vinaigrette rounds out the dish, giving it balance and acidity.

*Serves 4 to 6*

**ISLAND SQUASH SALAD**

**2 cups peeled and cubed cho cho**

**2 cups peeled and cubed yellow squash**

**3 cups arugula**

**salt and freshly cracked black pepper to taste**

**¼ cup toasted and salted pumpkin seeds**

**CHAMPAGNE VINAIGRETTE**

**⅓ cup champagne vinegar**

**1 clove garlic, smashed**

**1 teaspoon Dijon mustard**

**⅔ cup extra-virgin olive oil**

Blanch the cho cho and yellow squash in a pot of salted boiling water for about 2 minutes until slightly softened, making sure not to overcook. Run under cold water to stop the cooking, and spread out on a tray or sheet of parchment to cool.

To make the vinaigrette, whisk the vinegar, garlic, and mustard together in a small bowl. Add the olive oil in a slow, steady stream, whisking continuously until the mixture is thick.

When the squash has cooled, transfer it to a medium mixing bowl. Add the arugula, and season with salt and pepper. Add a few tablespoons of the dressing (to taste), and toss. Top with the toasted pumpkin seeds. Serve at room temperature with extra dressing on the side.

# CURRIED EGGPLANT AND POTATO WITH ROTI

O ur second island home, Trinidad, boasts an astonishing array of Indian-influenced vegetarian dishes. West Indian roti and curries are very different from the traditional northern or southern Indian versions, but they are equally tasty. This roti (flatbread) recipe hails from Guyana, and the curried eggplant (baigan) is inspired by the delicious Indian dishes of Trinidad and Tobago. Pair this curry with Tamarind-Raisin Ketchup (page 243), Sevens Mango Chutney (page 240), or a cool yogurt raita (page 38).

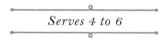

*Serves 4 to 6*

### CURRY

1 ½ tablespoons vegetable oil

1 tablespoon madras curry powder

1 tablespoon geera (cumin seed)

1 teaspoon garam masala

1 tablespoon coriander seed

¼ teaspoon finely chopped wiri wiri or Scotch bonnet pepper

1 small onion, diced

2 cloves garlic, crushed

2 plum tomatoes, diced

1 eggplant (baigan), about 1 to 2 pounds, peeled and cubed

3 small potatoes, cubed

½ cup canned coconut milk

2 tablespoons chopped culantro

¼ teaspoon salt

dash freshly cracked black pepper

### ROTI

3 cups all-purpose flour

¼ teaspoon salt

¾ cup vegetable oil, plus more for cooking

¼ cup shortening

To make the roti, mix the flour, salt, and 1¼ cups water to form a soft dough; let sit for 15 minutes.

Mix ¾ cup vegetable oil and the shortening together in a bowl.

On a floured surface, roll the dough into a rectangular shape about ⅛ inch thick. Brush the oil mixture liberally over the dough, making sure the entire surface of the dough is oiled. Starting from the longer side, roll the dough into a long, tight roll (similar to the process for cinnamon rolls). Slice into six pieces. Seal the loose end of each dough roll so it doesn't open. Place the rolls seam side down on parchment paper, and allow to rest for 30 minutes.

Heat a tawah (similar to a griddle), frying pan, or crepe pan over medium-low heat. Place a roll of dough flat side down on the floured surface, and roll it into a flat, thin circle. Continue with the remaining rolls. Place them in the warm pan. Liberally brush each roll with oil, cook 1 minute, then flip. Brush the other side with oil, and cook for another minute. Cover and shake the pan—this will cause the roti to fluff up. Remove to a warm place until you are ready to serve.

To make the curry, heat 1½ tablespoons vegetable oil in a saucepan over medium-high heat. When the oil is hot, add the curry powder, geera, garam masala, and coriander seeds, and cook, stirring, for about 3 minutes. Add the hot pepper, onion, and garlic, and cook for another 2 minutes. Add about 3 tablespoons of water, and scrape the pot with a wooden spoon so any stuck-on curry will release from the bottom of the pan. When the liquid evaporates, add the tomatoes, eggplant, potatoes, coconut milk, culantro, and salt and pepper. Bring to a simmer and allow the coconut milk to reduce a bit, then cover the pot and reduce the heat to the lowest simmer. Stir occasionally and keep an eye on things; the vegetables will release some natural juices, which should be enough for the baigan to cook without burning, but if you notice that it starts to stick to the bottom of the pan, your heat may be a bit too high. If that happens, reduce the heat and add 1 or 2 tablespoons of water. Cook for about 25 minutes or until the potato is fork-tender and the eggplant starts to dissolve.

Serve the curry hot with warm roti and sauces and sides of your choice.

# OKRA
## *with Scotch Bonnet, Cilantro, Coconut, and Lime*

Many people tell us that they dislike okra because it's too slimy. (It's true that traditional preparations in the islands often include steamed or stewed okra, which may not be palatable to all.) Our very favorite way to eat okra, however, is the northern Indian dish called bhindi masala: crisp, fresh okra is sautéed in a perfectly seasoned blend of tomatoes and traditional Indian spices. In our West Indian version, we sauté the okra in batches in coconut oil with garlic and ginger, then cook it with tomato, and top it with lime juice and some fresh coconut flakes. We say give okra a second chance—it may surprise you.

*Serves 6*

2 tablespoons coconut oil, divided

3 cloves garlic, chopped, divided

1 teaspoon chopped ginger, divided

1 medium yellow onion, chopped, divided

1 red bell pepper, sliced, divided

1 handful fresh thyme leaves, divided

1 Scotch bonnet pepper, seeded and minced, divided

4 cups sliced okra (sliced on the bias about ½ inch thick), divided

1 tablespoon salt, divided

freshly cracked black pepper to taste

3 plum tomatoes, roughly chopped

1 cup roughly chopped fresh cilantro, divided

juice of 2 small limes

¼ cup unsweetened coconut flakes

Heat 1 tablespoon of the coconut oil in a sauté pan over medium heat. Add half the garlic, ginger, onion, bell pepper, thyme, and Scotch bonnet pepper, and sauté for about 3 minutes, until the onions are soft. Add half the okra, ensuring that the pan is not overcrowded (cooking the okra in batches helps it to crisp up). Increase the heat to high, and sauté for about 5 minutes. Remove the contents from the pan and set aside.

Repeat the process with the remaining coconut oil, garlic, ginger, onion, bell pepper, thyme, Scotch bonnet pepper, and okra.

Once the second batch of okra has cooked for 5 minutes, return the first batch to the pan. Season with salt and black pepper. Add the tomatoes and half the cilantro, and sauté for 4 minutes. Reduce the heat and cook for about 10 more minutes, adding a small amount of water if necessary. Add some fresh cilantro toward the end of cooking, but leave some for a garnish. Transfer the okra to a serving dish, and garnish with the remaining cilantro, a squeeze of lime juice, and coconut flakes.

# CUCUMBER, TOMATO, AND ONION RAITA

The cool and creamy condiment known as raita pairs wonderfully with spicy Indian dishes like our Curried Eggplant and Potato (page 34) and Okra with Scotch Bonnet, Cilantro, Coconut, and Lime (page 37). Although raita is not typically consumed as part of the Indian cuisine of the Caribbean region, it balances and complements our Indian dishes particularly well.

*Makes 3 cups*

1 large yellow onion

1 large plum tomato

1 large cucumber, peeled

1 to 2 green chilies

1 cup full-fat plain yogurt

1 teaspoon
roasted cumin powder

1 tablespoon garam masala
(optional)

salt to taste

½ cup lime juice

chopped mint leaves,
chopped cilantro, and lime
wedges for garnish (optional)

Finely chop the onion, tomato, cucumber, and green chilies, and set aside. Whisk the yogurt until creamy and smooth. Stir in the chopped veggies and the roasted cumin powder. Mix thoroughly. Place in the refrigerator to chill. Just before serving, add the garam masala, salt, and lime juice. For a special presentation, garnish with mint leaves, cilantro leaves, and lime wedges.

# SPICY RED PEPPER PESTO

This spicy but slightly sweet and creamy pesto made regular appearances on summer menus in our café, restaurant, and catering business. Most often, we would serve it tossed with room-temperature pasta, roasted cherry tomatoes, garlic, and fresh basil, and topped with shredded Parmesan cheese. Simple, flavorsome, and fresh, the pesto also works well as a dip, spread, or crostini topping. Because it is so versatile it's a great item to keep on hand. Do as we did and serve it with pasta; whip together a light lunch by spreading some on a flatbread and topping it with sun-dried tomatoes, onions, fresh basil, and goat cheese; or serve it with crackers and cheese as a quick starter.

*Serves 6*

8 cloves garlic

1 teaspoon olive oil

6 large red bell peppers

½ to 1 small Scotch bonnet pepper, seeded

1 handful fresh basil

½ cup toasted sliced almonds

1 cup grated Parmesan cheese

¼ cup unsweetened coconut flakes

½ cup extra-virgin olive oil

salt and freshly cracked black pepper to taste

Preheat the oven to 400°F. Arrange the garlic cloves in a square of foil, and drizzle with the olive oil. Seal the foil, and place in the oven to roast for 30 minutes.

To roast the peppers, cut them in half lengthwise, remove the core and seeds, place them cut side down on a baking sheet, and roast them alongside the garlic for 25 to 30 minutes. Or, if you have a gas stove, you may roast the whole bell peppers over an open flame on the stove top, turning occasionally; remove the peppers from the flame when the skin is charred, but not burnt, about 10 minutes. Cover the roasted peppers with plastic wrap, and allow to cool for about 15 minutes. When they're cool, peel the skin off the peppers; do not rinse them with water, as doing so will remove flavor. Wipe the peppers with a paper towel, and cut them into strips.

Combine the roasted garlic, roasted bell peppers, Scotch bonnet pepper, basil, almonds, Parmesan, and coconut flakes in a food processor or blender. Pulse until everything is chopped and mostly combined—it should look crumbly. Next, turn on the processor and add the olive oil in a steady stream until the pesto is slightly runny and fully combined. Add salt and pepper to taste.

# TRINI CHOKAS
## *Tomato Choka and Coconut Choka*

The chokas of Trinidad are a well-known inheritance from the island's Indian heritage. A choka is a topping or sauce that is typically consumed in a very simple manner: on top of bread, with roti, as a side dish, or as a garnish for more elaborate meals. To make a choka, seasonings are cooked in very hot oil, which allows them to intensify in flavor. The hot seasoned oil is poured over a cooked vegetable of some kind. Choka can be made with roasted eggplant, pumpkin, or even coconut. The following two recipes can form the basis for many different flavor combinations. Serve warm, at room temperature, or chilled. Store in a sanitized container in the refrigerator for up to 1 week.

## TOMATO CHOKA

*Makes 1½ cups*

¼ cup olive oil

1 medium yellow onion, minced

2 cloves garlic, minced

1 Scotch bonnet pepper, minced

1 bunch basil, chopped

1 bunch cilantro, chopped

12 plum tomatoes, peeled, seeded, and diced fine

salt and freshly cracked black pepper to taste

Heat the oil in a sauté pan over medium heat. Add the onion, garlic, and Scotch bonnet pepper, and cook until softened, about 3 minutes. Combine the basil and cilantro with the tomatoes, and pour the hot oil over the tomato mixture. Season to taste with salt and pepper.

# COCONUT CHOKA

1 dry coconut (or substitute
3 cups unsweetened coconut
flakes, lightly toasted)

4 tablespoons Green Seasoning
(page 249)

2 teaspoons minced garlic

1 tablespoon minced onion

2 tablespoons Caribbean
hot pepper sauce

2 Scotch bonnet peppers,
seeded and finely chopped

1 teaspoon salt

freshly cracked black pepper
to taste

Preheat the oven to 350°F.

Using a screwdriver, poke holes in all three eyes of the coconut, and drain the water into a bowl. (Chill the coconut water, and drink it later for a refreshing treat.) With a hammer, sharply rap the drained coconut in several places until the shell cracks. Break open the coconut. Use a blunt tool like a large metal spoon to pry the coconut flesh from the shell. Remove the brown skin from the flesh with a vegetable peeler. Cut the flesh into large pieces. Arrange the pieces of coconut on a large baking sheet. Roast the coconut until the edges are brownish-black, about 10 minutes (do not burn).

Remove the coconut from the oven and allow to cool. Scrape off the burnt pieces as much as possible, and wipe with a paper towel. Chop into 2-inch pieces, and grind using a spice grinder or food processor. (If you're using prepared coconut flakes, after toasting them, grind them in the spice grinder or food processor.)

Transfer the ground coconut to a bowl, and add the Green Seasoning, garlic, onion, hot pepper sauce, Scotch bonnet peppers, and salt. Mix thoroughly with your hands until combined. Adjust the seasonings with salt and pepper.

# PEPPER GRILLED CHEESE
## with Caramelized Onions and Fresh Pepper Jelly

There are so many varieties of bread and cheese that you never need to make the same grilled-cheese sandwich twice—but we bet you'll crave this one again and again. The flavor profile for this version is deliberately reminiscent of a Trinidadian pepper roti, in which a similar blend of spicy peppers is melted inside a cheese-filled roti. We like to make our grilled-cheese sandwich on Jamaican hardo bread, and we always add some spice: here, we include caramelized onions, and we spread the bread with Dijon mustard, a hot pepper jelly, and a mixture of cheeses. Serve extra pepper jelly on the side for good measure.

### Serves 4

1 tablespoon olive oil

2 medium yellow onions, sliced

salt to taste

1 tablespoon minced ginger

¼ teaspoon minced
Scotch bonnet pepper

8 slices hardo bread
(or any firm, moist white bread)

4 teaspoons Dijon mustard

4 ounces Gruyere
cheese, grated

2 ounces mozzarella
cheese, grated

2 ounces provolone
cheese, grated

4 teaspoons spicy pepper jelly,
plus more for serving

4 teaspoons butter, divided,
plus more for cooking

4 tablespoons grated
Parmesan cheese

Turn on the broiler, or preheat the oven to 450°F.

Warm the olive oil over medium heat in a sauté pan. Add the onions, sprinkle with salt, and add the ginger and Scotch bonnet pepper. Cook until the onions are browned and wilted, about 8 minutes. Remove from the pan.

To assemble the sandwiches, spread four slices of hardo bread with Dijon mustard. On each slice of bread, layer 1 ounce Gruyere cheese, a quarter of the onion mixture, ½ ounce mozzarella, and ½ ounce provolone. Spread pepper jelly on the other four slices of bread, and place on top of the sandwiches. Spread the tops of each sandwich with 1 teaspoon of butter.

Melt about 1 teaspoon of butter in a nonstick pan over medium heat. Once the pan is warmed and the butter melted, place the sandwich, nonbuttered side down, in the pan. Press on the sandwich with the back of a spatula throughout the cooking process; when the bread is nice and caramelized, flip the sandwich and repeat on the other side. Once the cheese begins to melt inside the sandwich and the outside is crispy, remove the sandwich from the pan and place it on a baking tray.

*(Continued)*

To finish, top each sandwich with 1 tablespoon of Parmesan cheese, and broil (or bake) it in the oven until the Parmesan cheese is melted and slightly brown, about 2 to 8 minutes depending on your oven. Cut each sandwich diagonally, and serve with pepper jelly on the side.

# SESAME-ROASTED GARLIC AND EGGPLANT CAVIAR

To say we love eggplant would be an understatement. Any way you can make it, we will take it! What makes this recipe so unusual is the combination of charred eggplant with sesame oil, roasted garlic, ginger, and a touch of sugar. It is a delightful dip or topping for crostini, and would be a wonderful addition to a cheese board.

*Serves 8*

2 medium eggplants

16 cloves garlic

½ cup plus 4 tablespoons sesame oil, divided

1 teaspoon brown sugar

1 medium yellow onion, finely chopped

1 tablespoon minced ginger

2 tablespoons minced Scotch bonnet pepper

1 tablespoon rice wine vinegar

1 large handful chopped culantro

salt and freshly cracked black pepper to taste

Culantro Pepper Oil (page 250)

Scotch Bonnet Oil (page 250)

Preheat the oven to 375°F.

Cut slits in the eggplants, and stuff them with 4 whole garlic cloves per eggplant. Rub 2 tablespoons of sesame oil on the outside of the eggplants. Toss the remaining 8 garlic cloves with salt in 2 tablespoons of sesame oil. Place the eggplants and the 8 loose garlic cloves on a small baking sheet. Roast the eggplants and the garlic cloves, turning the eggplants occasionally, until the skin looks thin and the interior is soft, about 35 minutes. Remove the baking sheet from the oven. Cut the eggplants in half lengthwise, and use a spoon to scoop the cooked flesh (including the garlic cloves embedded in the eggplants) into a bowl. Mash the eggplant until it is smooth. Roughly chop the loose roasted garlic cloves, and stir them into the mashed eggplant.

Warm a medium sauté pan over high heat. Add the remaining sesame oil to the pan. When the pan is hot, stir in the brown sugar and cook for about 1 minute; add the onion, ginger, Scotch bonnet pepper, and rice wine vinegar. Stir in the culantro.

Pour the onion mixture, including the cooking oil, over the mashed eggplant, and stir well. Add salt and pepper to taste. Drizzle with Culantro Pepper Oil and Scotch Bonnet Oil. Serve hot or at room temperature as a dip.

# ROASTED TOMATOES AND EGGPLANT
## *with Spiced Cilantro Yogurt and Feta*

Roasted tomato and eggplant is always a perfect pairing. In this recipe we roast the tomatoes and layer them over crispy fried eggplant. The addition of a cool cilantro-yogurt dressing and fresh herbs takes this dish over the top.

*Serves 6 to 8*

1 large eggplant

6 to 7 medium plum tomatoes

1 medium red onion, quartered

2 to 3 cloves garlic, minced

3 tablespoons basil chiffonade, divided

3 tablespoons chopped cilantro leaves plus more for garnish, divided

3 tablespoons chopped mint, divided

6 tablespoons olive oil, divided

salt and freshly cracked black pepper to taste

¼ cup flour (for dredging)

¼ cup crumbled feta cheese

SPICED CILANTRO YOGURT

1 cup Greek yogurt

2 teaspoons lemon juice

1 clove garlic, smashed

½ teaspoon cayenne pepper

½ teaspoon paprika

1 tablespoon chopped dill

1 tablespoon chopped cilantro

1 small red chili pepper, seeded and minced

salt and freshly cracked black pepper to taste

*(Continued)*

To make the Spiced Cilantro Yogurt, combine all the ingredients together in a bowl. Refrigerate until ready for use.

Preheat the oven to 375°F. Slice the eggplant into ¼-inch thick rounds, arrange in a shallow baking dish, and sprinkle with salt. Set aside for 20 to 30 minutes as the eggplant purges.

In the meantime, cut the tomatoes into quarters or fifths. Transfer to a bowl, and add the red onion, garlic, and 1 tablespoon each of basil, cilantro, and mint. Add 3 tablespoons of olive oil, and toss everything together. The tomatoes should be glossy; if they aren't, add a bit more oil. Season with salt and pepper. Place the tomatoes on a baking tray, slide the tray into the preheated oven, and cook for 30 to 35 minutes, until they are soft and juicy (not dry).

While the tomatoes roast, wipe the water from the purged eggplant with a paper towel. Dredge the eggplant slices in flour, lightly coating each side. Heat 2 tablespoons olive oil in a skillet on high heat, and pan fry the eggplant in batches, about 2 minutes per side. As you remove the eggplant slices from the oil, place them on paper towels to drain any excess oil.

When the tomatoes are ready, toss them with another tablespoon of olive oil and the remainder of the basil, mint, and cilantro (reserve some cilantro for a garnish).

To serve, arrange the fried eggplant slices on a platter, and top with the warm roasted-tomato mixture. Drizzle yogurt dressing across the entire platter; top with fresh cilantro and a sprinkling of feta.

# ZABOCA TOAST
## with Coconut and Pumpkin Seeds

It seems that eating avocado for breakfast has long been a tradition in the West Indies. In her book on life in the islands, published in 1834, Mrs. A. C. Carmichael described the "alligator pear" or "zaboca pear" as a "pleasant wholesome fruit.... When ripe, it is soft and mellow, and the inside exactly resembles fine yellow butter....It is generally eaten for breakfast, either with sugar and lime juice, or with salt and pepper." Our ancestors may have appreciated the health-giving qualities of avocado and coconut fats. This modern avocado breakfast dish combines the various ingredients' flavor and texture profiles—tart, sweet, salty, creamy, crunchy, mellow, spicy—to create a subtle medley bursting with flavor that will surely wake up your taste buds. For an extra-hearty base, look for a crusty country-style bread laden with nuts and seeds. Serve as a healthy brunch or breakfast item, or slice the bread into thin triangles, toast until crispy, and serve as a crostini for a cocktail party.

*Serves 4*

1 large avocado, peeled, pitted, and chopped

1 bunch scallions, thinly sliced

1 handful of cilantro, chopped (reserve some for garnish)

2 teaspoons fine sea salt

1 teaspoon freshly cracked black pepper

juice of ½ lime

4 slices crusty whole-grain bread

1 handful unsweetened coconut flakes

1 handful salted pumpkin seeds

drizzle of Scotch Bonnet Oil (page 250)

In a small bowl, mash the avocado together with the scallions, cilantro, sea salt, pepper, and lime juice to taste. Toast the bread until it is warm and crispy on the outside. Spread the avocado mixture generously on top of the warm bread; sprinkle with coconut flakes and toasted pumpkin seeds. Drizzle with Scotch Bonnet Oil and fresh cilantro.

# CHEESY MUSHROOM TOAST

Goat cheese, heavy cream, and brown sugar sweeten this savory mushroom sauté. Spread atop a garlic baguette and crowned with Parmesan, this becomes an all-around scrumptious side dish, appetizer, or snack.

*Serves 2*

1 12-inch whole-grain baguette

3 tablespoons room-temperature butter, divided

1 tablespoon plus 1 teaspoon minced garlic

2 tablespoons chopped parsley, divided, plus more for garnish

salt and freshly cracked black pepper to taste

½ cup minced yellow onion

4 cups sliced assorted mushrooms (we like button, cremini, and shiitake)

¼ cup sherry or white wine

½ tablespoon brown sugar

1 ounce soft goat cheese

3 tablespoons heavy cream

¼ cup grated Parmesan cheese, for garnish

Heat the oven to 350°F degrees.

Slice the baguette into two 6-inch-long pieces, and then slice each piece lengthwise down the center.

Mix 1½ tablespoons butter with 1 teaspoon minced garlic, 1 tablespoon parsley, and a little salt. Spread the garlic butter on the bread slices, and arrange the slices butter side up on a baking sheet. Toast for about 5 minutes, but do not allow the bread to get too crispy.

Melt the remaining 1½ tablespoons butter in a saucepan over medium heat. Add the onions and the remaining 1 tablespoon garlic, and cook for about 3 minutes, until the onions are soft. Add the mushrooms, and cook for 3 more minutes. Add the sherry and brown sugar, and simmer for 1 minute. Remove the pan from the heat. Stir in the goat cheese, heavy cream, and 1 tablespoon parsley, and season with salt and pepper.

Remove the toasts from the oven, and top with the hot mushrooms and the remaining sauce from the pan. Garnish with Parmesan cheese and a sprinkling of parsley.

# AVOCADO AND PLANTAIN SALSA
## *with Breadfruit Chips*

**B**eing lucky enough to have a fine avocado tree in your garden is considered a blessing! But you would have to viciously guard your tree because, as we say in Jamaica, "Every man woulda want fi tief di pear," which translates to "Everybody will want to steal your pears [avocados]." And trust us—they do. This dish is a novel and tasty hors d'oeuvre for a cocktail or dinner party, and the perfect addition to any summer party menu. Zesty, sweet yet savory, the salsa is a wonderful accompaniment to one of our local staples: breadfruit, prepared here as chips. This item was a hit at a Sunday brunch we curated for the Jamaica Food and Drink Festival at the National Gallery of Jamaica. Our guests begged for the recipe, so here it finally is; we hope you enjoy eating it as much as we love making it.

*Serves 6*

1 large breadfruit, whole and unpeeled (if breadfruit is unavailable, substitute 2 pounds sweet potatoes)

4 cups plus 2 to 3 tablespoons vegetable oil

flaked sea salt to taste

3 to 4 ripe plantains, peeled and diced into ¼-inch cubes

3 to 4 ripe but firm avocados, diced

3 plum tomatoes, diced

½ cup diced bell pepper

1 small red onion, diced

2 tablespoons basil chiffonade

2 tablespoons chopped cilantro

2 jalapeno peppers, seeded and diced

1 tablespoon lime juice

2 tablespoons olive oil

½ teaspoon cumin

½ teaspoon coriander

salt and freshly cracked black pepper to taste

*(Continued)*

To make the breadfruit chips, slice the breadfruit in half, leaving the skin on and the core intact. Turn each half over so that the flat side lies face down on the cutting board, and, working from the sides toward the center, slice the fruit about ⅛ inch thick. (If you're using sweet potato, slice into rounds, discarding the ends.)

Heat 4 cups of vegetable oil in a thick-bottomed sauté pan over medium-high heat. Working in batches, arrange breadfruit slices in the hot oil in a single layer, making sure to avoid overcrowding the pan. Deep fry the breadfruit until golden-brown (3 to 4 minutes per side). Remove from the oil when the slices look slightly translucent. Drain on paper towels, and sprinkle with flaked sea salt while hot. Hold at room temperature until ready to serve.

To make the salsa, heat 2 to 3 tablespoons vegetable oil in a sauté pan over high heat; add the diced plantain, and pan fry until browned on all sides, stirring occasionally. When finished, remove the plantain to a plate lined with paper towels; allow to cool.

Transfer the fried plantain to a large bowl. Add the remaining ingredients, season with salt and pepper, and gently toss, making sure to avoid mashing the avocado. Transfer to a serving bowl, place in the center of a platter, and surround the bowl with breadfruit chips.

# AVOCADO-GINGER SPRING ROLLS
## *with Lemongrass-Citrus Dipping Sauce*

We like to play with our ingredients, creating variations on dishes by modifying their texture and traditional method of cooking. Although we love this avocado-ginger filling tucked inside a hot and crispy Thai-style spring roll, it works equally well deep fried in a wonton skin. Try mixing it up for variety. Imagine fresh buttery avocado, sweet ripe plantain, crunchy corn kernels, tart lime, and the exotic sweetness of Asian sesame oil, all rolled up in a snappy-crisp wrapper and served piping hot with a lemongrass dipping sauce. Need we say more?

*Serves 8 to 10*

1 tablespoon sesame oil

¼ cup corn kernels (canned or thawed from frozen)

1 cup diced ripe plantain

2 tablespoons diced red bell pepper

1 small red chili pepper, thinly sliced on the bias

2 tablespoons diced scallion

1 teaspoon minced ginger

1 large ripe avocado, mashed (leave a few lumps for texture)

2 tablespoons chopped cilantro

juice of 1 lime

salt and freshly cracked black pepper

16 to 24 spring roll or wonton wrappers

1 egg

oil for deep frying (2 to 3 cups)

LEMONGRASS-CITRUS DIPPING SAUCE

½ cup orange juice

6 tablespoons white vinegar

4 tablespoons coconut aminos or tamari

1 teaspoon brown sugar

2 tablespoons minced peeled fresh ginger

1 tablespoon sesame oil

4 tablespoons chopped lemongrass (or a handful of whole leaves bruised by rubbing them together)

4 tablespoons chopped cilantro

*(Continued)*

Heat the sesame oil in a sauté pan over medium heat. Add the corn, plantain, red bell pepper, chili pepper, scallion, and ginger. Sauté for 2 minutes; remove from the heat and place in a medium bowl. Add the smashed avocado, cilantro, and lime juice. Stir until the ingredients are combined, and season to taste with salt and pepper.

Assemble the spring rolls. Make an egg wash by whisking the egg with 2 tablespoons water. Spoon 2 tablespoons of filling at one end of a wrapper. Fold in the sides of the wrapper, and, starting with the end containing the filling, roll up the wrapper. Seal the seam by brushing it with a little egg wash; set the roll aside, seam side down. Continue until all the filling is used up. Layer the spring rolls, seam side down, between sheets of waxed paper. Cover and refrigerate until ready to fry.

Make the dipping sauce. Combine all ingredients except the cilantro in a medium saucepan. Bring to a boil, reduce the heat to medium, and simmer for 5 to 10 minutes until the sauce is reduced and slightly thickened. Stir in the cilantro, and simmer for another minute. Remove from heat.

Fry the spring rolls. Heat the vegetable oil in a thick-bottomed saucepan or wok over medium heat. Working in batches (and making sure to avoid overcrowding the pan), add the spring rolls to the hot oil, and fry until they are golden on the outside. Drain on paper towels. Serve immediately with the dipping sauce alongside.

# ACKEE TACOS
## *with Island Guacamole*

While shooting the photos for our first cookbook, *Caribbean Potluck,* our food stylists, Christine Albano and Nora Singley, came up with the novel idea that ackee would make a terrific taco filling. We love ackee and have prepared it in a variety of unconventional ways (as a dip, in a pasta sauce, in lasagna, on a pizza), but it had never occurred to us to use it as a filling for tacos. Boy, was that a fantastic idea! Though it is Jamaica's national fruit, ackee is cooked and used as a vegetable. It is an unusual ingredient that we feel should be explored and consumed way more often than it is. With a subtle, almost nutty taste, it is an exciting addition to vegetarian menus. We love the fresh ackee available in markets in Jamaica, but canned ackee is a fine substitute if you can't get it fresh.

*Serves 4 to 6*

### ISLAND GUACAMOLE

3 medium avocados, peeled, pitted, and sliced

1 to 2 plum tomatoes, seeded and diced

3 tablespoons diced red onion

½ cup diced pineapple or mango

1 tablespoon lime juice

1 tablespoon orange juice

1 teaspoon orange zest

1 teaspoon minced Scotch bonnet pepper

2 tablespoons olive oil

3 to 4 tablespoons chopped cilantro

salt and freshly cracked black pepper to taste

### ACKEE FILLING

2 to 3 tablespoons coconut oil or other vegetable oil

1 small yellow onion, diced

1 plum tomato, diced

2 cloves garlic, diced

4 tablespoons diced bell pepper

¼ teaspoon seeded and minced Scotch bonnet pepper

1 stalk scallion

2 dozen frozen ackee or 2 cans ackee, drained (or 2 cups ackee, cooked from fresh)

1 teaspoon thyme leaves

½ teaspoon chili powder

salt and freshly cracked black pepper to taste

12 taco shells (either soft or crunchy)

⅔ cup grated sharp cheddar cheese

1 cup shredded lettuce or purple cabbage

1 large handful chopped fresh cilantro

salsa (optional)

sour cream (optional)

*(Continued)*

Make the guacamole. Dice or mash the avocado depending on your preference; it can have a more salsa-like texture if preferred. Add the remaining guacamole ingredients, gently stirring to combine. Refrigerate until you are ready to assemble the tacos.

Make the ackee filling. Heat the oil in a sauté pan over medium-high heat. Add the onion, tomato, garlic, bell pepper, Scotch bonnet pepper, and scallion, and cook until the ingredients are soft, about 3 minutes. Add the ackee, thyme, chili powder, salt, and pepper, gently folding the ingredients together. Cook for 5 to 8 minutes or until the mixture is heated through; remove from heat.

Serve assembly-line style, with the ackee mixture, guacamole, grated cheese, shredded lettuce or cabbage, cilantro, salsa, and sour cream (if using) in colorful bowls next to a basket of soft or hard taco shells. Alternately, serve a large platter of already assembled tacos: fill each shell with a few tablespoons of ackee, layer with lettuce, guacamole, and cheese, and top with a mound of fresh cilantro for a mouthful of exotic flavor. Serve with salsa and/or sour cream if you wish.

# ACKEE LASAGNA

Delicate ackee makes a wonderful lasagna filling. In this recipe, two cheeses combine with the creamy, coconut-flavored ackee sauce in a subtle and glorious way. Serve with a fresh salad and a glass of rosé.

*Serves 8 to 10*

12 lasagna noodles

2 tablespoons olive oil, plus more for noodles

1 small yellow onion, diced

1 stalk scallion, diced

3 cloves garlic, minced

½ teaspoon minced Scotch bonnet pepper (flesh only, no seeds or pith)

2 tablespoons diced bell pepper

2 tablespoons fresh thyme leaves

2 small plum tomatoes, peeled, seeded, and diced

3 cups canned ackee, drained (or cooked from fresh)

salt and freshly cracked black pepper to taste

1 cup canned coconut milk

2 cups heavy or whipping cream

2 cups grated mozzarella cheese

1 cup grated Parmesan cheese

Preheat the oven to 375°F.

Boil the lasagna noodles until al dente in salted water according to the package directions. Drain the noodles, run them under cold water, and toss them with a little olive oil so they don't stick together.

Heat 2 tablespoons of olive oil in a saucepan over medium heat. Add the onion, and sweat for about 5 minutes (don't allow the onions to brown). Add the scallion, garlic, Scotch bonnet pepper, bell pepper, and thyme; cook until the peppers are soft, about 5 minutes. Add the tomatoes; cook, stirring, for about 3 minutes. Fold in the ackee. Season with salt and pepper. Cook until the ackee is well seasoned and the flavors combined, about 5 minutes; do not stir too often.

Add the coconut milk, and bring the mixture to a boil. Add the heavy cream, return the mixture to a boil, lower the heat to a simmer, and allow the sauce to reduce for about 5 minutes. Season again to taste with salt and pepper; remove from heat.

Spread about ½ cup of the ackee sauce on the bottom of a 9 x 9-inch baking pan or casserole dish. Arrange three lasagna noodles to cover the sauce. Top with one-third of the remaining ackee sauce, spreading to cover the layer below. Layer with one-third each of the mozzarella and the Parmesan. Repeat the layers, ending with a layer of noodles. Top with the last of the mozzarella and Parmesan. Bake for 35 to 40 minutes, until the cheese is golden-brown and bubbly.

# CHO CHO "APPLE" CRISP

Growing up in the 1970s, we lived in both Jamaica and Trinidad. It was an idyllic time of pure, sweet, wild childhood memories. Our days were filled with fun explorations—climbing fruit trees, and generally running free in nature. Back then, imported food supplies in the West Indies were severely limited; we certainly never saw imported fruits, vegetables, sweets, or snacks on Jamaican or Trinidadian supermarket shelves until about the 1990s. At the same time, however, Caribbean women remained very much aware of the trends and norms of societies other than ours, and they were ingenious in using local ingredients to create "foreign-tasting" gourmet dishes. Our mother was a master at this feat; we remember her making international (to us!) dishes like apple pie, donuts, and beef stroganoff. We had no idea that the "apple" pie we were eating was actually made with cho cho, our local squash. This vegetable is bland enough to take on the flavor of whatever you cook it with, so you simply poach the squashes whole in apple juice, cinnamon, cloves, allspice, and brown sugar, slice them thinly like apples, and bake them in a pie crust. In this recipe, we add a crispy, sugary oat topping. This dessert will both surprise and satisfy you.

*Serves 8*

1 Basic Pastry Crust (page 165) or premade pie crust, unbaked

5 to 6 medium cho cho (chayote)

2 cups apple juice

4 cloves

10 whole allspice berries

2 cups plus 1 tablespoon brown sugar, divided

¾ cup plus 5 tablespoons flour, divided

2 teaspoons lime juice

2 teaspoons cinnamon, divided

¼ teaspoon nutmeg

dash of salt

⅓ cup unsalted butter, cubed

¼ cup sliced almonds, toasted

2 tablespoons oats

Preheat the oven to 400°F.

Prepare the pie crust. If using a frozen premade pie crust, allow it to thaw.

Peel the cho cho. In a large saucepan over medium heat, bring the apple juice, cloves, and allspice berries to a boil with 1 tablespoon brown sugar. Add the whole, peeled cho cho, and simmer for about 10 minutes. Do not overcook. Remove the cho cho from the liquid, cool, and slice thinly.

Mix together 1½ cups brown sugar, 5 tablespoons flour, lime juice, 1 teaspoon cinnamon, nutmeg, and a dash of salt. Combine with the cooked, sliced cho cho. Line a 9-inch pie pan with the pie crust; pour in the cho cho mixture. Set aside.

Combine ½ cup brown sugar and ¾ cup flour. Add the butter, 1 teaspoon cinnamon, almonds, and oats; blend well. Sprinkle the topping over the cho cho filling. Bake for about 40 minutes. Allow the crisp to set up for 10 minutes before slicing. Serve warm with a scoop of ice cream.

# CHAPTER 3

# SPROUTS & STARCHY FRUITS

*Hearts of Palm, Artichoke Hearts, Pumpkin,*
*Banana, Plantain & Breadfruit*

IN THE CARIBBEAN, WE HAVE A LOVE AFFAIR WITH STARCHY FRUITS THAT CANNOT BE DENIED. FRUITS LIKE GREEN BANANA, GREEN PLANTAIN, breadfruit, and pumpkin take center stage at the Caribbean table.

This produce was originally brought to the islands by planters as a cheap form of sustenance that could supplement the starchy provisions like yam that were a part of the slave diet. Accordingly, banana walks, plantain groves, and breadfruit trees were present on most if not all estates; plantain and banana trees were present in all provision grounds. The breadfruit, introduced from Tahiti, was not initially favored by the slaves, who preferred the texture of the starchier and heavier ground provisions. Plantain was well appreciated by all.

Most of these ingredients, whether breadfruit, plantain, banana, or pumpkin, are eaten simply—boiled or roasted over an open flame and topped with butter and salt. Prepared in these traditional ways, they are absolutely delicious. Densely flavorful, nutritious, high in fiber, and gluten free, they provide a fantastic alternative to the typical starchy sides of the Western diet. But we also love to experiment with them. They make great chips when fried; they bake, braise, and stew well; and they combine gloriously with traditional sauces in dishes of all kinds—from curries to cheesy gratins. In this chapter we share some of our favorite ways to work with our starchy island fruits.

> Plantains green, plantains ripe, plantains turned. All are appreciated by the West Indian and are popular with our visitors. Green, they are boiled or roasted. The people put the green plantains, and also the green bananas, in their soups or eat them with their salt fish.…"Turned" is when they are between green and ripe, and they go excellently well with salt fish or eaten boiled or roasted with butter put inside them.
>
> —*The Jamaica Cookery Book,* 1893

# CURRIED GREEN BANANA
## *with Pineapple and Raisins*

We first had curried green bananas a few years ago, on a visit to the lovely isle of Dominica. Although residents of all the region's islands consume green bananas, they tend to mash them with butter, boil them, or stew them, like in our Cream of Callaloo Soup (page 108). This innovative preparation impressed the heck out of us (as did Dominica, by the way). The sweetness of the pineapple and raisins balances the spice and tartness of the curry, and coconut milk brings everything together in a delectable way.

*Serves 4*

1 tablespoon coconut oil

1 teaspoon finely chopped ginger

¼ cup chopped onion

1 teaspoon brown sugar

6 green bananas, peeled and sliced

2 tablespoons chopped culantro (or substitute cilantro)

1 teaspoon ground garam masala

1 teaspoon ground turmeric

1 Scotch bonnet pepper

6 whole allspice berries

½ cup fresh pineapple pieces (½ inch dice), (optional)

½ cup raisins

¼ cup canned coconut milk

½ cup unsweetened coconut flakes

salt to taste

lime juice to taste

2 tablespoons chopped cilantro leaves, for garnish

Warm the coconut oil in a deep saucepan over medium heat. Add the ginger and onion, and cook for 1 minute. Stir in the brown sugar and cook until it has dissolved. Add the green banana, culantro, garam masala, and turmeric, and stir until the bananas are coated with the seasonings. Add 1½ cups water, the whole Scotch bonnet pepper, and the allspice berries. Bring to a boil, then reduce the heat to low. Cover and simmer for 15 minutes.

Next, add the pineapple (if using), raisins, and coconut milk, and simmer until the bananas are soft and the sauce has reduced (about 10 minutes). Stir in the coconut flakes, and season with salt and lime juice. Garnish with cilantro leaves.

# GRILLED GREEN BANANA AND PLANTAIN WITH BUTTER

In most islands of the West Indies, people eat bananas and plantains in both their green and ripe states. This delicious recipe presents a simple and fantastic way to eat green bananas and green or "turned" plantains. (No longer green but not quite ripe, turned fruit is starchy rather than sweet.) Make this a part of any barbeque menu, and you and your guests will rave.

*Serves 4 to 6*

8 to 10 green bananas

4 large green or "turned" plantains

3 to 4 tablespoons butter

salt

Preheat the grill to medium-high.

Peel the bananas and plantains. The skins will be starchy and sticky, so use gloves if you like. Rinse the fruit with water, and pat dry with a paper towel.

Leave the bananas whole. Cut the plantains in half, and then slice them lengthwise down the center. Lay the bananas and plantains on the heated grill. Allow the fruit to cook for 5 to 8 minutes, and then turn them. Cook for another 5 to 8 minutes or until brown. The plantains will take longer to cook than the bananas. Once the fruit is cooked through, arrange it on a platter. Dot it with butter and sprinkle with salt. Eat right away.

# PLANTAIN AND CHEESE EMPANADILLAS

This delightful pastry is a blend between a Jamaican patty and a Venezuelan empanada; however, in this recipe we switch out ground beef for a spicy, cheesy plantain filling. Add to it a "Trini"-style garlic dipping sauce, and the result is spectacular. Here, we include instructions for making both cocktail-size and slightly larger empanadillas. Serve them as either an hors d'oeuvre or a first course.

*Makes 8 large or 16 small empanadillas*

2 tablespoons olive oil, divided

½ cup diced ripe plantain

1 tablespoon diced garlic

2 tablespoons diced scallion

½ red bell pepper, seeded and diced

½ cup cooked corn kernels

1 teaspoon diced Scotch bonnet pepper

4 tablespoons chopped cilantro

½ teaspoon cumin

1 teaspoon honey

1 teaspoon lime juice

½ cup heavy cream

salt and freshly cracked black pepper to taste

½ cup grated Monterey Jack cheese

2 sheets prepared puff pastry (17.3 ounces each)

flour, for rolling

1 egg, lightly beaten

Garlic-Lime Sauce (page 243)

Preheat the oven to 375°F.

Heat 1 tablespoon olive oil in a sauté pan over medium heat. Add the plantain and sauté for about 5 minutes until golden-brown; remove from the pan. Heat another tablespoon of olive oil, and add the garlic, scallion, bell pepper, corn, Scotch bonnet pepper, cilantro, cumin, honey, and lime juice. Cook for 2 minutes until fragrant. Add the cream, heat through, and season to taste with salt and pepper. Remove from the heat and stir in the cheese and the cooked plantain. Place the mixture in the refrigerator to chill.

Unfold 1 pastry sheet on a lightly floured surface. Roll it into a 16 x 12-inch rectangle. Cut into eight (3-inch) or four (6-inch) circles or squares. Repeat with the remaining pastry sheet, making a total of sixteen cocktail-size or eight larger empanadillas.

*For cocktail-size empanadillas,* spoon 1 to 1½ teaspoons filling onto half of each 3-inch circle or square of pastry. *For larger empanadillas,* use 1 to 1½ tablespoons filling per 6-inch circle or square. Brush the edges of the pastry with water. Fold the pastry over the filling, and crimp it with a fork to seal.

Arrange the empanadillas on a sheet pan lined with parchment paper. Brush the tops with the beaten egg. Bake for 30 minutes or until the outsides are golden-brown. Serve with Garlic-Lime Sauce.

NOTE: You can freeze the unbaked empanadillas in a sealed container for up to two weeks; place waxed paper between the layers, and completely thaw the pastries before baking.

# ROASTED RIPE PLANTAIN
## *with African Pepper Compote*

Memories of the homeland were never far from the minds of our displaced Afro-Caribbean ancestors. Despite isolation from friends, family, tribes, and community, they brought with them a shared memory and a collective knowledge of how and what to eat. This knowledge has been passed down over generations, and it never ceases to amaze us how intricately connected we still are to our motherland, Africa. With dishes like this one, inspired by a popular African street food, it is easy to see that the roots of our dining habits are deeply entrenched in a shared heritage with our ancestors from across the seas. Our friend Nadine from the Ivory Coast speaks so passionately about the delicious street food from her homeland that it makes us drool. Here, the combination of sweet plantain, spicy pepper compote, creamy avocado, and tart lime makes for a simple and fresh snack or side. Add the crunch of roasted peanuts, and the result becomes a totally different take on the typical roasted provisions of the Caribbean.

### *Serves 6*

2 whole ripe plantains

1 cup raw shelled peanuts, with the papery skins still on

2 medium avocados

juice of 2 limes

½ teaspoon paprika

¼ teaspoon cinnamon, (optional)

¼ teaspoon cayenne pepper

1 teaspoon sea salt

African Pepper Compote (page 248)

Preheat the oven to 400°F.

Place the plantains, with the skins still on, on a baking sheet, and pop it in the oven. Roast them for 35 to 40 minutes, until cooked through. (Alternatively, you can cook the whole, unpeeled plantains on a grill over a medium flame.) Keep the plantains warm until it's time to serve them.

While the plantains are roasting, spread the peanuts on a smaller sheet pan, and place them in the oven as well. After 10 minutes, remove the peanuts from the oven, and set aside, keeping them warm.

Slice the avocados in half, remove the pit, and scoop the flesh out of the skins. Roughly mash the flesh, and arrange it on a serving plate. Squeeze lime juice over the avocado, and dust it with paprika, cinnamon (if using), cayenne, and sea salt.

Roughly chop half the peanuts, and sprinkle them over the avocado. With the skins still on, slice the plantains in half, and add them to the platter. Dollop or drizzle the plantains with African Pepper Compote. Garnish the platter by sprinkling the remaining whole roasted peanuts over the top.

# RIPE PLANTAIN GRATIN
## *with Gruyere*

This French-inspired twist on a simple baked plantain combines the savory richness of a Mornay sauce with the sharpness of Gruyere cheese and the sweet undertones of ripe fruit. Preparing vegetables or savory fruit au gratin transforms any of the region's starchy vegetables into a delicious side dish. In St. Lucia, for example, they make an astonishing breadfruit gratin. To change up this fantastic recipe, try substituting breadfruit, yam, or cassava, and use different cheeses like chèvre, cheddar, or mozzarella. Any way you make it, you can be prepared for sighs of contentment, moans of delight, and perhaps even exclamations of joy from those at your table—yes, it's simply that good!

*Serves 8 to 10*

4 ripe plantains

4 tablespoons vegetable oil

2 tablespoons butter

1 tablespoon minced onion

1 teaspoon finely diced garlic

2 teaspoons fresh thyme leaves

1 teaspoon diced scallion

2 teaspoons flour

1 cup milk

1 cup whipping cream

¼ cup white wine

3 ounces Gruyere
cheese, grated

salt and freshly cracked
black pepper to taste

2 ounces Parmesan
cheese, grated

2 tablespoons panko
breadcrumbs

Preheat the oven to 475°F.

Peel the plantains, and cut them lengthwise into slices about ⅓ inch thick. Heat the oil in a frying pan over low heat, and, working in batches, fry the plantain slices until brown (don't overload the pan). Drain on paper towels.

Melt the butter in a saucepan over medium-low heat. Add the onion, garlic, thyme, and scallion, and cook for 1 minute. Add the flour and cook for about 2 minutes, until the flour is no longer raw. Gradually add the milk and cream to the saucepan, whisking as you do, and cook, stirring, until the sauce thickens. Add the wine, and stir to combine. Turn off the heat, and stir in the Gruyere. Season to taste with salt and pepper.

Arrange the fried plantains and the white sauce in alternating layers in a baking dish. Finish with the white sauce. Sprinkle the Parmesan cheese and breadcrumbs on top. Bake for 30 minutes, until the top is golden and crusty.

# OVEN-ROASTED PUMPKIN FLATBREADS

## *with Goat Cheese, Cilantro-Coconut Pistou, and Sweet 'n' Salty Pumpkin Seeds*

We love the way the creamy sweetness of island pumpkin, when roasted, combines with the tartness of soft goat cheese. For these flatbreads, we spread the base with a coconut pistou (page 248) and top that with succulent roasted pumpkin, goat cheese, fresh mint, and olive oil. This fantastic party of flavors gets roasted in the oven until the cheese melts, and finished with crunchy pumpkin seeds. Flatbreads are one of the easiest and quickest lunches or party snacks that you can make. If you're especially in a rush, you can use ready-made flatbread dough—but our homemade dough is worth the wait when you've got the time.

*Serves 4 to 6*

**HOMEMADE FLATBREAD DOUGH (OR USE PREMADE FLATBREAD DOUGH)**

4¼ cups flour plus more for kneading and rolling

1 ounce salt

1 packet instant yeast

¼ cup olive oil, divided

**OVEN-ROASTED PUMPKIN TOPPING**

1 tablespoon olive oil

½ onion, chopped

1 clove garlic, diced

2 tablespoons chopped fresh mint

2 tablespoons chopped fresh cilantro

1 pound calabaza pumpkin, peeled, seeded, and cut into ⅛-inch thick slices

1 teaspoon salt

¼ teaspoon freshly cracked black pepper

1 bunch scallions, washed and roots trimmed

Cilantro-Coconut Pistou (page 242), at room temperature

**SWEET 'N' SALTY PUMPKIN SEEDS**

½ cup pumpkin seeds

½ teaspoon fine sea salt

1 teaspoon brown sugar

**TO SERVE**

2 ounces chèvre (or other soft goat cheese)

¼ to ½ cup grated Parmesan cheese

mint or cilantro leaves, for garnish

*(Continued)*

Make the flatbread dough. Blend the flour and salt in the bowl of a stand mixer fitted with the dough hook until thoroughly incorporated (about 1 minute). In the meantime, put the yeast in another bowl, and whisk in 1 cup of warm water, then 3 tablespoons of olive oil. Let the yeast rest until the liquid begins to foam, about 10 minutes; pour the mixture into the center of the flour. Using the dough hook, mix the flour and yeast solution until incorporated. Add 2¾ cups cold water to the flour, and mix again until the dough pulls together in a single, unified mass. Turn the dough out onto a lightly floured surface, and knead for 6 to 8 minutes, or until it is smooth and no longer sticky. Brush a clean stainless steel bowl with the remaining 1 tablespoon olive oil, and place the ball of dough in the bowl. Cover with a clean cloth, and let rise at room temperature until it has doubled in size.

Preheat the oven to 400°F. When the dough has risen, divide it into eight balls. On a lightly floured surface, roll out each ball into an oval shape, about 6 to 8 inches by 4 to 5 inches. (Note: The balls of dough can be individually wrapped in plastic and frozen for up to two months.) Slide the flatbreads onto baking sheets (or directly onto the oven rack), and bake for 6 to 8 minutes, just until they start browning. Or cook them on a char grill. Set the baked flatbreads aside for assembly.

Make the Oven-Roasted Pumpkin Topping. Preheat the oven to 400°F. In a large bowl, combine the olive oil, onion, garlic, mint, and cilantro. Add the pumpkin slices, and toss to coat. Season with the salt and pepper, and transfer to a baking tray. Place in the oven and cook for 20 to 25 minutes, until the pumpkin is soft. Add the whole scallions to the tray after 10 minutes, and allow to finish roasting.

While the pumpkin and scallions are roasting, prepare the Sweet 'n' Salty Pumpkin Seeds. Toast the pumpkin seeds in a sauté pan on the stove top over medium heat for about 3 minutes, tossing regularly. Add the salt and brown sugar, and cook for about 1 minute more. Add 1 teaspoon water, and cook, stirring, until the sugar is melted and the water evaporated. Spread the seeds on waxed paper to cool.

Once the pumpkin and scallions are finished roasting, remove from the oven and reduce the temperature to 375°F. To assemble the flatbreads, spread the pistou on the bread, top with the roasted pumpkin and scallions, and add dollops of chèvre. Return the assembled flatbreads to the oven and bake for about 10 minutes, until the flatbreads are warm and the goat cheese is melted. Garnish with Parmesan cheese, sweet 'n' salty pumpkin seeds, and mint or cilantro leaves.

# EGGPLANT AND PLANTAIN PARMESAN
## with Two Sauces

T wo of our favorite things in the world, plantain and eggplant, are perfect companions in this unusual dish that resides somewhere between an eggplant Parmesan and a lasagna. Add both white sauce and spicy tomato sauce, goat cheese, and mozzarella, and the result is a creamy, cheesy deliciousness that will have you hooked from the first bite.

### Serves 8 to 10

**2 large eggplants**

**1 teaspoon kosher salt**

**2 large ripe plantains**

**¼ cup olive oil, divided**

**¾ cup flour**

**1 cup White Sauce (page 110) divided into three ⅓ cup portions**

**2 cups Scotch Bonnet Tomato Sauce (page 76) divided into four ½ cup portions**

**1½ pounds fresh mozzarella, sliced into ¼-inch slices**

**1⅓ cups grated Parmesan cheese**

**8 ounces soft goat cheese**

Preheat the oven to 350°F.

Slice the eggplants into ¼-inch to ½-inch-thick rounds. Lay the eggplant slices on a rack over a rimmed sheet pan (or on several layers of paper towels). Sprinkle both sides of the eggplant rounds lightly with salt. Set aside, allowing the eggplant to release moisture for 20 to 30 minutes. While the eggplant slices are resting, prepare the remaining ingredients.

Peel the plantains and cut them into slices about 4 inches long and ½ inch thick. Warm 1 tablespoon olive oil in a sauté pan over medium-high heat, and pan fry the plantains until caramelized and cooked through (about 1 minute per side).

Rinse the purged eggplant and pat dry. Coat on both sides with flour. Warm 1 tablespoon olive oil in a sauté pan, and pan fry the eggplant slices in batches until they are golden on each side, adding more olive oil as necessary.

Assemble the ingredients like a lasagna, as follows. Spread a little of the white sauce over the bottom of an 8- to 10-inch casserole dish or cast-iron skillet. *For the first layer:* Arrange a third of the eggplant rounds in a single layer, over the white sauce. Top with a fourth of the tomato sauce, and then half the sliced mozzarella, a quarter of the plantains. Follow with a third of the remaining white sauce and ⅓ cup Parmesan cheese. *For the second layer:* Repeat the layering, this time using half the goat cheese (instead of the mozzarella). *For the third layer:* Repeat the layering, this time using the remaining mozzarella. *For the top layer:* Finish with a layer of plantains, and top with the last of the tomato sauce, the last of the goat cheese, and the final ⅓ cup Parmesan cheese.

Bake, uncovered, for 35 to 40 minutes or until the top is golden-brown and bubbly. Remove from the oven and let sit for 10 minutes before cutting and serving.

# SCOTCH BONNET TOMATO SAUCE

This recipe, which adds dimension to any dish that calls for a tomato base, is our go-to tomato sauce. Spicy and bursting with Scotch bonnet flavor, it is particularly flavorful in our Eggplant and Plantain Parmesan with Two Sauces (page 74) but is also delicious on its own as a pasta sauce. Try it when making your next vegetable lasagna, or simply toss it with the pasta of your choice for a quick and easy dinner. It will keep refrigerated for up to 1 week.

*Makes 4 cups*

2 tablespoons olive oil plus more to finish

1 small yellow onion, diced

1 Scotch bonnet pepper, chopped

4 cloves garlic, chopped

1 tablespoon fresh thyme leaves

12 medium plum tomatoes, peeled, seeded, and diced, juice reserved

1 15-ounce can good-quality whole tomatoes, chopped, juice reserved

salt and freshly cracked black pepper to taste

Heat the olive oil in a medium saucepan over medium heat. Add the onion, Scotch bonnet pepper, garlic, and thyme. Sauté for 5 minutes. Add the plum tomatoes and their juice, and cook for about 8 minutes. Add the canned tomatoes and their juice. Bring to a boil. Reduce heat to low and simmer for 20 minutes. Season with salt and pepper. Remove from the heat and, using an immersion blender, puree until smooth. Return to the heat, add a drizzle of olive oil, and adjust the seasonings as needed.

# ROASTED HEARTS OF PALM AND ARTICHOKE HEARTS DIP

Be warned: this is not a typical baked dip, but with its creamy and rich combination of flavors, it is just as delicious as one. Artichokes and hearts of palm are roasted in the oven to perfection then blended with mayonnaise, Dijon mustard, Parmesan cheese, Scotch bonnet pepper, and lime. Serve it with pita chips as a great item for predinner cocktails or a light snack.

*Serves 6*

1 15-ounce can hearts of palm

1 15-ounce can artichoke hearts

1 teaspoon paprika

2 teaspoons chopped garlic

1 tablespoon fresh thyme leaves plus 1 teaspoon for topping

salt and freshly cracked black pepper to taste

2 tablespoons olive oil

½ cup mayonnaise

2 teaspoons Dijon mustard

1 tablespoon fresh lime juice

½ cup grated Parmesan cheese plus ¼ cup for topping

½ teaspoon Scotch bonnet pepper sauce

¼ cup panko breadcrumbs

Preheat the oven to 425°F.

Drain the hearts of palm and artichoke hearts, and pat dry with a paper towel; combine them in a bowl. Season with paprika, garlic, 1 tablespoon thyme, salt, and pepper, and toss with olive oil. Spread on a sheet pan, and roast for 15 to 18 minutes until the vegetables are lightly browned.

Remove the seasoned hearts from the oven and transfer to a food processor (keep the oven on—the blended dip will go back in to brown before serving). Add the mayonnaise, Dijon mustard, lime juice, ½ cup Parmesan, Scotch bonnet pepper sauce, salt, and pepper to taste. Pulse until blended but still slightly chunky. In a small bowl combine ¼ cup Parmesan, panko breadcrumbs, and 1 teaspoon thyme. Transfer the pureed dip to a medium-sized ovenproof baking dish or bowl, and top with the Parmesan-panko mix.

Return to the oven to bake for 15 minutes or until the top is golden and the dip is bubbly.

# FIRE-ROASTED BREADFRUIT
## *with Flaked Sea Salt and Honey*

Roasted breadfruit is our absolute favorite Jamaican starch. Although finding it outside the islands might take a little effort, it's well worth seeking out. Look for it at Caribbean markets. Brought to Jamaica from Tahiti, breadfruit was thought to be easy sustenance on plantations, so trees were planted all across the islands. In the West Indies, breadfruit is typically thrown directly on an open flame or charcoal fire and roasted until the outer skin is charred and black. While the outer skin blackens, the inside steams and takes on a soft and doughy texture, like bread—hence the name. The charred exterior is peeled away, and the insides, piping hot, are topped with butter and salt. Ready-to-eat, preroasted, whole breadfruit is available for sale from street and produce vendors all across the island as a convenient grab-and-go accompaniment for any meal. When cooked over an open flame, the breadfruit takes on a delicious smoky flavor that is hard to replicate in an oven; we suggest using a charcoal barbeque grill or wood fire if available. In this unique presentation we take our love of breadfruit to higher heights with the outstanding combination of butter, sea salt, and honey. Try it for a new spin on breakfast.

### *Serves 4 to 6*

**1 breadfruit (3 to 4 pounds)**

**4 tablespoons salted butter (½ stick)**

**flaked sea salt, to taste**

**2 tablespoons Jamaican logwood honey (or any runny honey)**

Remove and discard the stalk. Using a sharp knife, cut two incisions into an X at the opposite end.

To cook directly over charcoal, preheat a charcoal grill to high. Once the coals are hot and glowing, nestle the breadfruit stem-side down in the coals, gathering as much coal around the fruit as possible. Cook, turning the breadfruit from time to time, until the skin is charred and the flesh soft, between 40 and 60 minutes depending on the size and ripeness of the fruit. You can test for doneness by inserting a skewer or knife. Once the center is soft, the breadfruit is cooked. You can follow the same procedure to cook the breadfruit over a wood fire, nestling the fruit into the hot coals.

To cook the fruit on a gas stove, place it directly on a burner lit to medium, stem-side down. Roast the bottom of the breadfruit for 30 minutes. Next, use a mitt or cloth to turn the fruit upside down on the burner, and roast for another 30 minutes. Then turn it on its side, rotating it periodically. Allow the breadfruit to cook until the exterior is black. The outside should be black and charred and the inside soft and cooked through when pierced with a knife.

If using a gas grill or oven, preheat to medium-high or 400°F. Place the breadfruit in the center rack of the oven, or the middle of the grill, away from the direct heat, and roast until well browned on the outside and soft in the center, 1 to 1½ hours.

After the breadfruit has cooled for about 30 minutes, but while it is still warm inside, hold the fruit by the stem end in your open palm on a paper towel (this can get messy). With a sharp knife and starting at the top, peel it over a garbage pail or other vessel, using a circular motion as though you were peeling an orange. Allow the skin to fall away, preventing the black char from getting on the peeled breadfruit. Alternately, you can stand the breadfruit on its top on a cutting board and cut away the skin in strips in a downward motion, starting at the stem side. Remove the center (the heart). Slice the fruit; spread liberally with butter, sprinkle with flaked sea salt, and drizzle with honey. Serve hot.

# ROASTED BREADFRUIT
## *with Sauteed Peppers,*
## *Cho Cho, and White Wine*

This is another simple and satisfying way to eat "roast breadfruit," as we call it in Jamaica. The sauté of bell peppers, onions, and cho cho in butter and wine is colorful and adds texture and a light sauce to the breadfruit, keeping the fruit moist and succulent. Delectable. This is a unique side dish that adds exotic variety to any meal, simple or grand.

*Serves 6*

1 medium breadfruit, roasted and peeled (see page 78)

1 cup julienned cho cho

4 tablespoons butter

1 cup bell pepper strips, multiple colors

½ cup sliced onions

1 teaspoon thinly slivered habanero pepper, seeds and membrane removed

4 tablespoons fresh thyme leaves, divided

salt and freshly cracked black pepper to taste

¼ cup dry white wine

sprigs of thyme for garnish (optional)

Slice the roasted breadfruit and keep it warm in a low oven while you prepare the remaining ingredients.

Bring a small pot of salted water to a boil. Add the cho cho, and cook for 5 to 6 minutes. Strain immediately and set aside.

In the meantime, melt the butter in a skillet over medium heat. Add the bell peppers, onions, habanero, and half the thyme, and sauté for five minutes or until the onions are translucent and soft. Add the cooked cho cho, and toss to coat. Add the remaining thyme, season with salt and pepper, and then add the wine. Cook for about 1 minute.

Arrange the sliced breadfruit on a platter. Pour the cho cho mixture over the breadfruit, and top with sprigs of thyme. Serve immediately.

# OMA CHEPA'S
# PUMPKIN PANCAKES

O ur lovely friend from Curacao, Dani, shared her grandmother Oma Chepa's delightful recipe for pumpkin pancakes with us. Eaten as either a sweet or a savory side dish, these versatile pancakes are yet another example of how resilient Caribbean women utilized what they had available to make complete and wholly satisfying meals. According to Dani, the art lies in finding the right heat to fry the pancakes to a "well-cooked" state on the inside without keeping them too long on the stove, to avoid making them greasy. Serve them individually as a sweet snack, or omit the sugar and eat with Caribbean dishes such as steamed callaloo, fried fish, or salt cod. Savory or sweet preparations work equally well, but we really love this recipe as a dessert, topped with cinnamon sugar, Curacao liqueur, and maybe even a scoop of ice cream.

*Serves 4*

¼ cup raisins, (optional)

1 cup dark rum, (optional)

1 pound fresh pumpkin
(about 4 cups raw, peeled
and cubed, or 1 cup cooked
and mashed)

1 teaspoon salt plus more
for seasoning

7 ounces all-purpose flour

2 teaspoons baking powder

1½ teaspoons cinnamon, divided

½ teaspoon ground allspice
(optional)

5 tablespoons granulated sugar,
divided (optional)

¼ cup milk

¼ cup coconut oil

2 eggs

vegetable oil for frying

TO SERVE (OPTIONAL):

butter

rum-raisin or vanilla ice cream

Curacao liqueur

If using, soak the raisins in the rum a couple of hours in advance.

Peel the pumpkin and remove the seeds and stringy flesh. Cut into small pieces. Fill a large saucepan with enough water to cover the pumpkin (4 to 6 cups), add 1 teaspoon salt, and bring to a boil over high heat. Add the pumpkin cubes and boil for approximately 15 minutes until soft. Mash the pumpkin with a fork or potato masher.

In a bowl, mix the flour, salt to taste, and baking powder (if you want them sweeter, add ½ teaspoon cinnamon, the allspice, and 3 tablespoons sugar). In a separate bowl, whisk together the milk, oil, and eggs. Slowly add the wet ingredients to the dry ingredients, stirring, until the mixture starts looking like pancake batter. Don't overmix; the batter should have a few lumps.

Drain the raisins (if you're using them). Stir the mashed pumpkin and rum-soaked raisins into the batter. Heat the frying oil in a large skillet over medium heat, and fry 2 to 3 pancakes at a time. Use at least 2 tablespoons batter per pancake, depending on the desired size. Serve warm.

If adding the sweet toppings, combine 1 teaspoon cinnamon with 2 tablespoons granulated sugar. Top each pancake with a pat of butter and a sprinkle of cinnamon sugar. If you wish, add a scoop of ice cream and a splash of Curacao liqueur.

# BANANA-DATE PROTEIN SMOOTHIE

Aprotein shake makes for an easy and light breakfast, especially as the summer months start to heat up. For a special treat on a leisurely afternoon, add the optional rum. The addition of rum or rum essence is inspired by our grandfather Hugh Holness, also known as "Gampi." Gampi made delicious creamy, blended, milky drinks for us as afternoon snacks. His special recipe included cinnamon, nutmeg, vanilla, and a splash of rum for "good health." This protein-rich smoothie is more nourishing than Gampi's milkshakes, but the flavors—and the wish for good health—come right from his tradition.

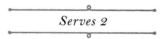

*Serves 2*

2 medium ripe bananas, frozen (peel the bananas before freezing them)

¼ cup pitted dates, soaked in hot water

2 cups chilled coconut or almond milk

2 teaspoons natural almond butter

1 scoop natural pea-protein powder

½ teaspoon cinnamon

1 teaspoon vanilla extract

1 teaspoon rum or rum extract (optional)

4 ice cubes

dash of nutmeg

Combine all ingredients in a blender, and purée on high until smooth, about 1 minute. Divide between two glasses, and top with a sprinkle of nutmeg. Best if served immediately.

# PUMPKIN CUPCAKES
## *with Cream Cheese Icing*

Cupcakes are always a treat, and unusually flavored ones are even better. We served a delectable carrot cake during the early days of our little bistro, Café Bella on Hillcrest Avenue in Kingston. These cupcakes remind us of that creation, combining carrot and pumpkin for a moist, tasty indulgence that we top with cream cheese icing. Perfect with coffee, or tea, or for any occasion that meets your fancy.

*Makes 12 cupcakes*

2 cups all-purpose flour

2 teaspoons baking powder

½ teaspoon baking soda

½ teaspoon salt

1 teaspoon cinnamon

4 eggs

1 cup granulated sugar

½ cup brown sugar

½ cup coconut oil

½ cup melted butter

2 cups grated carrots

1½ cups mashed pumpkin

1 cup shredded
unsweetened coconut

### ICING

8 ounces cream cheese,
room temperature

½ cup (4 ounces) butter,
room temperature

1 teaspoon vanilla

2 cups confectioners' sugar

shredded sweetened coconut,
for garnish

12 fresh cherries, for garnish

Preheat the oven to 350°F.

Sift together the flour, baking powder, baking soda, salt, and cinnamon. In a separate mixing bowl, combine the eggs, granulated sugar, and brown sugar; beat for about 2 minutes until well combined. Add the coconut oil and melted butter; mix well. Stir in the grated carrots, pumpkin, and coconut until well combined. Gradually add the dry ingredients, mixing well after each addition.

Line a muffin tin with paper cupcake liners; fill each cup about ⅔ full with batter. Bake for about 20 minutes or until a toothpick inserted into the center of a cupcake comes out clean. Place the muffin tin on a cooling rack. Allow the cupcakes to cool completely.

While the cupcakes cool, make the icing by beating the cream cheese and butter together until soft and combined; add the vanilla and confectioners' sugar, and beat until smooth. Ice the cooled cupcakes, and garnish each with coconut flakes and a cherry on top.

# CHAPTER 4

# GREENS, LEAVES & SHOOTS

*Callaloo, Pak Choi, Lettuce, Arugula,*
*Cabbage, Broccoli & Cauliflower*

IN THE CARIBBEAN, WE EAT GREENS IN A VARIETY OF SIMPLE AND DELICIOUS PREPARATIONS THAT ARE UNLIKE WHAT YOU'LL FIND ANYWHERE ELSE IN THE world. A hearty stew or soup made of local greens (amaranth leaves or dasheen bush, for example), starchy provisions, and salted meat or fish was a staple dish in the slave diet on almost all the islands of the West Indies. Each island has its own version of this dish with a particular mix of ingredients and seasonings: pepper pot soup, from Jamaica, uses amaranth leaves, coconut milk, salt pork, yam, and flour dumplings; Trinidadian callaloo is made with dasheen leaves, pumpkin, okra, peppers, and coconut milk; callaloo from St. Lucia incorporates crab with fish, okra, and dumplings for a truly delicious treat. (Our own nontraditional greens soup is the delicious Cream of Callaloo Soup, found on page 108.) Prepared in an intuitive manner out of necessity, these stewed greens of varying forms and interpretations represent a perfectly nutritious dish.

By far the most popular green in many islands is callaloo, a sort of umbrella term that covers a variety of different leaves depending on the island. A good pot of callaloo steamed in a little butter, oil, or coconut milk, and seasoned with garlic, onions, tomatoes, and hot pepper, is a nutritiously divine dish. Bok choy (spelled *pak choi* in Jamaica) and cabbage are prepared in a similar way. All three of these vegetables are commonly eaten in Jamaica at breakfast, lunch,

or dinner, either as part of the meal or as the meal itself when combined with salted fish and a starchy ground provision.

We also love salads, and now that locally grown organic greens are readily available everywhere in the islands, tossed salads served as a main course are common in many homes and restaurants.

In this chapter, we share our favorite nontraditional recipes for greens of all kinds: from salads to soups to updated one-pot dishes and sides that celebrate our beloved island greens.

[The meal] consists of green plantains, eddoes or yam, made into soup, with an abundance of creole peas or beans, or the eddoe leaf, the calialou, or perhaps a plant which grows indigenous, and particularly among the canes; it is known by the name of weedy-weedy; I never could learn that there was any other appellation for it: it also nearly resembles spinach....The soup is boiled very thoroughly, and forms a substantial mess, being of the consistency of thick potatoe soup. It is well spiced with country peppers; and cooked, as they cook it, is a most excellent dish indeed.

—Mrs. A. C. Carmichael, 1834

# ISLAND GREENS
## *with Avocado, Mint, and Mango*

Fresh, sweet, and bursting with flavor, this is a fabulous salad for our hot West Indian summers, when mango season is in full swing. Our biggest decision always is which variety of mango to use; usually the Julie or Bombay mango wins out as they are our favorites and each has its own distinct essence. The king of all mangoes (at least for us) is the Bombay mango—it is very sweet with a slight tartness and an almost aromatic note. The flesh is silky but firm, not mushy. Julie mangoes are sweeter with an equally firm skin, but they lack that aromatic or tart flavor. This recipe works well with whatever variety of mango you can find. The vinaigrette, which uses mango puree as the base, is particularly scrumptious. The crisp zest of fresh mint, cilantro, bell peppers, slices of mango, and feta cheese combine to make this a delicious accompaniment to any meal.

*Serves 8 to 10*

**MANGO VINAIGRETTE**

½ cup mango puree, preferably from fresh mango

⅓ cup white cane vinegar or cider vinegar

1 teaspoon Dijon mustard

1 clove garlic, diced

⅔ cup extra-virgin olive oil

salt and white pepper to taste

**ISLAND GREENS SALAD**

1 pound mixed greens

handful of combined mint and cilantro leaves

1 mango, peeled and thinly sliced

¼ small red onion, thinly sliced

1 cucumber, julienned

1 red bell pepper, julienned

1 ripe avocado, sliced

4 ounces feta cheese, crumbled

freshly cracked black pepper

salted plantain chips to garnish (page 133)

To make the mango vinaigrette, whisk together the mango puree, vinegar, mustard, and garlic. In a steady stream, gradually add the olive oil, whisking continuously, until the mixture thickens and emulsifies. Season to taste with salt and white pepper.

To assemble the salad, arrange the greens on a chilled platter or on individual plates. Garnish with the cilantro and mint, mango, onions, cucumber, bell pepper, and avocado. Top with the crumbled feta and pepper. Just before serving, drizzle the salad with a liberal amount of mango vinaigrette, and garnish with the plantain chips. (Or combine all the salad ingredients in a large bowl, reserving some feta for garnish, and season with salt and pepper. Before serving, toss with the mango vinaigrette, and garnish with plantain chips and remaining feta).

# BUTTER LETTUCE, AVOCADO, AND CHIVE SALAD

We have been making versions of this simple but divine salad since our university years. Summer holidays in Jamaica were not complete without a dinner party hosted at our parents' home in Kingston, the official fete house, hang-out spot, and liming center for a multitude of local and foreign friends during our highly social high school and college years. Vacation ended with a big dinner before we had to go our separate ways to get back to the reality of school life. When Jamaican avocado is in its high season in the summer, this clean and refreshing salad is at its best. What makes the salad so special is the step of rubbing garlic inside a wooden salad bowl, which adds pungent flavor. (Even if you don't have a wooden salad bowl, the salad will still be delicious!) Add a dusting of Parmesan or goat cheese if you want even more flavor (or, for any meat eaters, add bacon or pancetta).

*Serves 4 to 6*

**LEMON-MUSTARD VINAIGRETTE**

2 to 3 tablespoons white wine vinegar

1 tablespoon lemon juice

½ teaspoon dry mustard or 1 teaspoon Dijon mustard

½ to 1 clove garlic, minced

½ cup olive oil

salt and white pepper to taste

**BUTTER LETTUCE SALAD**

4 heads butter lettuce

1 large or 2 small avocados

1 bunch chives or 2 stalks green onion

1 large clove garlic, peeled

salt and freshly cracked black pepper to taste

Wash and dry the lettuce, and allow it to crisp in the refrigerator for at least half an hour before preparation.

Prepare the dressing by whisking together the vinegar, lemon juice, mustard, and minced garlic. In a steady stream, gradually add the olive oil, whisking continuously, until the mixture thickens and emulsifies. Season to taste with salt and white pepper. Set aside.

Peel and cube the avocado, and finely chop the green onion or chives. Smash or flatten the garlic clove with the back of a knife or spoon, and rub the garlic all over the bottom and sides of a wooden salad bowl. Once the inside of the bowl is coated with garlic, roughly tear the lettuce leaves, and add them to the bowl with most of the chives and half the avocado. Season with salt and black pepper, add the dressing, and toss gently but well, making sure the avocado stays firm. When all the leaves are coated with dressing, top with the remaining avocado and a sprinkle of chives.

# BABY GREENS
## with Lentils, Roasted Peppers, Crispy Chickpeas, and Ortanique-Thyme Vinaigrette

The combo of lentils and greens has got to be one of our favorite healthy lunches of all time; it is super easy to whip up and somehow manages to be both light and filling at the same time. Here, hearty lentils and delicate greens are tossed with a vinaigrette made from ortanique juice. Ortanique, a cross between an orange and a tangerine, was developed in Jamaica in the 1920s. (If you can't find ortaniques, oranges will do.) Topping the salad with feta and spicy Trini-style channa (crispy fried chickpeas) transforms this simple, clean dish into a wonderful lunchtime treat.

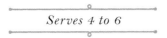

*Serves 4 to 6*

### ORTANIQUE-THYME VINAIGRETTE

1 tablespoon fresh thyme leaves

juice of 3 large ortaniques or oranges

2 tablespoons white cane vinegar or white wine vinegar

½ teaspoon salt

1 tablespoon granulated sugar

freshly cracked black pepper to taste

6 tablespoons olive oil

### BABY GREENS AND LENTIL SALAD

2 cups cooked lentils

¼ cup roasted red bell pepper strips

2 tablespoons minced red onion

salt and freshly cracked black pepper to taste

10 cups mixed baby greens

4 ounces soft goat cheese

½ cup Crispy Trini-Style Channa (page 118)

*(Continued)*

Make the vinaigrette by whisking together the thyme, ortanique/orange juice, vinegar, salt, sugar, and black pepper. In a steady stream, gradually add the olive oil, whisking continuously, until the mixture thickens and emulsifies. Set aside.

In a large salad bowl combine the lentils, bell pepper strips, and red onion. Season to taste with salt and pepper, add thyme vinaigrette to taste (just enough to saturate the lentils), and toss. Add the greens to the bowl, and toss with the lentils, adding more dressing if necessary. Any leftover dressing can be stored in the refrigerator. Serve topped with goat cheese and Crispy Trini-Style Channa.

# CRUNCHY PAK CHOI SALAD

Pak choi, although commonly consumed cooked, makes an awesome salad. This recipe is our version of one made famous by our friend the caterer Anna Kay Zaidie, who sadly is no longer with us. Every time we make this salad we think of her beautiful spirit and all the joy she created with her scrumptious food and desserts. The crunch of the raw greens, combined with a zesty ginger vinaigrette and toasted almonds, is addictive, and it works either on its own as a great meal or as an accompaniment. Feel free to use any kind of almonds—whole, slivered, raw, toasted, spiced, honey-roasted— or mix it up and replace the almonds with cashews or peanuts. You will probably have leftover vinaigrette, which you can store in the refrigerator and use with any kind of salad.

*Serves 4 to 6*

**SESAME-GINGER VINAIGRETTE**

¼ cup sesame oil

½ cup rice wine vinegar

2 tablespoons water

1 tablespoon soy sauce

1 to 1½ tablespoons grated fresh ginger

1 clove garlic, peeled and smashed

⅔ tablespoon agave nectar or honey

salt and freshly cracked black pepper to taste

**PAK CHOI SALAD**

1 pack ramen noodles

½ cup almonds

1 pound pak choi

1 large carrot

1 yellow bell pepper

2 green onions or scallions, chopped

salt and freshly cracked black pepper to taste

Preheat an oven or toaster oven to 250°F.

Combine all vinaigrette ingredients in a bowl, whisk, and set aside.

Break up the ramen noodles into small pieces, and toast them on a baking sheet until golden and crisp, about 10 minutes. If desired, toast raw almonds in the oven or on the stove top until lightly browned; leave them whole, or gently crush them into pieces with a rolling pin or the bottom of a sturdy frying pan.

Separate the pak choi leaves, wash them, and pat dry. Gather the leaves into a bunch, and slice them thinly crosswise (across the veins) from leaf to stem, using both the white and the green parts. Julienne the carrot and bell pepper to a similar size.

Combine the pak choi, carrot, bell pepper, and green onion in a bowl. Add the toasted noodles and half the toasted almonds. Toss the ingredients together with about half the vinaigrette; season with salt and pepper to taste. If the salad needs more dressing, feel free to add more. Sprinkle the reserved almonds over the top, and serve.

# ARUGULA
## *with Plantain and Parmesan*

Arugula is one of our favorite greens, and the organic variety we get in Jamaica is complex, with an incredibly intense peppery flavor, a firm stalk, and a sturdy texture. It makes a delightful base for a main-course salad, especially paired with sweet, ripe plantain and the sharp bite of Parmesan. With its citrusy honey-Dijon vinaigrette, this salad makes us think of long and leisurely lunches in the countryside. It would be a natural to serve alfresco at a summertime-in-Provence-themed meal: imagine a beautiful table loaded with fresh flowers, a bottle of crisp rosé, a basket of warm, cheesy Coco Bread (page 161), bowls of olives, Spicy Red Pepper Pesto (page 39), Tomato Choka (page 40), and rounded off with an indulgent dessert of coconut Gizzadas (page 201).

### Serves 2

**HONEY-DIJON VINAIGRETTE**

1 teaspoon Dijon mustard

1 teaspoon honey

1 tablespoon white balsamic vinegar

1 tablespoon sour orange juice

1 clove garlic, peeled and smashed but left uncut

2 tablespoons olive oil

2 tablespoons fresh basil chiffonade

salt to taste

**ARUGULA SALAD**

1 tablespoon olive oil

1 cup cubed ripe plantain

5 cups torn arugula

sea salt and freshly cracked black pepper to taste

½ cup shaved Parmesan cheese

To prepare the vinaigrette, combine the mustard, honey, balsamic vinegar, and orange juice in a small bowl with the smashed garlic, and whisk until combined. Add the olive oil one teaspoon at a time, whisking after each addition until the dressing is thick and emulsified. Stir in the basil leaves, and season with salt. Allow the vinaigrette to rest for at least 1 hour at room temperature.

For the salad, warm the olive oil in a medium sauté pan over medium heat for about 1 minute. Add the plantain, and sauté until golden-brown, about 4 minutes. Remove the plantain cubes from the pan and spread them on a paper towel, allowing them to cool slightly.

Combine the arugula and plantain in a medium-sized salad bowl, season with salt and pepper, and toss lightly with the vinaigrette to taste. Top with shaved Parmesan and serve.

# ISLAND GODDESS KALE COBB SALAD

There is something supremely satisfying and old school about a classic Cobb salad. In our book, anything that contains both avocado and cheese must be a hit! We also love green goddess dressing, but this version is very different from the California original. Instead of the classic combo of mayonnaise, herbs, lemon, and anchovy, our island goddess dressing uses a deliciously creamy combination of ginger, tahini, honey, and citrus. It freshens up the traditional Cobb with the addition of some island flavor and ingredients: a base of hearty kale topped with our beloved avocado, toasted cashews, chopped papaya, cheese, and fresh coconut "croutons."

*Serves 2*

### COCONUT "CROUTONS"

1 dry coconut, drained, meat removed, and cut into 1-inch cubes (for tips on working with a whole coconut, see recipe for Coconut Choka, page 41)

1 tablespoon olive oil

sea salt to taste

### ISLAND GODDESS DRESSING

2 tablespoons olive oil

juice of 2 limes

juice of 1 orange

2 tablespoons chopped parsley

2 tablespoons chopped chives

1 teaspoon chopped ginger

1 teaspoon chopped garlic

handful of cilantro leaves

1 tablespoon tahini

1 teaspoon honey

salt and freshly cracked black pepper to taste

### KALE SALAD

4 cups washed and torn kale

1 small papaya, seeded, peeled, and diced

½ cup cashews, toasted and chopped

1 large or 2 small avocados, sliced

½ cup cheese of choice (we like ricotta salata or burrata)

*(Continued)*

Preheat the oven to 375°F.

Toss the cubed coconut with 1 tablespoon olive oil. Season with sea salt, spread on a baking sheet, and roast until golden-brown, about 10 to 15 minutes.

While the coconut croutons are roasting, make the dressing. Combine all the dressing ingredients except the salt and pepper in a food processor, and blend until smooth. Season to taste with salt and pepper. Thin with a little water as necessary.

Arrange the kale in two bowls. Top with papaya, cashews, avocado, cheese, and coconut croutons. Serve with the Island Goddess Dressing on the side or drizzled over the top.

# ROMAINE HEART SALAD

Avocado, roasted corn, toasted almonds, blue cheese, tomatoes, and scallion provide a veritable cornucopia of texture and flavor atop this salad's crunchy base. Easy to assemble, it would serve as an excellent plated first course for a dinner party; it would work equally well at a buffet served on a platter. The lemon-dill dressing is so yummy that you will want to use it for many other purposes. Crudité platters, chips, wraps, sandwiches—all would be greatly enhanced with the addition of this divine dressing.

*Serves 4*

### HARDO BREAD CROUTONS

5 slices Jamaican hardo bread
(or firm white bread),
cut into ½-inch cubes

¼ cup olive oil

4 sprigs thyme, chopped

1 clove garlic, finely minced

sea salt and freshly cracked
black pepper to taste

### LEMON-DILL RANCH DRESSING

2 to 3 stalks scallions or chives

¼ cup dill leaves

1 tablespoon Dijon mustard

2 cloves garlic

¾ cup mayonnaise

½ cup Greek yogurt

½ cup sour cream

2 tablespoons lemon
or lime juice

1 tablespoon olive oil

1 teaspoon lemon or lime zest

2 teaspoons salt

1 teaspoon freshly cracked
black pepper

### ROMAINE HEART SALAD

2 heads romaine lettuce, halved,
or 1 head iceberg, quartered

½ cup diced scallion

¾ cup roasted corn kernels

½ cup diced tomato

½ cup toasted almonds

1 cup diced avocado

¾ cup crumbled blue cheese

2 tablespoons chopped
fresh dill for garnish

*(Continued)*

To make the croutons, preheat the oven to 400°F. Toss the bread with the olive oil, thyme, garlic, salt, and pepper. Spread on a baking tray. Bake for 20 to 25 minutes until browned on the outside and crispy.

To make the dressing, blend all the dressing ingredients together in a food processor. Hold in the refrigerator until ready to use.

To make the salad, place half a head of romaine (or a wedge of iceberg) onto an individual serving plate. Spoon a generous amount of dressing over the middle of the lettuce, drizzling it across the plate. Top with 1 to 2 tablespoons of each of the following: scallion, roasted corn, tomato, and almonds, allowing the ingredients to fall onto the plate. Add croutons and avocado, sprinkle with 3 to 4 tablespoons blue cheese, and garnish with chopped fresh dill.

# SPICED COOKED CABBAGE

Cabbage is a popular vegetable choice for many island people. We shred and serve it raw as a salad on the side of hot meals, we make coleslaw, and we prepare it for breakfast, usually served with some boiled food ("food" is a mix of boiled dumplings, green banana, yam, or sweet potato) and cooked saltfish. In this recipe, we explore a slightly different preparation, one that's full of Indian spices for a novel take on this usually bland vegetable.

*Serves 4 to 6*

2 tablespoons coconut oil

2 tablespoons butter

½ cup chopped onion

3 to 4 medium cloves garlic, chopped

1 tablespoon chopped ginger

1 teaspoon turmeric

1 teaspoon ground cumin

1 teaspoon ground coriander

1 teaspoon garam masala

1 medium head white cabbage, shredded

½ medium head red cabbage, shredded

salt and freshly cracked black pepper to taste

cilantro sprigs, for garnish

Heat the oil and butter in a large sauté pan or heavy-bottomed saucepan over medium-high heat. When the pan is hot, add the onions and cook until translucent, about 3 minutes. Add the garlic and ginger, and cook for about 1 minute, stirring, until aromatic. Add the turmeric, cumin, coriander, and garam masala, and sauté for 1 minute, stirring to incorporate into the onions, garlic, and ginger. Add the shredded cabbage, and season with salt and pepper. Stir to combine the ingredients and distribute the spices evenly into the cabbage. Reduce the heat to medium, and cook for about 10 minutes, stirring occasionally, until the cabbage is soft. Serve immediately, garnished with fresh sprigs of cilantro.

# CALLALOO
# IN COCONUT MILK

Callaloo is a leafy, spinach-like vegetable that has a distinctively Caribbean origin. The *Amaranthus viridis* variety, found in Jamaica and better known as Chinese spinach or Indian kale, should not be confused with the callaloo found in the eastern Caribbean, which refers to the leaves of the dasheen plant. Collard greens or curly-leaf kale makes a good substitute. In this recipe we steam the callaloo in coconut milk, ginger, and garlic for a clean-tasting and wholesome side dish.

*Serves 6*

1 tablespoon coconut oil

2 tablespoons chopped onion

1 teaspoon minced ginger

1 teaspoon minced garlic

1 teaspoon slivered Scotch bonnet pepper (or habanero)

1 medium bell pepper, sliced into strips

2 tablespoons thyme leaves

1 bunch callaloo, cleaned and chopped (or substitute collard greens or curly-leaf kale)

¼ cup canned coconut milk

salt and freshly cracked black pepper to taste

Heat the coconut oil in a sauté pan over medium heat. Add the onion, ginger, garlic, and Scotch bonnet pepper, and sauté for about 3 minutes. Add the bell pepper and thyme, and cook for another 3 minutes. Add the chopped callaloo leaves, stirring well to combine. Add the coconut milk, and season with salt and pepper. Reduce the heat to low and cover the pan, allowing the callaloo to steam for about 10 minutes, until it turns bright green and is cooked through.

# LEEK, BRIE, AND THYME SOUP AU GRATIN

## *with Aged Caribbean Rum*

A s young restaurant owners when we opened our first fine-dining establishment back in 1998, we had no idea what to expect; nor were we sure what our customers would want to eat, so we allowed ourselves to be guided by our own palates, passions, and cravings. And we have *always* had a passion for French onion soup. When we decided to put onion soup au gratin on the menu, we knew we needed to create a version that would be delicious and unique, but easy enough to execute for our daily dinner menu. The result was this delightful twist on traditional French onion: the subtle combination of leeks with the slight sweetness of the aged Caribbean rum and the richness of melted brie makes for a deeply satisfying and filling soup. The medley is pureed until creamy and smooth and topped with crunchy, cheesy toasted bread. It became a number-one seller on our menu—and we guarantee it will be just as well loved at your table.

*Serves 4*

1 tablespoon butter

1 small onion, minced

1 stalk celery, diced

1 small carrot, diced

5 cups thinly sliced leeks, white parts only

2 tablespoons fresh thyme leaves plus more leaves and sprigs for finishing

2 teaspoons granulated sugar

salt to taste

¼ to ½ cup aged rum (10 to 15 years old), sherry, or sweet white wine

4 slices whole-grain country-style bread or 1 whole-grain baguette, sliced on the bias into rounds

8 ounces Brie cheese, rind removed and interior cubed, plus 1 ounce for finishing

¼ cup grated Gruyere cheese

white pepper to taste

*(Continued)*

Melt the butter in a heavy saucepan over medium-low heat. Add the onions, celery, and carrot, and cook, stirring, for about 5 minutes until the vegetables are tender and the onions are translucent but not browned. Add the leeks, 2 tablespoons of thyme, and sugar; stir until the leeks are well coated with butter. Sprinkle with a little salt, cover, and cook over low heat until the leeks are soft, about 10 minutes. Uncover and continue to cook, stirring from time to time, for 5 to 10 minutes more until the leeks are golden; do not allow them to brown.

Stir in the rum, and cook for about 1 minute. Add 6 cups water. Bring to a boil. Reduce the heat to low, and simmer uncovered for about 20 minutes. Cover and simmer for another 20 minutes.

When the simmer time is almost over, preheat the oven to 400°F. Top each slice of bread with a pat of brie, a sprinkle of Gruyere, and a few leaves of thyme, and bake on a foil-covered baking sheet until the cheese is melted and bubbly, about 6 minutes.

When the soup has finished simmering, remove from the heat and puree with an immersion blender, or puree in batches in a stand blender and return to the pot. Stir in 8 ounces of brie, mixing until the cheese is melted and the soup creamy. Add white pepper to taste, and more salt as necessary.

Ladle the soup into four crocks or soup bowls. Top each with a toasted bread garnish and a sprig of thyme, and serve immediately.

# CREAM OF CALLALOO SOUP

Soups featuring callaloo are found throughout our region. This exotic and delightful version was a very popular weekly special at our restaurant, Café Bella. It incorporates many typical island ingredients—callaloo leaves, green banana, green papaya, ginger, garlic, brown sugar, and coconut milk—in a somewhat unconventional way. The result is heavenly: savory and creamy with hints of ginger, cilantro, and coconut, served, if you wish, over starchy green bananas.

*Serves 4*

1 tablespoon butter

1 tablespoon plus 2 teaspoons olive oil, divided

1 large yellow onion, chopped

1-inch slice ginger, peeled and minced

3 large cloves garlic, chopped, plus ½ teaspoon minced garlic

6 okra pods, sliced into 1-inch slices

1 cup cubed green papaya

1 tablespoon brown sugar

4 cups chopped, washed callaloo (or substitute spinach)

salt and freshly cracked black pepper to taste

1 15-ounce can coconut milk

1 bunch cilantro, chopped, with some reserved for garnish

1 bunch thyme

6 boiled green bananas (page 275), sliced (optional)

unsweetened coconut flakes, for garnish

Heat a large heavy saucepan or soup pot over medium heat. Add the butter and 1 tablespoon olive oil. When the butter is melted, add the onion, ginger, and 3 cloves of chopped garlic, and sauté for about 2 minutes, until the onions are translucent. Add the okra, green papaya, and brown sugar. Cook, stirring frequently, for about 1 minute. Add the callaloo, season with salt and pepper, and cook for 2 minutes. Add the coconut milk, cilantro (reserving some for a garnish), thyme, and 1½ cups water, and bring to a boil. Reduce heat, cover, and simmer 20 to 30 minutes.

When the soup is almost done, warm the remaining 2 teaspoons olive oil in a small sauté pan over medium-high heat. Add ½ teaspoon minced garlic and the boiled green bananas. Sauté about 5 minutes or until warmed through, making sure to avoid overbrowning the garlic.

Remove the soup from the heat, remove the thyme, and puree until smooth, either with an immersion blender or in a stand blender in batches. Return to the pan to heat through, and adjust seasonings.

Place a spoonful of sautéed bananas in the bottom of four soup bowls, and ladle the callaloo puree over the bananas. Garnish with coconut flakes and cilantro.

# AUNT MARJORIE'S CALLALOO GRATIN

We have prepared this versatile green in a multitude of ways over our years in catering, but our favorite is the callaloo and cheese gratin we enjoy every Christmas at our Aunt Marjorie's caroling party. It may be because the holidays in the Caribbean are such a joyful and festive time, or it may be because the dish is flavored with the memories of so many Christmases lovingly shared with old friends and family singing our hearts out. Whatever the reason, Aunt Marjorie's callaloo gratin is unforgettable. Serve this dish at your own holiday feast, or any time you crave a warm comfort food.

*Serves 6 to 8*

1 medium onion

4 cloves garlic

1 Scotch bonnet pepper

4 stalks scallion

2 to 3 plum tomatoes

2 tablespoons chopped fresh thyme

2 tablespoons butter

10 to 12 cups chopped callaloo (about 2 pounds whole leaves), or substitute kale

1½ teaspoons salt

½ teaspoon freshly cracked black pepper

2 cups White Sauce (page 110)

1¼ cups grated sharp cheddar cheese, plus more for topping (optional)

½ cup grated Parmesan cheese, plus more for topping (optional)

Preheat the oven to 350°F.

Roughly chop the onion, garlic, Scotch bonnet pepper, scallion, and tomatoes.

Heat a large pot with a lid over medium heat; add the butter. Once the butter is melted, add the chopped vegetables and the thyme and cook, stirring occasionally, about 5 minutes or until soft. Add the callaloo, and stir to combine all the ingredients. Add the salt and pepper. Add ¼ cup water, and cover the pot. Turn the heat to low and steam the vegetables for 7 to 10 minutes, checking the pot and stirring occasionally. Once the callaloo is soft, turn off the heat. Add the white sauce and the cheeses, and mix well to coat the vegetables, seasoning with more salt and pepper if desired.

Transfer the mixture into a deep baking dish. If you wish, sprinkle more cheese on top. Bake the callaloo for 25 to 30 minutes. The gratin should be firm and moist, not dry or runny. Remove from the oven, and allow to set up for 10 minutes before serving.

# WHITE SAUCE

For extra flavor and depth, our version of this classic sauce adds seasonings in the form of scallion, onion, and garlic to the flour roux.

2 tablespoons butter

¼ onion, minced

1 teaspoon fine-diced garlic

2 teaspoons fresh thyme leaves

1 teaspoon chopped scallion

2 teaspoons flour

2 cups milk

1 cup whipping cream

salt and freshly cracked black pepper to taste

Melt the butter in a saucepan over medium-low heat. Add the onion, garlic, thyme, and scallion, and cook, stirring, for 1 minute. Add the flour; cook, stirring continuously, for about 2 minutes until the flour is cooked through. Gradually add the milk and the cream, whisking as you do, and cook, still stirring, until the sauce thickens. Season with salt and pepper.

# ONE-POT PIE

## *with Callaloo, Plantain, Goat Cheese, and Cornmeal Crust*

P ot pie has got to be one of the most satisfying and mouthwatering comfort foods ever created. In this version, we pair goat cheese with Jamaican classics like plantain, corn, and callaloo in a cornmeal-Parmesan crust. We love that it plays on the Caribbean tradition of "one pot" cooking; with savory fillings encased in a pastry crust, it is also a nod to the ever-popular Jamaican patty.

*Serves 6*

### CORNMEAL-PARMESAN CRUST

1 stick cold butter

1½ cups all-purpose flour plus more for rolling

½ cup yellow cornmeal

½ teaspoon sea salt

¾ cup Parmesan cheese

### FILLINGS (CALLALOO AND PLANTAIN)

2 tablespoons olive oil, divided

2 cloves garlic, diced, divided

1 small yellow onion, chopped, divided

2 tablespoons chopped red bell pepper, divided

1 or 2 Scotch bonnet peppers, seeded and diced, divided

2 tablespoons fresh thyme leaves, divided

2 scallions, diced, divided

4 cups callaloo chiffonade

½ cup heavy cream, divided

2 cups cubed ripe plantain (1-inch cubes)

salt and freshly cracked black pepper to taste

½ cup canned corn kernels

2 tablespoons chopped cilantro

### SAUCE

1 tablespoon butter

1 tablespoon chopped scallion

¼ cup dry white wine

½ cup heavy cream

½ cup whole milk

1 tablespoon fresh thyme leaves

2 tablespoons grated Parmesan cheese

### FOR ASSEMBLY

8 ounces fresh mozzarella cheese, cut into ½-inch cubes

½ cup grated Parmesan cheese, divided, some reserved for the top of the pie

½ cup goat cheese

1 egg, beaten

*(Continued)*

TO MAKE THE CRUST: Cut the chilled butter into very small pieces. Mix the flour, cornmeal, and sea salt in a food processor; add the butter, and pulse until the mixture is a sandy texture that resembles breadcrumbs. Transfer to a bowl, and add half the Parmesan cheese, mixing with a fork or knife until combined. Measure out 4 tablespoons of ice-cold water, and add to the flour mixture a little at a time until the dough sticks together, mixing just long enough to create a mass. Do not overmix. Wrap the dough in plastic wrap or place in a plastic bag; hold it in the refrigerator for at least 20 minutes. Remove one hour before use to bring to room temperature.

TO MAKE THE CALLALOO FILLING: Heat 1 tablespoon olive oil in a large sauté pan over medium heat. Add half the garlic, onion, bell pepper, Scotch bonnet pepper, thyme, and scallion; cook for about 5 minutes until soft. Add the callaloo and cook down for about 8 minutes, until it turns bright green. Stir in ¼ cup heavy cream. Remove from heat and allow to cool. Season with salt and pepper to taste.

TO MAKE THE PLANTAIN FILLING: Heat 1 tablespoon olive oil in another sauté pan over medium heat, and add the remaining garlic, onion, bell pepper, Scotch bonnet pepper, thyme, and scallion; sauté for about 1 minute. Add the plantain and cook, stirring occasionally, for another 5 minutes. Add the corn and cilantro, and sauté for another minute. Add ¼ cup heavy cream, and season to taste with salt and pepper.

TO MAKE THE SAUCE: Melt 1 tablespoon butter in a saucepan over medium heat. Add 1 tablespoon chopped scallion. Add the white wine, and cook, stirring, until the wine is evaporated. Stir in the heavy cream and whole milk. Bring to a simmer. Allow to simmer for about 5 minutes, until the sauce is reduced. Stir in the thyme and Parmesan cheese.

TO ASSEMBLE THE POT PIE: Preheat the oven to 375°F. On a lightly floured surface, roll out two-thirds of the pastry into a large circle, and use it to line the base and sides of an 8-inch pie dish or casserole. Layer half the plantain mixture in the bottom, then distribute half the mozzarella and a sprinkle of Parmesan on top of that. Cover with half the callaloo mixture, then half the goat cheese and more Parmesan. Repeat the layers in the same order with the remaining plantain filling, mozzarella, Parmesan, callaloo filling, goat cheese, and more Parmesan. Pour the sauce over the assembled pie.

On a lightly floured surface, roll out the rest of the pastry into an 8-inch round; lay it on top of the pie, trimming away any excess pastry and crimping the edges to seal well. Score an X in the middle of the top crust with a sharp knife. Brush the top of the pie with the beaten egg, scatter with the rest of the Parmesan, and chill for at least 20 minutes. Bake for 30 to 35 minutes until the pastry is golden-brown on top. Allow to cool in the pan for 10 minutes before serving.

GREENS, LEAVES & SHOOTS

# BROCCOLI, CAULIFLOWER, AND CASHEW TEMPURA
## *with Citrus-Miso-Rum Glaze*

The novelty of crisp-fried tempura cashews is something you won't soon forget. We jazz up our tempura batter by preparing it with chilled coconut milk. As if that isn't enough, the piping-hot veggies and nuts are drizzled straight from the pan with a delightful citrus-miso-rum glaze. Fair warning: the combination of flavors and textures in this dish is unforgettably addictive and can easily become an obsession.

*Serves 4*

### MISO GLAZE

½ **cup sake or sherry**

½ **cup dark rum**

6 **tablespoons white or yellow miso paste**

1 **cup orange juice**

4 **tablespoons chopped cilantro**

2 **tablespoons brown sugar**

4 **teaspoons dark sesame oil**

### TEMPURA

4 **cups coconut oil or vegetable oil**

1¼ **cups all-purpose flour**

2 **tablespoons cornstarch**

½ **teaspoon baking powder**

¼ **teaspoon salt**

1 **can refrigerated coconut milk**

2 **cups broccoli florets**

2 **cups cauliflower florets**

1 **cup raw cashews**

¼ **cup chopped scallion**

To make the miso glaze, combine the sake and rum in a small saucepan, and bring to a boil over high heat. Boil for about 40 seconds or until the liquid is reduced by half, being careful to avoid reducing it too much. Reduce the heat to low, and whisk in the miso paste, orange juice, cilantro, and brown sugar. Continue whisking over low heat without letting the mixture boil. When the sugar has dissolved, remove from heat and whisk in the sesame oil. Allow the mixture to cool.

Heat the coconut oil in a deep-fryer or a wok to about 350°F.

To make the tempura batter, mix together the flour, cornstarch, baking powder, and salt; stir in the cold coconut milk until just combined. Don't overmix—a few lumps are okay.

Working in batches, dip the broccoli florets in the batter to coat, then carefully place them in the hot oil. Turn the florets from time to time to ensure that they cook evenly on all sides. Fry for 1 to 2 minutes or until the tempura coating is crisp and golden-brown. Remove with a slotted spoon, transferring them to a plate lined with paper towels. Repeat the process with the cauliflower florets, and then the cashews.

To serve, you can either combine the still-warm vegetables and cashews with the chopped scallion in a bowl and toss them in just enough glaze to coat; or assemble the veggies on a platter, sprinkle fried cashews over the top, and drizzle with the glaze and chopped scallions. Serve immediately with any extra glaze on the side.

# CHAPTER 5

# BEANS, PULSES & LEGUMES

*Black Beans, Gungo Peas, Chickpeas, Lentils,*
*Red Peas & Black-Eyed Peas*

With the limited choice of proteins available to them and the ease with which plant life thrived in the warm, wet weather, glorious sunshine, and nutritious island soil, it's no surprise that our ancestors relied on beans and pulses to add needed protein to their diets. In the traditional African diet, pulses were consumed with regularity—they were relatively easy to prepare, were accessible, possessed a good shelf life, and were satisfying and hearty. All throughout the Caribbean islands, beans and pulses appear in a myriad of familiar ways that pay homage to our African ancestry: they are paired with rice in dishes like Trinidadian pelau, Jamaican stew peas, or Cuban black beans and rice, put into hearty stews and soups like gungo pea soup, pounded and formed into fritters like akkra, or eaten alongside a flatbread like Trinidadian doubles.

Jamaica's red pea soup ranks on the top of our list of heavenly comfort foods. It is actually made with kidney beans, not peas. (In true Jamaican fashion, all beans and pulses are called "peas," even if they are actually beans.) Red pea soup is always on the menu at Saturday soup, a tradition that many islanders still follow of friends and family dropping by for a lunch that always runs into late afternoon and is accompanied by lots of noise, laughter, and good-humored debate about island life. Our take on this standby is on page 122—we hope it will find its way into your family traditions, too.

> [Slaves] cultivate a variety of the pulse tribe in their grounds—Lima beans, the common kidney, or French bean.... The gub-a-gub, or black-eyed pea, is also excellent; and the value of all these is the same as the Lima bean.... The pigeon-pea is an uncommonly nice vegetable: its cultivation is easy, and every estate is full of pigeon-pea bushes....They bear so richly, that [one] can pick in ten minutes as many peas as would serve for soup for dinner to four or five grown persons.
>
> —Mrs. A. C. Carmichael, 1834

# CRISPY TRINI-STYLE CHANNA

During our childhood years spent living in Trinidad, channa was one of our favorite snacks, and it still is today, some thirty years later. Fried chickpeas that are seasoned with pepper, spices, and chadon beni (culantro), channa is sold in every shop or grocery store across the island. It is downright delicious. Spicy, crunchy, and salty, channa is a superb substitute for nuts at a lime (a social gathering involving drinks).

*Serves 6*

1 pound dried chickpeas

6 cloves garlic

½-inch piece ginger, peeled

1 Scotch bonnet pepper, pith and seeds removed

¼ cup chopped culantro (or cilantro)

1 tablespoon salt

1 teaspoon lime zest

1 cup vegetable oil

Soak the chickpeas overnight in water, making sure that all peas are submerged.

Drain the chickpeas and pat them dry with a paper towel.

To make the seasoning mix, combine the garlic, ginger, Scotch bonnet pepper, culantro, salt, and lime zest in a food processor. Pulse until the mixture forms a fine paste. Alternatively, smash the ingredients together in a mortar and pestle. Transfer to a large bowl.

Heat the oil in a deep sauté pan over medium-low heat. Once the oil is hot, working in batches, add the chickpeas, and deep fry until golden-brown, about 5 to 6 minutes. Remove the peas from the oil, and place them on paper towels to drain for a minute or so. Toss them in the seasoning mix. Allow to cool. Store in an airtight container for an easy party snack.

# CURRIED CHICKPEAS
## *with Mango Chutney*

Curried chickpeas make an easy, low-maintenance lunch or dinner, and are a go-to when we don't want to think about what to cook. We love adding lots of herbs and spices to our curries, but once you've prepared your ingredients, the dish itself comes together with little fuss or fancy technique. Our special touch of swirling in mango chutney at the end adds a slight sweetness that complements the savoriness. Serve a generous portion of chickpeas over a mound of basmati or jasmine rice, top with toasted coconut and cashews, and you have yourself a meal that will never fail to satisfy.

*Serves 6*

3 tablespoons butter or vegetable oil

1 onion, diced

3 cloves garlic, diced

2 teaspoons grated ginger

1 tablespoon turmeric or curry powder

1 teaspoon ground cumin

1 teaspoon ground coriander

1 teaspoon chili powder

3 cans chickpeas, drained

¼ cup coconut milk

¼ cup yogurt or heavy cream

2 tablespoons tomato paste

salt and freshly cracked black pepper to taste

2 tablespoons mango chutney (purchased or from recipe on page 240)

3 tablespoons chopped mint

3 tablespoons chopped cilantro

3 to 4 tablespoons chopped cashew nuts

4 tablespoons unsweetened coconut flakes, toasted

Heat the butter or oil in a saucepan over medium-high heat. Add the onions, garlic, and ginger, and cook for about 3 minutes until soft and fragrant. Add the turmeric or curry powder, cumin, coriander, and chili powder, and cook for 2 minutes. Add the chickpeas, and stir to coat them in the seasonings. Add the coconut milk, yogurt or cream, tomato paste, and a little water. Season with salt and pepper. Bring to a boil, then reduce the heat, cover, and simmer for 15 to 20 minutes, adding some water if the sauce dries out. After about 15 minutes, swirl in the mango chutney, mint, and cilantro, and cook for another 5 minutes.

Serve with a piping-hot bowl of jasmine or basmati rice, and top with chopped cashews and toasted coconut.

# CHICKPEAS
## *with Cilantro and Coconut*

We first ate this delicious dish at a southern Indian restaurant, where we were told that these piping-hot, perfectly spiced chickpeas are served in brown paper cones as a beachside snack in certain parts of India. From the minute they appeared, we knew we were headed to the magical land of culinary bliss! This dish features so many beloved spices and ingredients that are also common to the Caribbean islands—grated coconut, green mango, fresh cilantro—that we had to create our own version. Whether taken to the beach for a picnic or eaten straight out of the pot, it's simply perfect.

*Serves 2*

1 tablespoon coconut oil

2 small red chili peppers (whole)

½ medium yellow onion, chopped

2 Scotch bonnet peppers, coarsely chopped

1 tablespoon diced fresh ginger

½ teaspoon chili powder

¼ teaspoon turmeric

1 10-ounce can chickpeas, drained and rinsed

salt to taste

2 tablespoons chopped cilantro, some reserved for garnish

½ "turned" (not quite ripe) mango, peeled and grated

½ "turned" papaya, peeled and grated

2 tablespoons grated dry coconut (unsweetened)

4 limes, cut into wedges

In a sauté pan, heat the coconut oil over medium heat. Add the red chili pods, onion, Scotch bonnet pepper, ginger, chili powder, and turmeric. Cook for about 2 minutes. Add the chickpeas, and sauté until all the ingredients are combined and the chickpeas are well coated with seasonings. Reduce the heat to low, and cook for 2 minutes more. Season to taste with salt. Stir in the cilantro, reserving some for a garnish. Serve topped with the grated mango and papaya, coconut, fresh cilantro, and lime wedges.

# RED PEA PUREE
## *with Avocado*

Every time she eats red pea soup, Michelle is reminded of 1992's Hurricane Andrew. Stranded in Miami, she sought out Janie and Peter Trench, friends who are truly like family. To stay safe, the Trench family, with Michelle in tow, relocated with "bag and pan" to the home of fellow Jamaicans living in Miami. Properly secured and barricaded in, these seasoned hurricane veterans prepared to wait out the storm… with a simmering pot of red pea soup on the fire. As the winds howled Michelle ate what she calls one of the best dinners—and best red pea soups—of her life: rich, filling, and made even more decadent with chopped avocado on top. Despite the gale-force winds whistling outside and her trepidation at being without family, she was comforted to the tips of her toes—not only by the amazing generosity of our fellow Jamaicans who took her in, but by the salty, creamy deliciousness that is Jamaican red pea soup.

### *Serves 6*

1½ cups dried kidney beans (also known as "red peas")

1 tablespoon coconut oil or vegetable oil

1 onion, chopped

2 stalks scallion, chopped

3 cloves garlic, peeled and smashed

1 teaspoon diced ginger

1 teaspoon diced pimiento pepper

¾ cup chopped pumpkin

1 carrot, chopped

1½ tablespoons chopped fresh thyme

3 quarts vegetable stock or water

1 whole Scotch bonnet pepper

1 potato, diced

⅔ cup coconut cream

2 teaspoons salt

freshly cracked black pepper to taste

1 avocado, diced

To shorten the cooking time, do a "quick soak": Rinse and sort the beans, place them in a large pot, and cover them with water by 2 inches. Bring the beans to a boil over high heat, boil them for 2 to 3 minutes, turn off the heat, and allow the beans to soak in the hot water for 2 to 3 hours.

Heat the coconut oil in a soup pot or large saucepan over medium heat. Add the onion, scallion, garlic, ginger, and pimiento, and sauté for about 4 minutes until fragrant. Add the pumpkin, carrot, and thyme, and cook for another 2 minutes. Drain the kidney beans. Add them and the vegetable stock or water to the pot, and bring to a boil. Reduce the heat to low, add the Scotch bonnet pepper, and cook for about 1 hour, until the peas are soft. Stir in the potato, coconut cream, salt, and pepper, and cook for another 20 minutes. Once the cooking is complete, remove the pepper and discard. Use an immersion blender to puree the soup until smooth, or transfer the soup in batches to a blender, and puree. Make sure all the ingredients are combined and no lumps remain. Thin the pureed soup by adding a bit of water if necessary.

Return the puree to the pot, simmer for a further 10 minutes, and adjust the seasonings. To serve, ladle into bowls, and top with avocado.

NOTE: We love to serve our red pea soup with thick slabs of buttered Jamaican hardo bread on the side. If you can't find hardo bread, any firm white bakery bread would be great.

# BLACK BEAN PLANTAIN BURGER WITH PIKLIZ

A great veggie burger is not always easy to come by, so we often make our own. We wanted to create a burger that would be dense enough to pan fry without falling apart and that would hold together when either served in a bun and mounded with toppings or eaten on its own. Besides the fact that black beans and plantain are a classic Caribbean flavor combination, the starchy ripe plantain makes a great binder for these yummy burgers. They are made even better with the addition of our fresh Red Onion, Tomato, and Habanero Relish (page 241) and the kick of the spicy Haitian Pikliz (page 229). We like to serve ours without a bun and with a salad on the side, but you can also serve it as a burger topped with avocado slices and Pineapple Pepper Sauce (page 247).

*Serves 4*

2 teaspoons plus 1½ tablespoons coconut oil plus more for pan frying the patties

1 cup chopped ripe plantain

1 can black beans, drained and rinsed

¼ cup oats

2 tablespoons finely chopped cilantro

2 tablespoons chopped scallion

1 tablespoon fresh lime juice

½ teaspoon minced Scotch bonnet pepper

salt and freshly cracked black pepper to taste

4 ounces goat cheese (or cheese of choice, optional)

Red Onion, Tomato, and Habanero Relish (page 241)

Haitian Pikliz (page 229)

4 whole-wheat burger buns, toasted (optional)

To make the burger patties, heat 2 teaspoons of coconut oil in a sauté pan over medium heat. Add the plantain and cook until golden-brown. Drain on paper towels.

Transfer the cooked plantain to the bowl of a food processor. Add 1½ tablespoons coconut oil, black beans, oats, cilantro, scallion, lime juice, Scotch bonnet pepper, and salt and pepper. Pulse in a food processor until just combined; the mixture can be slightly chunky. (If you don't have a food processor, you can combine the ingredients in a large bowl and mash them together with a fork or potato masher.) Add 1 to 2 tablespoons water as needed—the mixture should be firm, not wet. Form the mixture into 4 burger patties, place on a sheet pan lined with waxed paper, cover, and chill until ready to use.

To cook the patties, warm 1 teaspoon coconut oil in a sauté pan over medium heat. Add two burger patties, and cook until they're brown on one side, about 2 minutes. Flip the patties and finish cooking. Hold in a warm oven. Repeat with the remaining two burgers.

To serve, top the bean patties with goat cheese, tomato relish, and pickled cabbage. Serve either open-faced on a toasted burger bun, or serve without the bun and add a salad on the side.

# GOOD HOPE
# GUNGO PEA FALAFEL

This recipe is entirely credited to our friend and fellow chef Tammy Hart, who generously contributed this inventive take on falafel. We shared a wonderful meal with Tammy at her Good Hope country home one December afternoon, and these lovely falafels were the stars of the show. Her menu typified a blend of rustic and sophisticated in ingredients, style, and setting that is so quintessentially West Indian that we were moved to ask her to share her recipe. Here, chickpeas are replaced with delicious fresh Jamaican gungo peas (pigeon peas), which bear in profusion during the cool months of November, December, and January. Coupled with Spiced Cilantro Yogurt (page 47) and Trini-style Pineapple Chow (page 231), this dish, to us, is island flavor perfected. These scrumptious falafels can be served in a variety of ways: we love them on top of a great salad, or as part of a light lunch which would also include a salad, a cooked vegetable, and a light starch. They can also be dropped into a pita bread or a wrap, along with hummus and fresh veggies, to make a healthy sandwich.

*Serves 4*

1½ cup dry gungo peas (pigeon peas)

½ large onion, diced

4 cloves garlic

2 tablespoons chopped parsley

2 tablespoons chopped mint plus mint leaves for garnish

2 tablespoons chopped cilantro

1 tablespoon lemon zest

1½ teaspoons salt

1 teaspoon ground cumin

1 teaspoon paprika

1 teaspoon baking powder

1 teaspoon diced habanero, without seeds

4 to 6 tablespoons flour

¼ cup vegetable oil for frying

Spiced Cilantro Yogurt (page 47)

Pineapple Chow (page 231)

*(Continued)*

Place the gungo peas in a bowl, cover with water, and leave to soak overnight. Drain them well.

Using a food processor with the blade attachment, pulse the soaked gungo peas, onion, garlic, parsley, 2 tablespoons chopped mint, cilantro, lemon zest, salt, cumin, paprika, baking powder, and habanero, scraping the sides of the processor occasionally as the ingredients blend. Taste the mixture and add more salt if needed. Sprinkle in 4 tablespoons of flour, and pulse for as short a time as possible to avoid the mixture becoming too dry. If the mixture is too wet and crumbly to make a patty that will hold together, add slightly more flour.

Pour enough oil into a frying pan to cover the bottom about 1 to 2 inches, and heat the oil over high heat. While the oil is heating, shape the gungo pea mixture into 2-inch patties, using 1 to 2 tablespoons of the mixture for each. Once the oil is hot, pan fry the falafel patties, turning so that all sides become golden. Drain on paper towels.

Serve on a platter with yogurt dressing drizzled over the top, fresh mint to garnish, and a mound of pineapple chow in the middle.

# SAUTÉED GUNGO PEAS
## *with Tahini and Mint*

We were thrilled to discover a recipe in a nineteenth-century book on Jamaican cookery that speaks about serving gungo peas with butter and mint: "Boil about a shelled quart [of green goongoo] exactly as you would English peas, with a little mint if you can get it and just a pinch of soda at the last moment. Serve with a little butter and black pepper."[4] We often whip up a quick, hot bean dish: sauté beans or peas in olive oil with garlic and mint, and drizzle with tahini just before you take it off the flame. So what seemed to us another quick and healthy meal turned out to be a time-honored formula! Serve with a freshly tossed green salad, roasted plantain, and lightly sautéed vegetables for a healthy and satisfying meal.

### Serves 4

3 cups fresh gungo peas

2 tablespoons olive oil

1 small yellow onion, minced

2 cloves garlic, sliced

2 tablespoons chopped mint plus more for garnish

salt and freshly cracked black pepper to taste

2 tablespoons tahini

¾ cup crumbled feta cheese (optional)

Bring 6 cups of salted water to a boil. Add the peas, and boil for about 20 minutes until cooked through. Remove from heat, drain, and set aside.

In a medium sauté pan, warm the olive oil over high heat. Add the onion and garlic, and sauté for about 2 minutes. Add the gungo peas and mint and cook, tossing, until all the ingredients are combined. Season with salt and pepper, drizzle with tahini, and toss to coat. Remove from heat and transfer to a serving bowl, topping with feta and more mint. Serve immediately.

4.  Sullivan, 27.

# JAMAICAN AKKRA

Akkra are fritters made of black-eyed peas. Of West African origin, this dish made its way over to the Caribbean and Brazil during the slave trade. In the traditional versions, black-eyed peas are pounded with seasonings in a mortar and pestle and then pan fried in palm oil. Less widely consumed today, akkra was a wildly popular dish in nineteenth-century Jamaica—and it is so delicious, we can see why! Our modern variation includes ginger and scallion. Serve the akkra topped with various homemade condiments, as pictured. A platter of them provides an easy, casual snack for entertaining.

*Makes 25 to 30*

1 cup black-eyed peas

1 onion, chopped

5 tablespoons chopped scallion

2 teaspoons minced
fresh ginger

1 teaspoon minced
Scotch bonnet pepper

1 teaspoon minced garlic

1 tablespoon chopped parsley

1 tablespoon thyme leaves

2 tablespoons cornmeal

salt and freshly cracked black
pepper to taste

½ to 1 cup coconut oil
for deep frying

Garlic-Lime Sauce (page 243)

Pickled Cucumber (page 230)

Watermelon-Lemongrass
Chutney (page 238)

Place the black-eyed peas in a large bowl, and add water to cover. Soak overnight. The next morning, while the beans are still in the soaking water, rub them between your hands to remove their skins. The skins will rise to the surface of the water, where they can be skimmed off. Drain the beans.

Place the beans and the onion, scallion, ginger, Scotch bonnet pepper, garlic, parsley, thyme, and cornmeal in the bowl of a food processor. Process until smooth, adding just enough water (¼ to ½ cup) to form a thick paste. Season with salt and pepper.

Heat about 1 inch of oil in a sauté pan over medium-high heat until it shimmers. Working in batches, drop spoonfuls of the batter into the hot oil, and fry, turning, until they brown on all sides, 8 to 10 minutes. Remove to a plate lined with paper towels, and keep warm until all the batter has been used up. Transfer to a warmed platter. Top with Garlic-Lime Sauce, Pickled Cucumber, and Watermelon-Lemongrass Chutney.

# LIMA BEANS
## with Sesame, Ginger, and Cashew

Our real love affair with fresh lima beans began when a local organic farmer sent us a crop he had reaped for us to use at an event we were catering. To say that the texture of fresh lima beans is satisfying would be an understatement. This dish was a standout that evening. The added Asian twist of sesame, ginger, lime, and cashews will surely make your mouth sing! This makes a wonderful side dish but is also enjoyable served as a main-course salad over a bed of lightly dressed greens.

*Serves 6*

4 cups shelled fresh lima beans

½ cup sesame oil, divided

¼ cup finely diced onion

¼ cup finely chopped scallion

½ Scotch bonnet pepper, seeded and minced

4 cloves garlic, diced

2 tablespoons ginger

1 tablespoon chopped mint

1 tablespoon chopped cilantro plus more for garnish

salt and freshly cracked black pepper to taste

juice of 3 limes (about 4 tablespoons)

½ cup roughly chopped roasted cashews

Boil the lima beans in enough salted water to cover (about 2 quarts) for 15 to 20 minutes until tender. Drain.

Heat 2 tablespoons sesame oil in a large sauté pan over medium heat. Working in batches to avoid overcrowding the pan, sauté the lima beans until the skins split and they are slightly browned. Remove from the pan and set aside.

Heat 2 tablespoons sesame oil in the same pan. Add the onion, scallion, Scotch bonnet pepper, garlic, and ginger, and sauté about 2 minutes. Add the lima beans back to the pan, add the mint and cilantro, and season with salt and pepper. Toss to combine all ingredients. To serve, sprinkle with fresh lime juice and garnish with cilantro and cashews.

# LENTIL–SCOTCH BONNET SPREAD
## *with Green Plantain Chips*

I f you like hummus then you will relish this lentil spread, which is made following a similar approach. Our version adds Scotch bonnet pepper, onion, scallion, and cilantro to the traditional Mediterranean ingredients of chickpeas, olive oil, lime juice, tahini, and garlic. The result, if we may say so ourselves, is spectacular—smooth, piquant, and quite unlike anything else. Serve the spread with crispy green plantain chips, or use it on a sandwich or wrap. (You can use store-bought plantain chips instead—we won't tell.)

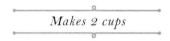

*Makes 2 cups*

**GREEN PLANTAIN CHIPS**

2 large green plantains

4 cups vegetable oil

sea salt and freshly cracked
black pepper to taste

**LENTIL–SCOTCH BONNET
SPREAD**

3 tablespoons extra-virgin olive
oil, divided, plus more to finish

1 yellow onion, chopped

2 cloves garlic, chopped

1 stalk scallion, chopped

1½ teaspoons minced Scotch
bonnet pepper, divided,
plus a whole pepper for garnish

1½ cups cooked green lentils

1 cup drained canned chickpeas

¼ cup lime juice

2 tablespoons chopped cilantro
plus more for garnish

1 tablespoon tahini

fine sea salt and freshly cracked
black pepper to taste

*(Continued)*

To make the chips, peel the plantains. Using a mandolin or a knife, slice the plantains very thinly into rounds. Soak the slices in salted water until ready to fry. Pat dry. Heat the vegetable oil in a large frying pan. When the oil reaches 375°F, drop the slices into the oil in small batches, taking care not to overcrowd the pan. Fry for 3 to 5 minutes per batch until crispy and golden, then remove and drain on paper towels. Season with sea salt and freshly cracked pepper, and keep in a warm, dry place until ready to serve.

To make the lentil spread, heat 2 tablespoons olive oil in a large pot over medium-high heat. Add the onion and cook, stirring occasionally, until soft, 5 to 7 minutes. Add the garlic, scallion, and minced Scotch bonnet pepper, and cook until fragrant, 1 to 2 minutes more. Add the lentils, season with salt, and warm through. Transfer the lentil mixture to the bowl of a food processor and let cool.

Add the chickpeas, lime juice, 2 tablespoons cilantro, tahini, 1 tablespoon olive oil, and salt and pepper to taste, and purée until smooth, adding a bit of water as needed. Scrape into a serving bowl, and garnish with cilantro, a drizzle of olive oil, and a whole Scotch bonnet pepper.

# LENTIL SALAD
## *with Feta, Orange, and Hazelnuts*

We love the medley of citrus dressing, orange zest, fresh herbs, lentils, and hazelnuts. This is a great lunch or dinner option, especially during the summer months, when lighter meals are desired.

*Serves 6*

2 cups uncooked brown lentils

1 red onion, finely diced

1 clove garlic, finely diced

3 tablespoons chopped mint plus more for garnish

2 tablespoons chopped parsley

2 tablespoons basil chiffonade

1 tablespoon orange zest

⅔ cup crumbled feta cheese, divided

½ cup roughly chopped roasted hazelnuts, divided

salt and freshly cracked black pepper to taste

### DRESSING

⅓ cup olive oil

2 tablespoons fresh lemon juice

3 tablespoons fresh orange juice

1 teaspoon Dijon mustard

1 clove garlic, whole but smashed

2 teaspoons chopped dill

salt and freshly cracked black pepper to taste

Bring 3 to 4 cups of water to a boil in a medium saucepan. Add lentils and cook for 15 to 20 minutes until soft. Once the lentils are cooked, pour through a sieve or fine colander to drain, and transfer to a large bowl to cool.

While the lentils cool prepare the dressing. Whisk together the olive oil, lemon juice, orange juice, mustard, smashed garlic, dill, salt, and pepper. Set aside.

To assemble the salad, add to the bowl of cooled lentils the red onion, diced garlic, 3 tablespoons mint, parsley, basil, orange zest, and dressing to taste. Stir to combine well. Add half the feta and half the hazelnuts, season with salt and pepper, and stir again. To serve, transfer the lentils to a shallow platter or bowl; top with remaining feta and hazelnuts and chopped mint.

# PINDA (PEANUT) STEW

Peanuts, also referred to as "pinda" in the local vernacular, grow profusely in Jamaica. Peanut punch, a sweet, creamy drink made with peanuts and sugar, is a common treat. Peanut vendors, pushing hand-made carts with built-in steamers or roasters, are a regular installation at stoplights across the island; they sell hot, salty peanuts in the shell served in brown paper cones. These roadside treats are the most common way we eat peanuts in Jamaica. And yet, though peanuts are a regular snack, we rarely cook with them. We take inspiration here from a delicious stew consumed in Ivory Coast that combines an array of fresh veggies in a rich and creamy peanut sauce. Serve the stew over fluffy white rice or couscous with plantains on the side.

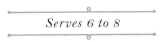

*Serves 6 to 8*

2 tablespoons peanut or
coconut oil

1 tablespoon brown sugar

1 medium yellow onion, minced

1 tablespoon minced ginger

3 cloves garlic, minced

2 tablespoons tomato paste

2 cups peeled, seeded, and
diced tomatoes

1 cup diced yellow squash

1 cup sliced zucchini

1 cup butternut or acorn squash

1 cup cubed white potato

½ cup chopped
green bell pepper

1 cup chopped carrot

1 cup natural, creamy peanut
butter (or use almond butter
if allergic to peanuts)

salt and freshly cracked
black pepper to taste

1 whole Scotch bonnet pepper

½ cup whole roasted peanuts or
almonds, for garnish

fried ripe plantain, for garnish
(optional)

*(Continued)*

Heat the peanut or coconut oil in a large saucepan or soup pot over medium-high heat. Add the brown sugar and cook for about 1 minute. Add the onion, ginger, and garlic, and sauté until translucent, 3 or 4 minutes. Stir in the tomato paste and cook for about 1 minute. Add the diced tomatoes and bring to a boil. Reduce heat to low and cook for about 5 minutes, stirring frequently. Add the yellow squash, zucchini, butternut squash, potato, bell pepper, and carrot, and cook, stirring occasionally, for about 3 minutes. Add enough water to the pot to give the dish the consistency of a stew (1 to 2 cups), and simmer for 5 minutes. Stir in the peanut butter, add salt and pepper to taste, and add the whole Scotch bonnet pepper. Partially cover, and cook for another 20 minutes, gently stirring from time to time and adding water as necessary to maintain a stew-like consistency. Adjust seasonings. To serve, garnish with roasted peanuts or almonds, and serve with fried plantains on the side, if desired.

## CHAPTER 6

# GRAINS

*Rice, Quinoa, Wheat & Corn*

EVERY ISLAND HAS ITS OWN VERSION OF WHAT IS ESSENTIALLY FRIED, BAKED, OR BOILED GRAIN: FLOUR, CORNMEAL, OR RICE. FESTIVAL (A deep-fried cornmeal dumpling like a hush puppy) and Johnny cakes from Jamaica, bakes from Trinidad and Guyana, jacks from Belize, yaniqueques from the Dominican Republic, and pastelles from Trinidad are just a few examples.

These flour- or cornmeal-based dishes actually originate from an early staple food of native communities across the Americas: bread or grain made from corn that provided sustenance and, if dried and cooked, could easily travel well over long distances. Dumplings and breads were made in a variety of forms; some versions were called "journey cakes" because of their "grab and go" nature. They were well suited to the daily life of travelers, who often had to take sustenance while working in the fields or trekking across the island or heading into town or market. A "journey cake," "bake," or "Johnny cake" was easily paired with a piece of salted fish or pork for a portable and filling snack.

A version of this dish is now prepared, in one way or another, all along the Atlantic coast, from Newfoundland to Jamaica. In the Caribbean, these deliciously hearty and rustic staples are served either as a snack on their own or paired with robustly seasoned fresh or salted fish; the sweet and bready texture of the fried or baked dough is a perfect complement to the intense tartness, spice, and flavor of the fresh, salted, or cured fish or meat. By far our favorite version of "dumplings" comes in the form of Trinidad's famed Maracas Bay beach snack known as bake and shark, much loved by locals and visitors alike. Simply put, there's nothing more soul-satisfying than biting into a piping-hot, fluffy bake, stuffed to capacity with crispy cornmeal-battered fried fish, lettuce, and tomato, and "lashed," as we like to say in the islands, with a liberal dose of tamarind sauce, hot pepper sauce, mustard, pickled onions, garlic sauce, and chadon beni (culantro) sauce. The wild beauty of Maracas Beach always astounds us, yet it's the explosion of flavor on the tongue at the first bite of this traditional snack that is permanently embedded in our memory.

# COUSCOUS

## *with Sweet Pot Herbs, Zucchini, Plantain, and Roasted Channa*

Couscous, made from durum wheat semolina, is a form of pasta common in the Middle East. It is one of our favorite grain-based foods to both cook and eat. The texture is ineffably gratifying, and so is the infinite variety of ways in which it can be served. In this delicious dish, we combine all our island favorites in the form of plantain, fresh "sweet pot" herbs, spicy Scotch bonnet, and lime. Top with piquant roasted chickpeas (or channa, as they are called in Trinidad) and toasted pistachios to make a complete meal.

*Serves 8*

1 can chickpeas, drained and rinsed

1 cup cubed pumpkin

½ medium zucchini, cubed

½ plantain or ½ yellow squash, cubed

1 cup halved cherry tomatoes

½ red bell pepper, chopped

½ green bell pepper, chopped

½ red onion, sliced

3 cloves garlic, peeled and left whole

½ cup olive oil

1 handful fresh oregano leaves, plus extra for garnish

1 handful fresh cilantro, plus extra for garnish

1 handful fresh mint, plus extra for garnish

1 handful thyme leaves

¼ cup Crispy Trini-Style Channa (page 118), for garnish, (optional)

½ cup toasted pistachios, roughly chopped, for garnish

COUSCOUS

1 box instant couscous

4 tablespoons lime juice

4 tablespoons olive oil

1 teaspoon minced garlic

½ teaspoon minced Scotch bonnet pepper

sea salt and freshly cracked black pepper to taste

*(Continued)*

Preheat the oven to 375°F.

Combine the chickpeas with the pumpkin, zucchini, plantain or yellow squash, cherry tomatoes, red and green bell pepper, onion, and garlic cloves in a large mixing bowl. Toss with ½ cup olive oil, oregano, cilantro, mint, and thyme. Season with salt and pepper. Spread evenly on a large baking sheet (or two smaller sheets). Roast for 40 to 45 minutes, stirring about halfway through, until the veggies are nicely caramelized.

Prepare the couscous according to package directions. When it has cooked, fluff it with a fork, and stir in the lime juice, 4 tablespoons olive oil, minced garlic, and minced Scotch bonnet pepper. Season with salt and pepper and allow to rest for 20 minutes.

Remove the roasted vegetables and chickpeas from the oven, and serve mounded on top of the couscous or tossed together with it. Top with channa, pistachios, and fresh herbs.

# KALE AND QUINOA SALAD
## *with Candied Sorrel, Pumpkin Seeds, and Almonds*

Sorrel in Jamaica is not the garden herb that you know in the United States. They are fresh hibiscus leaves that when steeped in water make a beautiful ruby-red juice. For this recipe we stew the sorrel/hibiscus in a simple syrup to create the texture and taste of dried or candied fruit. Pomegranate seeds make an equally delicious substitute. Hearty enough to serve as a main course, this salad is both healthy and satisfying; the medley of crunchy kale, quinoa, candied sorrel buds, nuts, and feta hits all the right notes. (You can also serve it as a side dish alongside a protein, for example, roasted salmon or grilled chicken.) Any kind of kale will do. Feel free to experiment and make this recipe work for you.

*Serves 4 to 6*

1 cup uncooked quinoa
(about 2½ cups cooked)

1 large bunch curly kale, washed
(about 4 to 6 cups prepped)

¼ cup thinly sliced red onion
or shallot

¼ cup diced red bell pepper

¼ cup roasted almonds, roughly
chopped, divided

¼ cup toasted pumpkin seeds,
divided

½ cup Candied Sorrel
Buds (page 187), torn into
small pieces, or substitute
pomegranate seeds

¾ cup crumbled feta cheese,
divided

salt and freshly cracked
black pepper to taste

### HONEY-MUSTARD VINAIGRETTE

4 tablespoons red wine vinegar
or lemon juice

2 teaspoons mustard

2 to 3 teaspoons honey

1 clove garlic, grated

⅓ cup olive oil

salt and freshly cracked
black pepper to taste

*(Continued)*

To prepare the quinoa, bring 2 cups of water to boil in a medium saucepan. Stir in the uncooked quinoa, season with a pinch of salt, and reduce the heat to a simmer. Cook for 15 to 20 minutes, until the quinoa is soft and the liquid is absorbed. Turn off the heat and fluff the quinoa. Allow the quinoa to cool.

To make the vinaigrette, whisk together the vinegar, mustard, honey, and garlic until combined. Add the olive oil in a steady stream, whisking constantly until the mixture is thick and emulsified. Season with salt and pepper and set aside.

To make the salad, bunch the kale leaves together, and horizontally slice them into thin strips, discarding the stems. Transfer the kale to a large bowl. Add the cooked quinoa, red onion, red bell pepper, half the almonds, half the pumpkin seeds, the candied sorrel or pomegranate seeds, ½ cup feta, the salad dressing, and salt and pepper to taste. Toss all ingredients together well, ensuring that the dressing is evenly distributed. To serve, arrange the salad in a large bowl or platter, and top with the remaining feta, almonds, and pumpkin seeds.

# BALINESE-STYLE BLACK RICE SALAD

An epic vacation to Bali in 2011 to celebrate our fortieth birthdays left us with mouthwatering memories of Balinese cuisine and an enduring love for the country's culture. The delightfully aromatic Balinese food was strangely reminiscent of Caribbean cuisine with its abundant use of coconut and tropical vegetables and fruits. This fresh salad of veggies, black rice, and sprouts, inspired by Balinese gado gado (a delicious mixed salad made with peanut dressing), is our homage to beloved Bali—a place of jasmine-scented bliss that often beckons.

*Serves 6 to 8*

2 cups cooked black rice

1 cup snake beans
cut into 1-inch pieces
(or substitute green beans)

1 cup bean sprouts

1 cup fresh broccoli,
lightly blanched

⅔ cup grated unsweetened
coconut, toasted

½ cup sliced bell pepper

½ cup thinly sliced or grated
green papaya or mango

handful fresh cilantro leaves,
plus more for garnish

1 tablespoon coconut oil

½ cup chopped onion

¼ cup chopped fresh red chilies

1 tablespoon sesame oil

4 cloves garlic, sliced

2-inch piece of ginger,
peeled and minced

½ cup roasted peanuts,
for garnish

½ cup watercress, for garnish

### PEANUT DRESSING

1 large red chili, seeded and
finely sliced

juice of 3 lime wedges
(about ¼ cup)

¼ teaspoon white pepper

2 teaspoons coconut sugar

½ cup peanut butter, thinned
with a little hot water

1 tablespoon sesame oil

1 tablespoon coconut milk

salt and freshly cracked
black pepper to taste

Bring 2 cups of water to a boil. Add the snake beans. Allow to cook for about 5 minutes. Drain the beans, and immediately rinse them under cold water to cool.

Toss together the cooked black rice, blanched beans, sprouts, broccoli, coconut, bell pepper, green papaya or mango, and cilantro. Heat the coconut oil in a sauté pan over medium heat. Sauté the onions and chilies for about 3 minutes, until the onions are soft. Add them to the vegetable-rice mixture. Heat the sesame oil in the same sauté pan, add the garlic and ginger, and fry over medium heat until crisp and golden. Set aside.

Whisk all dressing ingredients together in a small bowl. Pour half the dressing over the vegetables and rice and toss. Season with additional salt and pepper if needed. Plate the salad, drizzle with additional dressing to taste, and garnish with peanuts, watercress, cilantro, and crispy garlic and ginger.

# "TUN" CORNMEAL
## with Roasted Pumpkin
## and Garlic Confit

This simple dish, made from cornmeal seasoned with local spices and coconut milk, evolved out of necessity because cornmeal formed part of the weekly rations issued to slaves on plantations in the eighteenth and nineteenth centuries. In Jamaica, this substantial and delicious repast has typically been thought of as "poor man's food" and, erroneously in our opinion, is not usually considered worthy of inclusion in a more refined meal. Our recipe has you prepare the cornmeal polenta style for a finer presentation. (Alternately, of course, you can serve the cornmeal in a bowl hot from the pot as soon as it is finished cooking without shaping it.) We hope this dish proves its rightful place at any table!

### Serves 10

**ROASTED PUMPKIN**

1 cup cubed pumpkin

1 small red onion, chopped

2 cloves garlic

2 tablespoons olive oil

salt and freshly cracked black pepper

handful whole rosemary leaves

**CORNMEAL**

1 15-ounce can coconut milk

2 stalks scallion, chopped

handful fresh thyme leaves

1 whole Scotch bonnet pepper

2 cloves garlic, chopped

1 teaspoon salt

1 teaspoon freshly cracked black pepper

10 ounces cornmeal (about 2½ cups)

½ cup grated Parmesan cheese, plus more for garnish

¼ cup goat cheese

handful cilantro, chopped

handful basil, chopped, plus more for garnish

Tomato Choka (page 40)

Culantro Pepper Oil (page 250)

To make the roast pumpkin, preheat the oven to 400°F. Combine the pumpkin cubes with red onion and 2 whole cloves of garlic, and toss with the olive oil, salt and pepper to taste, and rosemary. Spread on a baking sheet and bake for 20 minutes or until the pumpkin is cooked through and the garlic and onion are caramelized.

To make the "tun" (or turned) cornmeal, bring the coconut milk and ½ cup water to a boil in a medium saucepan over medium heat. Add the scallion, thyme, 1 whole Scotch bonnet pepper, chopped garlic, salt, and pepper. Return to a boil, pour in the cornmeal, and stir continuously until smooth. Continue stirring until the cornmeal starts to thicken, about 10 minutes more. If it becomes too dense add a little more water, and continue to stir.

After 10 minutes, reduce the heat, cover the pot, and cook for another 10 to 15 minutes, until the cornmeal is dense but creamy in texture. Adjust the consistency by incorporating more water as needed. Once the cornmeal is finished cooking, stir in the roasted pumpkin, Parmesan cheese, goat cheese, cilantro, and basil. Remove and discard the Scotch bonnet pepper. Stir continuously until the cheese is melted. Add a bit of water if the mixture is too stiff. Remove from the stove. At this point, you can serve the cornmeal hot from the pot, or continue to prepare it polenta-style, as described next.

Spread the cornmeal on a sheet pan, about 1 to 2 inches thick. Place in the freezer to cool for about 10 minutes. Cut into desired shapes using a sharp knife or cookie cutter; remove from the sheet pan and store in a covered container between sheets of waxed paper until ready to serve.

To serve, warm a little olive oil in a nonstick pan over medium heat. Sear the tun cornmeal in the pan, about 2 minutes per side or until heated through. Top each piece as desired with tomato choka, fresh basil, Culantro Pepper Oil, and grated Parmesan.

# EMPRESS BOWL
## *Coconut Rice and Guyanese Dhal*

A friend from Guyana served us this bowl straight from the stove as a hearty and healthy lunch. We were starving at the time, and the warm and supremely satisfying combination of rice, soupy dhal, charred coconut, and delicious spicy okra made us want to hug her. We immediately recognized a kindred spirit: a nurturer who loves to feed and take care of people. She was generous enough to share her recipes for Guyanese-style dhal and Coconut Choka (page 41) with us. For our version, we include a seasoned coconut basmati rice and leave some of the dhal unblended to add texture and body.

### *Serves 6*

**COCONUT BASMATI RICE**

1 tablespoon coconut oil

1 teaspoon cumin seed

½ medium yellow onion, minced

3 cloves garlic, minced

1 tablespoon grated fresh ginger

5 tablespoons chopped
cilantro, divided

½ teaspoon salt

2 cups basmati rice
(or substitute jasmine rice)

1½ teaspoons turmeric

1 15-ounce can coconut milk

1 pinch saffron threads

¼ cup sliced almonds, toasted

**GUYANESE YELLOW DHAL**

1½ cups yellow split peas

1 medium onion, chopped

¼ cup chopped culantro
(chadon beni)

3 cloves garlic, chopped

3 tablespoons chopped
celery leaves

1 habanero or country pepper,
whole

1 teaspoon turmeric

½ teaspoon ground cumin

½ teaspoon curry powder

1 to 2 tablespoons salt
(or to taste)

**TO FINISH**

2 tablespoons coconut oil

1 tablespoon cumin seed

1 clove garlic, sliced

2 tablespoons minced shallot

2 tablespoons minced
green onion

4 cups Okra with Scotch Bonnet,
Cilantro, Coconut, and Lime
(page 37)

1½ cups Coconut Choka
(page 41)

fresh cilantro leaves for garnish

*(Continued)*

To make the rice, heat the coconut oil in a medium saucepan over medium heat. Add the cumin seeds and cook, stirring continuously, for about a minute or until fragrant. Stir in the onion, garlic, ginger, 2 tablespoons of cilantro, and salt. Cook for 5 to 7 minutes, stirring occasionally, until the onions have become golden and soft, but haven't yet browned. Add the rice and turmeric to the saucepan, and stir until evenly combined. Let the rice cook for 2 to 3 minutes, stirring frequently. Add the coconut milk, saffron, and 2½ cups of water, and stir to combine. Increase the heat to let the liquid come to a boil. Once boiling, reduce the heat to low and cover the saucepan. Simmer the rice until all the liquid has been absorbed, 15 to 18 minutes. Fluff the rice with a fork, stir in 3 tablespoons of cilantro, and top with the almonds.

To make the dhal, wash the split peas twice to remove any stones or debris. Bring 6 cups water to a boil; add the split peas, onion, culantro, garlic, celery leaves, and whole habanero pepper. Reduce the heat to medium, and add the turmeric, cumin, and curry powder. Add salt, stir, reduce the heat, and cover. Simmer for about 20 minutes until reduced. Remove the pepper carefully, making sure not to burst it.

Using a hand-held blender, blend about half the dhal, leaving some whole for body. Whisk the dhal and continue cooking, allowing to thicken for about 5 minutes more.

To finish, heat the coconut oil in a small sauté pan over medium heat, add the cumin seed and garlic, and fry until the garlic is golden and crisp, about 1 minute. Pour the sizzling-hot oil along with the garlic and cumin into the dhal. Stir in the shallot and green onion.

To assemble the Empress Bowls, spoon a cup of coconut rice into each bowl and top with a cup of dhal. Top each with ¾ cup okra and ¼ cup Coconut Choka, and garnish with fresh cilantro leaves.

# HAITIAN-STYLE DJON DJON RISOTTO
## *(Riz Djon Djon)*

Djon djon is a black mushroom native to Haiti. It has a flavor that cannot be replicated. Considered a delicacy, djon djon are often sold dried in local markets. The classic Caribbean dish riz djon djon (or black rice and mushrooms), made with long-grain rice, is typically served as a side dish. Our tribute to the traditional Haitian dish celebrates this unique West Indian ingredient in a totally irresistible format: a creamy, cheesy risotto that is made with arborio rice and incorporates the soaking liquid from the mushrooms into the vegetable stock. The result is a rich and smoky risotto that easily stars as the main course. (It is very difficult to find djon djon outside of Haiti. You can substitute dried porcini or shiitake mushrooms for an equally delicious variation.)

*Serves 4*

1 cup dried Haitian djon djon
(or other dried mushroom)

3½ cups good-quality
vegetable stock

3 tablespoons olive oil

1 medium yellow onion, diced

6 cloves garlic, sliced

1 teaspoon minced
Scotch bonnet pepper

1 cup arborio rice

2 sprigs thyme

½ teaspoon salt

¼ cup white wine

1 tablespoon butter

4 ounces goat cheese

2 tablespoons chopped parsley

freshly cracked black pepper
to taste

½ cup shaved
Pecorino Romano cheese

*(Continued)*

Clean the mushrooms and place them in a saucepan with 3 cups of hot water. Soak for at least 4 hours or overnight. Place half the soaked mushrooms with half the liquid in a blender and puree. Strain the puree and add it to the vegetable stock.

Drain the remaining mushrooms, pressing with a cheesecloth over a strainer to release all the liquid.

In a small saucepan, heat the mushroom-vegetable stock, and keep it at a very low simmer. In a separate, medium-sized saucepan, heat the olive oil over low heat; add the onion, garlic, and Scotch bonnet pepper and cook, stirring occasionally, until the onions are transparent (about 5 minutes). Add the mushrooms, rice, thyme, and salt, and cook, stirring, for 2 minutes. Add the wine and cook until it has evaporated. Add ½ cup of the stock to the rice, and cook, stirring continuously, until it is absorbed into the rice. Continue adding the stock ½ cup at a time, stirring constantly to allow it to absorb after each addition. Continue for 25 to 30 minutes until the rice is cooked through and has reached a thick, creamy consistency. If more liquid is needed, supplement with hot water. When the risotto is ready, remove it from the heat, and stir in the butter, goat cheese, parsley, and pepper. Serve the risotto topped with shaved Pecorino Romano.

# CREAMY TRINI CORN SOUP

**O**ur favorite West Indian soup, Trini corn soup, is consumed year-round in Trinidad, but our fondest memories of it are laced with lots of rum and laughter at the end of some fete during carnival time. This soup is unique, rich with flavor, and oh so satisfying due to the hearty base of potatoes, carrots, and split peas. Corn, Scotch bonnet pepper, chadon beni (culantro), thyme, and coconut milk are always delicious together, and the addition of chopped avocado makes it even better. Serve with a warm slice of Cheesy Scotch Bonnet Corn Bread (page 160), as pictured, and you are good to go!

*Serves 8 to 10*

2 tablespoons coconut oil
or olive oil

2 medium onions, chopped

3 to 4 cloves garlic, diced

1 pound potatoes,
peeled and quartered

2 carrots, chopped

¼ cup chopped celery

3 stalks scallion, diced

2 sprigs thyme leaves, chopped

2 teaspoons diced Trinidad
pimiento or country pepper

¾ cup yellow split peas

salt and freshly cracked
black pepper to taste

¾ cup coconut milk

1 whole Scotch bonnet pepper

6 cups corn kernels
(from 3 to 4 ears)

½ cup chopped cilantro or
culantro, plus more for garnish

**TO SERVE**

1 avocado

juice of 1 lime

1 teaspoon olive oil

Heat the oil in a large, deep pot over medium-high heat. Add the onion and garlic and cook for about 3 minutes until soft. Add the potato, carrot, celery, scallion, thyme, and pimiento, and cook for another 5 minutes, stirring occasionally. Add 2½ quarts of water and the split peas; season with salt and pepper. Add the coconut milk and the Scotch bonnet pepper. Return to a boil, reduce the heat, cover, and simmer for 45 to 50 minutes or until the peas are soft. Once the peas are soft, add the corn and cilantro or culantro and simmer for another 20 to 25 minutes. Once the corn is cooked, remove the soup from the heat. Using an immersion blender, puree the soup in the pot. Or, working in batches, transfer the soup to a stand blender and puree. Return the soup to the pot and adjust the seasoning with salt and pepper. Thin with a little water or coconut milk as necessary.

Dice the avocado; sprinkle it with lime juice, olive oil, and a little salt, and hold it in the refrigerator until assembly. To serve, ladle a generous helping of soup into a bowl, and top with a spoonful of avocado and a sprinkle of chopped cilantro.

# CHEESY SCOTCH BONNET CORN BREAD

Classic West Indian corn bread is actually more like a spoon bread that was traditionally baked in a skillet over an open flame. As with many of our island's baked goods, it is dense and hearty. In this version, we incorporate some West Indian flavor by adding Scotch bonnet, citrus zest, coconut oil, and cheddar cheese to round out the gritty and dense texture of the cornmeal.

*Serves 8 to 10*

1 cup all-purpose flour

1½ cups yellow cornmeal

3 tablespoons brown sugar

1½ teaspoons baking powder

½ teaspoon baking soda

½ teaspoon salt

¼ teaspoon black pepper

½ teaspoon cayenne

1 cup whole milk or buttermilk

2 tablespoons coconut oil

2 eggs, beaten

1 to 2 teaspoons orange zest

½ Scotch bonnet pepper, seeded and minced (about 1 teaspoon minced)

1 cup grated aged cheddar cheese

Preheat the oven to 400°F. Grease a loaf pan or a 9-inch square baking dish.

In a large bowl mix together the flour, cornmeal, brown sugar, baking powder, baking soda, salt, pepper, and cayenne. In a separate bowl, whisk together the milk or buttermilk, coconut oil, eggs, orange zest, and Scotch bonnet. Combine the wet and dry ingredients, and mix thoroughly. Add the grated cheese and mix again. Transfer the batter to the baking pan and bake for 20 to 25 minutes, or until a knife or toothpick comes out clean when inserted into the center of the corn bread. Remove from the oven, allow to cool for 10 to 15 minutes, slice, and serve warm, with butter if desired.

# COCO BREAD
## with Aged Cheddar and Crispy Garlic

One of the greatest pleasures in life is a warm coco bread straight out of the oven, served in the requisite brown paper bag, of course. If you haven't had coco bread, imagine a moist and doughy bread, neatly folded, with melted butter in the middle. A typical lunch for most Jamaican high school students includes a piping-hot Tastee patty stuffed into a warm coco bread—an irresistible combination for kids and adults alike. Ever since our own school days, we have been obsessed with the idea of stuffing things inside coco bread. Here our classic Jamaican coco bread pairs majestically with aged cheddar, crispy garlic, sea salt, and thyme to create doughy perfection.

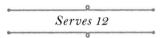

*Serves 12*

**6 cups bread flour**

**4½ tablespoons sugar**

**2½ teaspoons salt**

**4¼ tablespoons shortening**

**3⅓ tablespoons yeast**

**¼ cup olive oil, divided**

**4 cloves garlic, chopped**

**¼ cup salted butter, melted**

**2 tablespoons fresh
thyme leaves**

**½ cup grated aged cheddar**

**1 egg, beaten**

**coarse sea salt, for finishing**

Place flour, sugar, salt, shortening, yeast, and 2 cups water in the bowl of a stand mixer. Mix on low with the paddle attachment for 8 to 10 minutes. Cover with a dish cloth and allow the dough to proof in a warm place for 1 hour.

While the dough is proofing, heat 1 tablespoon olive oil in a sauté pan over medium-high heat. Add the garlic and sauté until it is golden-brown and crispy, 1½ to 2 minutes. Do not allow the garlic to burn.

After the dough has proofed for an hour, remove the cloth and punch down the dough with your fists. Using a sharp knife or a bench scraper, divide the dough into 4-ounce pieces. On a lightly floured surface, roll out each piece of dough into a 6-inch circle. Brush the top of each with butter, drizzle with olive oil, sprinkle with thyme leaves, and fold it in half. Roll out again, brush with butter, drizzle with olive oil, top with crispy garlic and aged cheddar, and fold again. Arrange the half circles of dough about 2 inches apart on baking sheets. Allow the breads to proof in a warm place for another hour.

When ready to bake, heat the oven to 350°F. Brush the coco breads on top with the beaten egg and sprinkle with sea salt. Bake for 20 minutes. The bread should be lightly golden on the outside and soft and moist inside.

# MAMACITA'S AREPAS
## *with Black Beans and Queso Blanco*

Arepas are a traditional Venezuelan bread made from harina pan (precooked corn flour). They are eaten in the same way that wheat bread is eaten: at breakfast with butter, or as a sandwich with various fillings. We were introduced to arepas many years ago at the home of a high school friend by her Venezuelan grandmother, Mamacita, and we have been hooked ever since. Whenever Mamacita visited there was an arepa feast, and we never missed it. Mamacita's typical fillings were spicy shredded beef, Venezuelan chicken salad with mayonnaise, grated queso blanco, and, our personal favorite, black beans, which she seasoned with oregano and a good dose of sugar. In our vegetarian version we leave out the oregano and create a spicy-sweet filling of black beans seasoned with habanero, brown sugar, and cumin. Served with queso blanco or ricotta salata, fried ripe plantain, sliced avocado, and cilantro, they are heaven in a mouthful. You can also enjoy arepas in simpler preparations: with butter alone or with butter and cheese, for a typical Venezuelan breakfast.

*Serves 6*

### FILLING

2 tablespoons olive oil

1 medium yellow onion, diced

2 tablespoons diced scallion

2 cloves garlic, minced

1 medium plum tomato, diced

3 tablespoons diced bell pepper

1 teaspoon diced habanero

1 can black beans,
drained and rinsed (or 1 cup dry
beans, cooked; see note)

2 bay leaves

2 tablespoons sugar

1 teaspoon ground cumin

1 teaspoon salt

freshly cracked black pepper
to taste

### AREPAS

1¼ teaspoons salt

3 cups harina pan or
precooked corn flour

2 tablespoons plus 1 to
1½ teaspoons vegetable oil

### TO SERVE

¾ cup grated queso blanco
(if unavailable, substitute feta
or ricotta salata)

¼ cup chopped cilantro,
for garnish

fried ripe plantain (optional)

sliced avocado (optional)

*(Continued)*

To make the filling, heat the olive oil in a saucepan over medium heat. Add the onion, scallion, garlic, tomato, bell pepper, and habanero, and sauté for about 3 minutes until soft and aromatic. Add the beans, and stir to combine all ingredients. Add ½ cup water and bring to a boil; then reduce heat to a simmer. Add the bay leaves, sugar, cumin, salt, and pepper, and cook for 20 minutes, tasting and adjusting seasonings as you go; the beans should be slightly sweet, so add more sugar if necessary.

To prepare the arepas, combine 3 cups lukewarm water with the salt in a large bowl, and stir until the salt dissolves. Mixing with your hands, gradually add enough corn flour to make a soft, moist dough that holds its shape and does not crack when molded. Ensure that the mixture is smooth and lump-free. Add 2 tablespoons vegetable oil, working it into the mixture with your hands, and adding cornmeal or water as necessary to maintain the dough's consistency. Divide the dough into six equal portions. Shape each into a ball, and then flatten them into 1-inch-thick pancakes. Hold them on a baking sheet.

Preheat the oven to 350°F. Place a rack in the middle of the oven. While the oven is heating, heat a frying pan or griddle, and add 1 to 1½ teaspoons vegetable oil. Cook the arepas for 3 to 4 minutes per side, flipping when they are golden-brown. Once all the arepas are cooked, place them in the heated oven, directly on the center rack (not on a baking sheet). Bake until the surface of the arepa is firm to the touch, about 15 minutes. Remove from the oven, cool, and split them down the center, like hamburger buns.

Assemble the arepas by filling each with 3 to 4 tablespoons black beans, 1 to 2 tablespoons of queso blanco, and fresh cilantro. If you wish, add fried plantain and avocado for another layer of wicked deliciousness.

**NOTE:** To make the filling with dried beans instead of canned, soak 1 cup of dried black beans for a few hours or overnight. Drain them well. After cooking the onion, scallion, garlic, tomato, bell pepper, and habanero, add the soaked beans, 2 cups of water, and bay leaves, and bring to a boil. Reduce the heat and simmer on low until the beans are tender, approximately 1 hour. Check for tenderness, as it may take longer. Once the beans are tender, season with sugar, cumin, salt, and pepper, and cook for another 10 minutes.

# BASIC PASTRY CRUST
## *for Savory or Sweet*

This simple pastry recipe is our go-to for many of the dishes in this book.

*Make 12 tart shells or one 8-inch pie crust*

**1 pound (3½ cups)
all-purpose flour**

**1 teaspoon salt**

**½ pound (1 cup) cold butter,
cut into ½-inch pieces**

Sift the flour and salt together into a bowl. Work the butter into the flour mixture with your fingers until it is incorporated into the dough and the mixture appears sandy in texture. Add 4 tablespoons ice-cold water, stirring it into the flour mixture until a dough forms; knead for a few turns to bring the dough together. Wrap well, and chill for three hours before using.

# CHAPTER 7

# SWEET FRUITS & FLOWERS

*Mango, Papaya, Berries, Citrus, Melon, Guava,
Pineapple, Passionfruit & Sorrel*

THE LUSH, TROPICAL CARIBBEAN ISLANDS ARE NATURALLY WELL FRUITED, SUPPLYING AN ABUNDANCE OF ALL KINDS OF fresh fruit. The variety of tastes, textures, and flavor profiles of local fruits boggles the mind.

Exotic tropical fruits are one of the greatest joys for an islander, and this seems to have been true even back in the 1800s. Fruit trees played a key role in nineteenth-century plantations, providing beauty, shade, and, most importantly, sustenance—particularly for slaves. Because they were allowed to grow their own fruit trees in the slave grounds, as well as pick produce from the estate trees, in the more lush tropical islands that possessed good soil (like St. Vincent, Jamaica, Trinidad, Tobago, and St. Lucia), slaves were never without a steady supply of fresh tropical fruits: mango, guava, banana, passionfruit (or granadilla), shaddock (or pomelo), papaya, and pineapple.

> Mangoes are of good variety. Common, Golden, Yam, beef, east Indian, Number Eleven, Harry, Black, Kidney, Plummy and so on….The number eleven is the best table mango. Some prefer the commoner sorts; and some people do not like them at all. The people live on them during the mango season.
>
> —*The Jamaica Cookery Book,* 1893

> The guava bush is indigenous to most of the islands of the West Indies, and every estate is more or less over-run with guavas. The St Vincent guavas are considered of a very fine quality, and when stewed with sugar, are not unlike the flavour of a strawberry.
>
> —Mrs. A. C. Carmichael, 1834

Another important role played by fresh fruit was its procurement for trade and sale at Sunday markets. When a seasonal fruit was overabundant, ladies processed it into jams, jellies, and preserves for use in the great house and for sale at market. A West Indian Sunday market in the nineteenth century would have been overflowing with a wide selection of fresh, plump tropical fruits attractively displayed by female vendors.

To this day, the tradition remains the same, except that market day is no longer limited to Sunday, and roadside fruit vendors are found scattered throughout the city and country streets. Our homes are never without a tasty selection of fresh tropical fruit; in order to ensure the freshest produce possible, we, like many islanders, have a favorite fruit vendor. A biweekly trip for the freshest selection of seasonal produce is a must in order to keep our pantries appropriately stocked.

# CARAMELIZED FENNEL AND GRILLED GREEN GUAVA WITH MINT

Fennel has such a distinct flavor that it can be hard to know how to prepare it. We love to bake or grill our fennel; combined with caramelized onions, it makes a delicious side dish. A recent trip to St. Kitts introduced us to an astonishing culinary discovery: green guava tossed in olive oil, seasoned with salt and pepper, and charred on a grill. The grilled green guava in this dish creates a wonderful medley of tart, clean flavors that balance the fennel and caramelized onion.

## Serves 6

4 tablespoons olive oil, divided

1 tablespoon salted butter, divided

4 fennel bulbs, sliced lengthwise (from stem end to root end) about ½ to ¾ inches thick

2 tablespoons brown sugar

1 medium red onion, thinly sliced

salt and freshly cracked black pepper to taste

handful fresh mint leaves plus more for garnish

8 ounces soft chèvre or goat cheese

2 large unripe guavas or 1 large "turned" (underripe) mango, peeled and sliced

Preheat the oven to 350°F.

Heat 1 tablespoon olive oil and 1 teaspoon butter in a large sauté pan over medium heat. Working in batches, add the fennel slices in a single layer, and allow to cook until one side is brown and the fennel is almost cooked through (1½ to 2 minutes); turn the fennel pieces over and caramelize the other side. Remove from the pan and arrange on a sheet pan. Once all the fennel is cooked, to the same pan add 1 tablespoon olive oil and 2 teaspoons butter and allow to melt. Add the brown sugar and red onions, season with salt, lower the heat, and allow the onions to caramelize, stirring frequently so they don't burn (8 to 10 minutes). When the onions are a rich brown color, remove from the heat. Spread the caramelized onions over the fennel, top with chopped mint, and season with salt and pepper. Spread dots of chèvre over the onions and fennel, and bake for 20 to 25 minutes.

While the onions and fennel are baking, warm the grill or a griddle pan over medium heat. Brush the green guava slices on both sides with the remaining olive oil. Place on the grill, and char for about 2 minutes; turn over and char the other side for another 2 minutes.

To serve, arrange the fennel topped with onions and goat cheese on a serving platter. Top with grilled green guava, and garnish with chopped mint leaves.

# WATERMELON CARPACCIO
## *with Arugula and Pecorino*

Carpaccio is a dish of thinly sliced raw meat or fish; this salad replaces the meat with refreshing, cool, crisp watermelon. To make sure your watermelon stays very fresh, thinly slice it crosswise, and dress it just before service so that it does not turn slimy, get soggy, or go "off" in texture. Watermelon carpaccios are often made with mint, but we prefer the peppery bite of arugula, the contrast of sharp pecorino, and a light drizzle of a citrus-balsamic reduction. This dish makes a delicious summer starter or an easy salad for a barbeque buffet.

*Serves 4*

**ORANGE-BALSAMIC REDUCTION**

¾ cup balsamic vinegar

¼ cup orange juice

1 tablespoon brown sugar

1 tablespoon honey

**WATERMELON CARPACCIO**

12 very thin slices watermelon

4 cups arugula

1 cup shaved
Pecorino Romano cheese

freshly cracked black pepper
to taste

Make the balsamic reduction by combining the balsamic vinegar, orange juice, sugar, and honey in a medium saucepan. Bring to a simmer over high heat. Reduce the heat to low and simmer for 20 to 30 minutes until the mixture is reduced to a syrupy consistency.

When you're ready to serve, arrange three slices of watermelon on each plate, and top with arugula. Sprinkle liberally with pecorino, drizzle with the balsamic reduction, and finish with fresh cracked pepper.

# BAKED BRIE EN CROUTE
## *with Sorrel Chutney and Pistachios*

Baked Brie is the perfect way to start a fabulous evening with friends. For our fantastic West Indian Brie en croute, we top the cheese with Jamaican sorrel chutney and pistachios, then wrap it in a pastry crust and bake it to golden perfection. Any type of fruit chutney will work, so experiment away with mango, peach, or papaya for other scrumptious versions.

*Serves 6*

**2 sheets prepared puff pastry (17.3 ounces each)**

**1-pound wheel Brie**

**¼ cup purchased sorrel or fruit chutney or Quick Sorrel Marmalade (page 236)**

**½ cup toasted pistachios**

**baguette or crackers to serve**

Preheat the oven to 425°F.

Roll out the puff pastry sheets, ensuring there is enough dough to completely wrap around the cheese. Wrap one sheet around the base and sides of the Brie, leaving the top uncovered. Spread the top of the Brie with sorrel chutney or sorrel marmalade. Cut the other sheet of pastry into strips, and arrange in a crisscross pattern over the chutney/marmalade to create a lattice top. Sprinkle with pistachios. Place the pastry-wrapped Brie on a baking sheet.

Bake for 15 to 20 minutes until the crust is golden-brown and the cheese is warmed and melted through. Serve immediately on a plate surrounded by baguette slices or crackers.

# STEWED GUAVA
## *with Red Wine*

**G**uava is deliciously sweet and tart and even more delectable when stewed, especially served warm with ice cream. After a particularly decadent lunch at a Jamaican country home, we were served a dessert of stewed guava accompanied with ice cream and homemade citrus shortbread. It was a revelation! In homage to fabulous Jamaican country cooking, we suggest serving this decadent dessert over our Coconut-Ginger Ice (page 196), or use your favorite premade ice cream.

*Serves 4*

8 ripe guavas

½ cup brown sugar

¼ cup orange juice

¼ cup red wine

1 tablespoon orange zest

dash cinnamon

dash nutmeg

4 sprigs mint, for garnish

Peel and quarter the guavas. In a saucepan, combine ¾ cup water, the brown sugar, orange juice, red wine, orange zest, cinnamon, and nutmeg, and bring to a boil. Add the guavas, and return to a boil. Boil for about 15 minutes or until the syrup thickens. To serve, ladle a generous serving of warm stewed guava and its liquid into a small bowl. Garnish with a sprig of mint.

# MANGO-PASSION FOOL

This old-school sweet harkens back to days gone by when dessert was as simple as fresh fruit swirled with cream. The dish known as "fool" is essentially that: some kind of fruit or fruit puree mixed with cream and custard. You can't go wrong with it, and, yes, we are fools for it. In this recipe, we love the decadence of the passionfruit and mango compote swirled into an unsweetened creamy custard. This makes a really tasty "kitchen dessert" (restaurant parlance for a simple dessert prepared in the main kitchen) for all occasions and can be served either as single portions or in a big glass bowl to be placed family style on the table or on a dessert buffet.

*Serves 6*

4 mangoes

2 passionfruit, halved, pulp and seeds scooped out (discard the peel)

½ cup sugar

juice of ½ lime

1 egg

½ cup milk

1 teaspoon vanilla

½ cup heavy cream

Peel the mangoes, remove the flesh from the seeds, and roughly chop. Place the mango, passionfruit pulp and seeds, sugar, lime juice, and ½ cup water in a medium saucepan over medium heat and bring to a boil. Reduce the heat to low, and simmer gently until the mixture is smooth and cooked through to a puree-like consistency, about 10 minutes. Strain the mango-passion puree through a sieve to remove the pulp and seeds, and beat with a wire whisk until smooth. Cool, cover, and hold in the refrigerator while you make the custard.

Break the egg into a bowl, and beat lightly with a wire whisk. Warm the milk over low heat—do not allow it to come to a boil. Stir a small amount of warm milk into the beaten egg to temper the egg. Add the egg/milk mixture to the remaining milk, still over the heat. Whisk constantly over very low heat until the custard thickens. Do not allow it to boil. Remove the custard from the heat, stir in the vanilla, and allow it to cool.

Whip the heavy cream until stiff peaks form. To serve, swirl the mango-passion puree and heavy cream into the custard. Do not blend thoroughly as it is supposed to look streaky. Pour the fool into glasses, individual serving dishes, or a large bowl, and chill thoroughly. Feel free to stir or top with fresh fruit for serving.

# TROPICAL ISLAND FRO YO

Ice cream is hugely popular in the West Indies, particularly on Sundays in Jamaica, when the national pastime is to head out with the family for a Sunday "cream." Our hot climes lend themselves to indulging in cold treats. Here we take a modern turn toward frozen yogurt. We love the tartness of the yogurt combined with the punch of exotic fruit flavors native to our region, like mango, guava, and passionfruit. Simple and refreshing, this recipe says hello sunshine and summer in a single bite. If you wish, serve with toppings like molasses, Sorrel Syrup (page 187), coconut flakes, toasted peanuts, fresh mango, pumpkin seeds, cashews, or pomegranate seeds.

*Each recipe serves 4 to 6*

## GUAVA, MANGO, OR PASSIONFRUIT FROZEN YOGURT

3¾ cups full-fat plain yogurt

¾ cup granulated sugar

¼ teaspoon fine sea salt

½ cup guava puree, mango puree, or passionfruit puree

Combine the yogurt, sugar, and salt in a chilled stainless steel bowl. Whisk together until the sugar and salt are completely dissolved. Stir in the fruit puree. Chill, covered, for a few hours. Scrape into the bowl of an ice cream machine, and follow the manufacturer's instructions for making ice cream. Once finished, transfer to a covered container, and rest in the freezer for at least 4 hours before serving.

## GINGER-LIME FROZEN YOGURT

3¾ cups full-fat plain yogurt

1 cup granulated sugar

¼ teaspoon fine sea salt

2 teaspoons grated fresh ginger

3 tablespoons lime juice

1 teaspoon lime zest

Combine the yogurt, sugar, and salt in a chilled stainless steel bowl. Whisk together until the sugar and salt are completely dissolved. Stir in the grated ginger, lime juice, and zest. Chill, covered, for a few hours. Scrape into the bowl of an ice cream machine, and follow the manufacturer's instructions for making ice cream. Once finished, transfer to a covered container, and rest in the freezer for at least 4 hours before serving.

# GRILLED PINEAPPLE UPSIDE-DOWN RUM CAKE

Rum cake—a simple moist vanilla cake saturated in rum—is a common dessert throughout the Caribbean. This decadent version combines that island standby with another classic: pineapple upside-down cake. Here, grilled fruit makes it anything but ordinary. The fresh pineapple slices are soaked in rum, dipped in brown sugar, and then charred on the grill. This stellar combo turns the cake into a moist and sticky delight.

*Serves 12 (makes one 10-inch round cake)*

### FOR THE TOPPING

6 to 8 cored slices pineapple, each ¼-inch thick

½ cup dark rum

1 cup brown sugar, divided

¼ cup unsalted butter, melted

### FOR THE CAKE

1½ cups butter, at room temperature

3 cups sugar

5 large eggs, at room temperature

2 teaspoons vanilla extract

3½ cups all-purpose flour

½ teaspoon baking powder

½ teaspoon salt

1 cup whole milk

### FOR THE RUM SYRUP

½ cup butter

1 cup granulated sugar

1 cup dark rum

Preheat the oven to 350°F.

To prepare the grilled pineapple topping, soak the pineapple slices in the rum for at least 5 minutes. Remove, and coat in a little brown sugar (about ½ cup). Heat the grill or griddle to medium-high, and grill the pineapple slices for about 2 minutes on each side.

Pour the melted butter into a 10-inch round cake pan. Sprinkle with the remaining ½ cup brown sugar, and top with the grilled pineapple slices. Set aside while you make the cake batter.

To make the cake batter, cream the butter and sugar together until the mixture is light in color and fluffy. Add the eggs, one at a time, whisking after each addition until combined. Stir in the vanilla. In a medium bowl, sift together the flour, baking powder, and salt. Slowly add the dry ingredients to the egg mixture, stirring until combined. Add the milk, stirring until there are no lumps in the batter. Pour the batter over the grilled pineapple in the cake pan. Bake for 40 to 45 minutes, until a knife or toothpick inserted in the center comes out nearly clean (a few moist crumbs clinging to the toothpick are okay).

While the cake is baking, make the rum syrup. Combine the butter, granulated sugar, and ¼ cup water in a small saucepan. Bring to a boil over medium heat; then reduce the heat and simmer for about 15 minutes until thickened. Remove from the heat and stir in the rum.

Remove the cake from the oven. While still cooling, pour the rum syrup over the cake a little at a time, so that it absorbs. Allow the cake to cool for at least 5 minutes, then invert it onto a cake stand or serving plate. Serve with ice cream.

# RASPBERRY–COCONUT CREAM SCONES

T ea with scones reminds us of our annual summer visits with our cherished Aunt Winsome, our father's cousin who lived in England. Summers spent at her lovely London abode always involved high tea, whether at home or at a charming English restaurant. This scone, studded with raspberries and coconut flakes, is a West Indian take on a traditional currant scone. It replaces the usual heavy cream with coconut cream. These treats are best enjoyed in the company of good lady friends and a pot of your favorite brew.

*Serves 12*

**2 cups flour**

**2 teaspoons baking powder**

**2 tablespoons sugar, divided**

**½ teaspoon salt**

**6 tablespoons cold butter, cut into small pieces**

**¾ cup raspberries**

**2 large eggs, lightly beaten**

**½ cup plus 1 tablespoon coconut cream or heavy cream**

**¼ cup sweetened coconut flakes**

Preheat the oven to 450°F.

Combine the flour, baking powder, 1 tablespoon sugar, and salt in a large mixing bowl. Add the pieces of butter, and work them into the flour mixture with your fingers until the mixture resembles coarse crumbs. Add the raspberries. Make a well in the center of the flour mixture. Add the eggs and ½ cup coconut cream or heavy cream, and mix with a wooden spoon until the dough comes together.

Drop the batter by large spoonfuls onto a cookie sheet. Brush with 1 tablespoon coconut cream, and sprinkle with the remaining tablespoon of sugar and the coconut flakes. Bake for 12 to 15 minutes, until lightly browned. Serve warm or at room temperature with preserves and butter or clotted cream.

# BEV'S KEY LIME PIE

One of the most vivid memories of our mother's cooking is her Key lime pie, a treat that she often baked throughout our childhood. We found her recipe on a handwritten card that clearly dates back to the 1970s. In true Caribbean form, she added gingersnaps to the traditional graham cracker crust. The condensed milk makes this pie quite rich and sweet, but the indulgence is worth it—if even for just a sliver!

*Serves 6 to 8 (makes one 8-inch pie)*

**FOR THE CRUST**

1 cup graham cracker crumbs

½ cup gingersnap crumbs

2 tablespoons granulated sugar

6 tablespoons melted butter

**FOR THE FILLING**

8 egg yolks

1 cup (8 fluid ounces) sweetened condensed milk

1 teaspoon lime zest

1 cup fresh lime juice

**FOR THE TOPPING**

1 cup whipping cream, chilled

1 teaspoon lime zest

Preheat the oven to 350°F.

Make the crust. Combine the graham cracker crumbs, gingersnap crumbs, sugar, and melted butter, and mix until well blended. Press the mixture into an 8-inch pie dish. Chill until ready to use.

Make the filling. Beat the egg yolks until they are thick and lemon colored. Add the condensed milk, and stir until combined. Stir in 1 teaspoon lime zest. Add the lime juice and stir well. Pour into the chilled crust, and bake for 30 minutes or until the filling is set. Remove from the oven and chill for 3 to 4 hours.

For the topping, whip the cream in a medium bowl until stiff peaks form. Spread the whipped cream over the cooled pie, and top with lime zest.

# MANGO, BLACKBERRY, AND PEACH PIE
## with Cornmeal Brown Sugar Crumble

A crumble is old-fashioned yet modern, rustic yet sophisticated, and always fulfilling in the way that only good comfort food can be. This dessert incorporates mango with blackberries and peaches as the filling. It would surprise some people to know that both blackberries and peaches grow in the hills of Jamaica; the local varieties tend to be smaller and more tart than supermarket produce and, with a little lime juice, provide great balance for our sweet Jamaican mango. The addition of some fresh island mint gives the filling a nice kick. For the top crust we make a variation of a traditional crumble topping, combining Caribbean staples like grated coconut and cornmeal with almonds, oats, brown sugar, and butter for a crispy, nutty, island-style crumble. Pair all this goodness with coconut cream, rum whipped cream, or coconut ice cream.

### Serves 6 to 8

1 Basic Pastry Crust (page 165)
or premade pie crust

**FOR THE FILLING**

2 cups cubed fresh mango

16 ounces fresh blackberries

4 medium peaches, thinly sliced
(can be peeled or unpeeled)

¼ cup granulated sugar

2 tablespoons fresh lime juice

2 tablespoons chopped mint

**FOR THE TOPPING**

⅓ cup brown sugar

⅓ cup butter, room temperature

⅓ cup old-fashioned oats

⅓ cup yellow cornmeal

3 tablespoons unsweetened
dried coconut flakes

3 tablespoons almonds

1 teaspoon cinnamon

**TO SERVE**

whipped cream, coconut cream,
or ice cream

mint leaves

brown sugar

*(Continued)*

Preheat the oven to 350°F.

Roll out your pie crust to a large round, and carefully lift it into an 8-inch pie dish. Allow the extra dough to lay over the sides of the dish, and flute or finish the edge of the crust only if you are so inclined—this crumble is Jamaican country cooking, proudly handmade, so we don't worry about making it look too neat and tidy.

To make the filling, combine the mango, blackberries, peaches, granulated sugar, lime juice, and mint in a large bowl. Allow to rest for 2 to 3 minutes, then pour the mixture into the pie crust.

To make the crumble topping, combine the brown sugar, butter, oats, cornmeal, coconut, almonds, and cinnamon in the bowl of a food processor. Pulse until combined. Spread the topping liberally over the fruit filling.

Bake for 1 hour or until the top is golden-brown and the fruit bubbly. Serve warm with a generous dollop of whipped cream, coconut cream, or ice cream, and garnish with mint leaves and a sprinkling of brown sugar.

# BERRY-COCONUT OVERNIGHT OATS

**O**ur breakfast of choice is overnight oats. It is quick, healthy, easy to make, and totally delicious. Plus, you can prep a few days' stock and store it in mason jars in the refrigerator so that a scrumptious breakfast is only one twist away. We love the combo of oats soaked in milk or yogurt, all dressed up with goodies like almonds, nut butter, spices, and honey, given a West Indian flair with grated coconut, otaheite apples, citrus, and fresh berries. (The otaheite apple or Malay apple isn't really an apple. It has a pear shape, and a large pit in the center of aromatic white flesh.) This recipe is very flexible, so experiment away with fruits, nuts, and toppings of your choice. To store the prepared oatmeal you will need a large bowl with a lid or cover, or you can make individual servings by using small mason jars. If you decide to make individual portions, divide the ingredients equally between the jars, and adjust the quantities if necessary.

*Serves 4*

2½ cups old-fashioned oats

2 cups almond milk or coconut milk

1 to 1½ cups Greek yogurt (plain or vanilla)

3 tablespoons fresh orange juice

1 teaspoon vanilla extract

¼ teaspoon almond extract

½ teaspoon orange zest

½ teaspoon cinnamon

¼ teaspoon nutmeg

3 to 4 tablespoons honey or agave nectar, divided

1 otaheite apple, grated or diced (or substitute Fuji apple)

1 cup blackberries, divided

1 cup blueberries or raspberries, divided

3 tablespoons smooth or crunchy almond or peanut butter

¼ cup unsweetened coconut flakes, toasted

¼ cup roasted almonds, chopped or whole

*(Continued)*

Place the oats in a bowl with the almond milk, yogurt, and orange juice, and mix well. If the mixture is dry add water or more almond milk; the liquid should cover the oatmeal. Add the vanilla extract, almond extract, orange zest, cinnamon, nutmeg, and 2 tablespoons honey or agave nectar, and stir to combine. Add the apple and half the berries, and gently mix again, tasting for sweetness; add more sweetener if necessary. Swirl in the nut butter, ensuring that it spreads throughout the mixture and doesn't lump up in one spot (you may need to thin out your nut butter with a bit of warm water or milk before swirling it in, if it is thick enough that it won't drizzle off a spoon). Finish this delicious breakfast treat by topping the oatmeal with a layer of coconut and almonds, or if preferred you can mix them into the oatmeal. Top with a drizzle of honey or agave nectar and a few more berries, and cover the bowl. Allow the oats to refrigerate overnight.

In the morning, divide the oatmeal into individual bowls and serve.

**NOTE:** Can't wait overnight? A faster version of this recipe would be to substitute quick oats for rolled oats; allow a soaking time of 1 hour.

# SORREL SYRUP
## *and Candied Sorrel Buds*

Sorrel buds make a great substitute for dried cranberries or dried pomegranate in savory and sweet recipes. The syrup, once cooled, should be stored at room temperature in a sanitized bottle or jar. It is great to use in desserts, over ice cream, on pancakes, in salad dressings, or in cocktails.

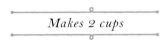

*Makes 2 cups*

**1 cup granulated sugar**

**2 cups whole fresh sorrel buds, washed (see note)**

Bring the sugar and 1 cup water to a boil over high heat in a wide-rimmed pot. Add the sorrel buds. Reduce the heat to low, and allow the mixture to simmer uncovered for about 1 hour until reduced. After about an hour, the sorrel buds should be candied, and the liquid should have acquired a syrupy texture. Using a slotted spoon, remove the sorrel buds from the syrup, and spread them on a rack to cool. Once cool, store the candied buds in an airtight container; they will keep for up to three weeks.

NOTE: See "Local Produce," in the back of the book, for more information about sourcing fresh sorrel buds.

# CHAPTER 8

# COFFEE, COCOA, NUTS & COCONUT

ALTHOUGH SUGAR PRODUCTION MAY HAVE DOMINATED AGRICULTURE IN THE WEST INDIES BECAUSE OF ITS DEMAND IN THE NINETEENTH-century world market, it was by no means the only type of farming practiced in the Caribbean. The majority of the slaves in the islands would have worked in sugar, but coffee, cacao, and coconut estates were also built on the back of African slave labor.

Sugarcane needed flat land, but coffee, cacao, and coconuts thrived in mountainous areas. Their cultivation allowed for the settlement of the interior, mountainous parts of the islands, which created more opportunities for industrious smaller planters who wanted to explore other industries. Caribbean coffee and cacao dominated the world market and were in very high demand in European coffee houses, chocolatiers, and chocolate houses.

Few things in life are more satisfying than the first sip of Blue Mountain coffee as the sun makes its ascent into the morning sky. Everything about the experience of drinking our cherished Jamaican coffee is sublime: the aroma wafting through the house in the quiet daylight, the delicious decision of whether to drink it pure and black or as café au lait increasing our anticipation. We love our coffee. Anyone who has not tried a cup of Blue Mountain coffee with condensed milk is missing out on a real treat. Condensed milk and evaporated milk are relics of the World War II era (when fresh milk was unavailable), but both continue to be very relevant in daily Caribbean life. Their addition to a cup of coffee or tea accompanied by scrumptious biscuits or cake is nothing short of perfection. In this chapter we share some of our favorite sweet recipes for coffee, coconut, and chocolate—might we suggest a fresh cup of Blue Mountain bliss to go along with them?

> The house is a good one, quite new. It is situated in the midst of mountains, out of which issue abundant streams of water; all of the sides of the mountains are planted with coconut trees, and coffee bushes. The coffee is a beautiful shrub, bearing a white flower on the stalk, and the leaf is a most brilliant green.
>
> —Lady Nugent's journal of her residence in Jamaica from 1801 to 1805

# CHOCOLATE-HABANERO MOUSSE
## *with Coconut-Rum Chantilly*

Tradition is always important, and nothing speaks to tradition better than chocolate mousse for dessert. It is so classic, so French, so delicate—what's not to love? Well, this version puts a Caribbean spin on the classic, with the addition of spicy habanero, smooth West Indian rum, and coconut. It is rich, dense with chocolate flavor, and rewarding in every way you can imagine.

*Serves 4 to 6*

### CHOCOLATE-HABANERO MOUSSE

2 cups roughly chopped semidark chocolate, divided

⅔ cup heavy cream

1 red habanero pepper, seeds and ribs removed, chopped

2 tablespoons dark rum

2 egg yolks

4 egg whites

2 tablespoons granulated sugar

### COCONUT-RUM CHANTILLY

2 cups heavy cream

1½ cups confectioners' sugar

½ cup coconut milk powder

2 tablespoons dark rum

chocolate shavings for serving

Make the mousse. Place 1½ cups of the chopped chocolate in a stainless steel bowl. In a medium, heavy saucepan, combine the heavy cream and the habanero, and bring to a boil. Remove from the heat, cover, and allow the mixture to rest for 15 minutes. After 15 minutes, return the cream to a boil. Stir in the rum.

Strain the habanero-rum cream directly over the chocolate, and stir well until the chocolate is melted. Add the egg yolks, stirring quickly until the mixture is glossy.

In a separate mixing bowl, beat the egg whites until they have doubled in size. Add the granulated sugar, and continue beating until the mixture is firm and fluffy and stiff peaks have formed. In three batches, gently fold the egg whites into the chocolate mixture, being careful not to overmix. Stir in the remaining ½ cup chocolate pieces. Transfer the mousse to a large glass bowl or individual dessert bowls. Chill for a few hours before serving.

Make the coconut-rum chantilly. Combine the heavy cream, confectioners' sugar, coconut milk powder, and rum in a blender, and blend on high until stiff peaks form.

Serve the mousse garnished with coconut-rum chantilly and chocolate shavings.

# RUM AND RAISIN BUDINO
## *with Candied Cashews and Citrus-Rum Sauce*

Every week, our grandmother Mavis, or Ma Ma, would make miniature dishes of delicate custard, a dessert that she had perfected, and keep them in her fridge in individual glass ramekins. Laced with a combination of caramelized-sugar syrup, nutmeg, dark rum, and raisins, her unique take on this traditional dessert was exceptional. We've taken Ma Ma's delicious custard and incorporated it into an unforgettable budino— creamy, rich pudding with a cookie crust (ours has ginger and cashew for a touch of island flavor, of course).

*Serves 8*

**GINGER CRUST**

10 crunchy oatmeal cookies or digestive biscuits

10 gingersnap cookies

½ cup roasted, salted cashews

2 tablespoons unsalted butter, melted

**RUM AND RAISIN BUDINO**

½ cup raisins

½ cup plus 2 tablespoons dark rum, divided

3 cups whole milk, divided

¼ cup cornstarch

pinch nutmeg

¾ cup (packed) dark brown sugar

½ teaspoon cinnamon

5 large egg yolks

3 tablespoons unsalted butter

1 teaspoon fine sea salt

**CANDIED CASHEWS**

1⅓ cups raw cashews

⅓ cup granulated sugar

1 tablespoon butter

**CITRUS-RUM SAUCE**

juice from 6 oranges, strained

½ cup plus 2 tablespoons confectioners' sugar

1 tablespoon orange zest

½ cup plus 1 tablespoon butter, softened

3 tablespoons dark rum

*(Continued)*

Have eight dessert bowls or ramekins ready.

To make the ginger crust, combine the oatmeal cookies, ginger cookies, and cashews in a food processor, and pulse until crumbled. Transfer to a mixing bowl, add the melted butter, and mix. Press approximately 3 tablespoons of the cookie mixture into the bottom of each ramekin. Cover and chill the crusts while you make the custard.

In a small bowl combine the raisins with ½ cup rum, and set aside to rest while you make the custard. Whisk ½ cup milk and the cornstarch together in a small bowl until smooth; set aside. Heat the remaining 2½ cups milk and a pinch of nutmeg in a small saucepan just to a simmer; set aside. In a heavy saucepan over medium heat, mix the brown sugar and the cinnamon in ¾ cup water, stirring constantly until the brown sugar is dissolved. Increase the heat to high and cook without stirring until thickened and dark in color.

Whisk the egg yolks in a large bowl until smooth. Gradually whisk in the hot nutmeg-infused milk, then whisk in the cornstarch-milk mixture. Once combined, slowly whisk in the cinnamon and brown sugar mixture. Return the custard to a saucepan and cook over medium heat, whisking constantly to prevent lumps, until the mixture thickens, about 3 minutes. Remove from the heat; whisk in the butter, the remaining 2 tablespoons rum, and the salt. If the custard is lumpy it can be passed through a strainer at this point.

Drain the raisins. To assemble the custards, spoon 1 tablespoon raisins on top of the crust in each ramekin. Pour approximately ½ cup of custard over the crust and raisins in each ramekin. Refrigerate for 4 to 5 hours to allow the custard to set.

While the custard is setting, make the candied cashews and the rum sauce. Preheat the oven to 350°F. Spread raw cashews on a baking tray, and roast for 10 minutes.

In a medium-sized heavy saucepan over medium heat, combine 1 tablespoon water with the granulated sugar and butter. Bring to a simmer, and allow the mixture to reach 245°F (should take 3 to 5 minutes and be light golden in color). Turn off flame. Add the roasted cashews and stir, until the nuts are well coated with the sugar mixture. Spread on a silicone sheet or a sheet pan lined with parchment paper. Return immediately to the oven for 5 to 6 minutes. After baking, allow the nuts to cool completely.

To make the orange-rum sauce, simmer the juice, confectioners' sugar, and zest over medium heat until reduced by half, about 5 minutes. Whisk in the butter a little at a time. Add the rum at the last minute. Serve the sauce warm or at room temperature.

When ready to serve, spoon 2 tablespoons of the rum sauce over each budino. Top with candied cashews.

# COCONUT-GINGER ICE

This dessert is inspired by a nineteenth-century Jamaican recipe for coconut ice cream that calls simply for four grated coconuts, sugar, and one pint of milk. The grated coconuts are squeezed of their juice to make a coconut cream, which is blended with milk, sweetened with sugar, and frozen.[5] Our plant-based version incorporates buttery vanilla, bright citrusy orange zest, and ginger for spice.

*Serves 4*

1 14-ounce can full-fat coconut milk, chilled

2 tablespoons liquid coconut palm syrup (or honey)

2 tablespoons grated fresh ginger

pinch of salt

1 tablespoon orange zest

1 teaspoon vanilla extract

Whisk together the coconut milk, palm syrup or honey, ginger, and salt in a chilled stainless steel bowl. Add the orange zest and vanilla extract, and stir to combine. Use a jug or a bowl with a spout to transfer the chilled mixture into the bowl of an ice cream maker. Make ice cream according to the manufacturer's instructions. Transfer to a covered container, and store in the freezer until ready to use.

5   Sullivan, 46.

# BLUE MOUNTAIN AFFOGATO

Affogato is a simple yet delicious Italian treat comprising vanilla gelato with a shot of steaming-hot espresso poured over the top. *Affogato* means "drowned" in Italian. In our West Indian version of this divine dessert, we "drown" vanilla ice cream in Jamaican Blue Mountain coffee, a shot of Tia Maria, and a sprinkle of chocolate shavings. It's easy, quick, and sure to please any dinner guest; it's even the perfect end to a delicious homemade dinner for one.

*Serves 4*

1 pint vanilla ice cream

8 tablespoons finely chopped bittersweet chocolate

8 tablespoons Tia Maria liqueur or dark rum

8 tablespoons hot, freshly brewed, strong Blue Mountain coffee

Have four tea or coffee cups ready. Spoon one large scoop of ice cream into each cup. Spoon 2 tablespoons each of chopped chocolate and liqueur or rum over the ice cream. Pour the coffee over all, and serve immediately.

# OLD-FASHIONED BLUE MOUNTAIN CHOCOLATE LAYER CAKE

When Suzanne's boys were little she didn't care if their friends preferred vanilla cake; she always served chocolate cake with chocolate frosting for their birthday parties because that's what she wanted to eat. Okay, so she was being a bit of a selfish mummy, but everyone was happy with the cake, and she threw rowdy, fun-filled birthday parties, so a good time was had by all. When making this recipe she sticks to tradition and always heeds the age-old cake-baking advice learned from the 1930s Jamaican newspaper columnist and homemaking expert "a Mother," who declared, "Cake making is most satisfactory conducted by one individual. Because the batter should be stirred continuously in one direction during the mixing—not first one way and then the other."[6] Suzanne's boys are now young men, but good old-fashioned chocolate cake makes us just as happy these days as it did when they were three and five. We hope you will make as many precious memories while enjoying it as we did.

*Serves 12 (makes a two-layer 9-inch cake)*

1¾ cups all-purpose flour, sifted
(sift after measuring)

¾ cup unsweetened
cocoa powder

2 teaspoons baking powder

1½ teaspoons baking soda

1 teaspoon salt

2 cups sugar

1 cup coconut milk
(or whole milk)

½ cup coconut oil

2 large eggs

2 teaspoons vanilla extract

1 cup hot, freshly brewed
Blue Mountain coffee

CHOCOLATE ICING

½ cup unsweetened cocoa

1 cup butter (2 sticks), softened

6 cups confectioners' sugar

½ cup whole milk

2 teaspoons vanilla extract

⅔ cup chocolate chips

chocolate shavings or chocolate
chips, for garnish

*(Continued)*

---

6. *Daily Gleaner, Our Women's Page*, "Bake Me a Cake as Fast as You Can."

Preheat the oven to 350°F.

Butter and flour two 9-inch cake pans and set aside. Sift the flour, cocoa powder, baking powder, baking soda, and salt into a bowl. Add the sugar, and stir thoroughly to combine. In a separate bowl whisk together the coconut milk, coconut oil, eggs, and vanilla extract. Add the wet ingredients to the dry ingredients, and mix on low to medium speed until the batter is well combined. Carefully add the hot coffee, and gently stir to combine.

Distribute the batter evenly between the two cake pans. Bake for 35 to 40 minutes or until a toothpick inserted in the center of each cake comes out nearly clean (a few moist crumbs clinging to the toothpick are okay). Cool completely on a wire rack.

While the cakes are cooling, make the chocolate icing. Sift ½ cup cocoa powder into a large bowl. Add the butter. Cream together the butter and cocoa powder until light and smooth. Add the confectioners' sugar, milk, and vanilla extract to the cocoa mixture, mixing at medium speed until it is smooth and creamy. Place the chocolate chips in the top of a double boiler over water that is simmering (not boiling), and stir until the chocolate is melted. Remove from heat, and add the melted chocolate to the butter and sugar mixture, stirring until smooth.

Once the cakes are cool, flip the pans upside down, tap the bottom of the pans lightly, and remove the cakes. To decorate and assemble, spread a generous portion of the chocolate icing on one layer. Place the second layer on top of the first, and frost the top and sides of the cake with the remaining frosting. Garnish with shaved chocolate or chocolate chips.

# GIZZADAS
## *with Chocolate and Almonds*

I n Jamaica, and all throughout the region, many sweet treats using coconut and sugar developed as a natural spinoff to sugar production. One sophisticated coconut and sugar dessert that would likely have been prepared in the planter's kitchen was called a gizzada, also called a "pinch me round" because the sides of the tart shell are "pinched." A gizzada is a sweet tartlet consisting of finely shredded coconut flavored with cinnamon, nutmeg, butter, rosewater or ginger, and brown sugar. We add a double kick of chocolate and crunchy almonds to take it up a notch.

*Serves 10*

1 cup brown sugar

2 cups grated unsweetened coconut

2 teaspoons vanilla extract

1 teaspoon nutmeg

1 teaspoon cinnamon

2 tablespoons butter

1 Basic Pastry Crust, unbaked (page 165)

¼ cup semisweet chocolate chips, melted over a double boiler

¼ cup sliced almonds

Preheat the oven to 350°F.

In a small saucepan, boil 1 cup water and the brown sugar together over low heat for 10 minutes or until the liquid thickens into a syrup. Add the grated coconut, vanilla extract, nutmeg, and cinnamon. Stir the ingredients thoroughly to prevent sticking. Bring to a boil, and cook for 20 minutes, stirring continuously. Add the butter, stirring constantly until the butter melts and disappears. Boil for another 7 minutes, stirring constantly. Remove the pan from the heat and allow the filling to cool.

Prepare the shells. Roll the pastry dough on a cutting board to a ¼-inch thickness. Use a cookie cutter (or an 8-ounce glass) to cut circles approximately 3½ inches to 4 inches in diameter. Cut as many circles as you can. Turn up and pinch (or crimp) the edges of each of the circles with your fingers to form rustic pastry shells. Place the shells on a greased baking sheet, and bake for 15 minutes. Remove the shells from the oven, and add filling to each. Drizzle with melted chocolate and top with almonds. Return to the oven, and bake the gizzadas for another 20 minutes.

# PECAN PIE
## *Infused with Rum*

Pecan pie reminds of us of the southern United States, but in particular of New Orleans. So much pecan candy and pecan pie abound in NOLA that we tend to overdo it a bit when we visit. This is our West Indian–inspired version of a pecan pie. Add some Jamaican rum, and oh boy is it good! Sometimes, for a country-style spin, we bake it in a skillet. This is our little homage to a beloved city…to NOLA with love.

*Serves 6 to 8 (makes one 8-inch pie)*

1 Basic Pastry Crust, unbaked (page 165)

½ cup granulated sugar

¼ cup dark-brown sugar

1½ cups dark corn syrup or Louisiana cane syrup

3 large eggs, lightly beaten

1½ teaspoons fine sea salt

1½ teaspoons all-purpose flour

2 tablespoons dark rum

1½ tablespoons unsalted butter, melted

1½ teaspoons vanilla extract

1½ cups pecan halves

Preheat the oven to 350°F and place a rack in the lower part of the oven.

Roll out the pie crust and carefully lay it into an 8-inch pie plate or 8-inch skillet. Trim and flute the edges of the pastry.

In a stainless steel bowl, mix the granulated and brown sugars together. Once combined, stir in the corn or cane syrup, eggs, salt, and flour. Continue stirring until everything is well combined (this should take about a minute). Stir in the rum, melted butter, and vanilla extract, and then fold in the pecans. Pour the pecan mixture into the pastry shell, and place the pie in the oven. Bake for at least 1 hour (up to 1 hour and 20 minutes), or until the pie is firm but soft in the center. Remove from the oven, and cool on a wire rack for at least an hour before slicing.

# EBONY AND IVORY
## *Double Chocolate–Pistachio Brownies and Coconut-Macadamia Blondies*

Suzanne loves brownies, but Michelle prefers blondies—so what could we do but include them both? We had both on the menu in our early Café Bella years. They were made with love by a charming Irish lady, who baked the most marvelous bars and brownies under the sun. (It was a challenge to refrain from eating the profits before the customers arrived for lunch.) No matter your preference, you are in for a treat: these bars are rich, decadent, and loaded with chocolate chips and nuts.

## DOUBLE CHOCOLATE–PISTACHIO BROWNIES

### *Serves 12*

½ cup all-purpose flour

½ teaspoon baking powder

2½ cups semisweet chocolate chips, divided

2 sticks unsalted butter (8 ounces), cut into pieces

3 extra-large eggs

1½ cups granulated sugar

1½ teaspoons instant coffee powder

1 tablespoon vanilla

1 cup pistachios

Preheat the oven to 350°F, and position a rack in the middle. Lightly grease a 9 x 13-inch baking pan, and line it with waxed paper.

Sift together the flour and baking powder in a small bowl. Combine 2 cups of the chocolate chips with the butter in a metal bowl, and set it over a pot of simmering water. Stir with a wooden spoon until the chocolate and butter are melted and glossy. Remove from the heat.

In the meantime, whisk the eggs. Add the sugar, coffee powder, and vanilla to the eggs, and whisk until combined. Add the egg mixture to the chocolate, and stir with a wooden spoon until it thickens, 2 to 3 minutes. Gradually add the flour mixture to the chocolate mixture, continuing to stir until well combined. Mix in the pistachios and the remaining chocolate chips.

Pour the batter into the pan, and smooth the top with a spatula. Tap the pan on the counter to remove air bubbles. Bake for 25 minutes or until a toothpick inserted in the center comes out clean. The brownies will be dense and chewy, so make sure to allow them to cool completely before cutting into squares. Store at room temperature in a sealed container.

# COCONUT-MACADAMIA BLONDIES

*Serves 12*

2 cups all-purpose flour

1 teaspoon baking powder

¼ teaspoon salt

2 sticks unsalted butter
(8 ounces), softened

2 cups packed light brown sugar

2 large eggs

2 teaspoons vanilla extract

¼ cup macadamia nuts

½ cup unsweetened coconut
flakes, toasted

¼ cup white chocolate chunks
or chips

Preheat the oven to 350°F and place a rack in the middle of the oven. Grease a 9 x 13-inch baking pan and line it with parchment paper.

In a mixing bowl, combine the flour, baking powder, and salt. In a separate bowl mix together the butter and brown sugar until smooth; add the eggs and vanilla, stirring to combine well. Stir in the flour mixture, macadamia nuts, coconut flakes, and white chocolate chips, ensuring that the chunky ingredients are distributed well throughout the batter. Pour the batter into the pan, and smooth the top. Bake for 20 to 25 minutes, until the top is golden and the sides are slightly crispy. Remove from the oven and allow to cool completely before cutting into squares. Store at room temperature in a sealed container.

# NUT-BUTTER LOAVES

Almond butter and peanut butter are staples in our homes. We use them on practically everything, from toast to oatmeal to yogurt. The days of old-school peanut butter and jelly sandwiches as the sole way to consume this delectable treat are long gone. Nut butters of today are sexy, delicious, full of flavor, and have all kinds of interesting ingredients blended in. Our rich and tasty butters reside halfway between a dessert and a nut butter. Deliberately more dense and flavorful than commercial ones, they are great as a topping for ice cream, in a smoothie, on top of oatmeal, or simply served as a healthy snack. Don't expect the texture of a typical peanut or almond butter, however; these yummy versions are so dense and delicious that we like to store them in the refrigerator (which allows the coconut oil to solidify) in a shallow rectangular container, yielding a "loaf" that can be turned out on a cutting board, served on a platter, or sliced with fresh fruit as an accompaniment.

*Each recipe serves 8*

## SEA SALT AND CINNAMON ALMOND BUTTER

2 cups roasted whole almonds

¼ cup coconut oil

1 to 2 tablespoons honey, agave nectar, or maple syrup

½ teaspoon cinnamon

¼ to ½ teaspoon coarse sea salt

¼ cup roughly chopped roasted almonds (optional)

Place the almonds in a food processor fitted with the blade; pulse a few times until they reach the consistency of meal. Add the coconut oil and blitz, scraping the sides regularly. Add your sweetener of choice: start with 1 tablespoon, pulse, and taste for sweetness. Continue pulsing until the almond meal forms a ball and is buttery in consistency, periodically scraping the sides of the processor. If you like your almond butter on the sweeter side, add the second tablespoon of honey at this point; then add the cinnamon and salt, and pulse until smooth and creamy.

Transfer the almond butter to a bowl, and stir in the chopped almonds if you like crunchy almond butter. If you prefer it smooth, skip this step. Transfer to a sanitized jar (see page 208), and refrigerate.

# CHOCOLATE PEANUT BUTTER

2 cups roasted fresh peanuts,
skins removed

5 tablespoons coconut oil

¼ cup cocoa powder

½ teaspoon coarse sea salt

2 tablespoons honey

½ cup water

If you want crunchy peanut butter, reserve ⅓ cup peanuts before blending, and roughly chop them.

Place all the ingredients in a food processor or Vitamix, and blend until smooth and shiny. Once rendered smooth, stir in the chopped nuts for a chunky peanut butter. Transfer to a sanitized jar and refrigerate.

# VANILLA-CASHEW BUTTER

2 cups raw cashews, roasted

3 tablespoons coconut oil

1 teaspoon vanilla

½ teaspoon sea salt

1 teaspoon honey

¼ cup coconut milk

2 tablespoons unsweetened
coconut flakes, toasted

Combine all ingredients except the coconut flakes in a Vitamix or food processor. Blend until smooth, remove to a bowl, and stir in the toasted coconut flakes. Transfer to a sanitized jar and refrigerate.

## How to Sanitize Glass Jars in Three Easy Steps

**Step 1:** Preheat the oven to 210°F. Thoroughly wash the jars in warm and soapy water, and rinse them well. Turn the jars upside down on a clean dishcloth, and allow to drain.

**Step 2:** Arrange the jars right side up on a sheet pan, making sure they are not touching each other. Place the sheet pan in the center rack of the oven, and leave the jars in the oven for 15 to 20 minutes. Remove from the oven and allow to cool.

**Step 3:** While the jars are in the oven, bring a saucepan of water to a boil; drop the lids and any rubber canning rings into the boiling water; boil for 15 to 20 minutes. Remove from the boiling water with tongs, and place on a clean dishcloth.

**Note:** To prevent the glass from cracking, one should never put cold ingredients into hot jars or hot ingredients into cold jars. Also, ensure that the lids are not old and rusty—only use new, clean lids for bottling and canning.

# CHAPTER 9

# RUM, BEVERAGES & FESTIVE RECIPES

RUM AND CARIBBEAN LIVING GO HAND IN HAND. RUM IS USED TO CELEBRATE, TO COMMEMORATE, TO BLESS, TO MOURN, AND TO HEAL. We drink and use rum for every occasion. A case of the common cold is treated with a dose of white rum warmed with honey and lime; a fever or headache is relieved by rubbing down the body or head with white rum; rum is liberally imbibed at occasions ranging from a new birth to a death to a fete to the blessing of a newly finished home or building. Rum is sprinkled on the ground to bless a space, to give thanks, to ward off evil spirits, to pay homage to ancestors. This tradition was inherited from our African slave forefathers and -mothers, who brought their spiritual practices with them when forced into a life of bondage on the West Indian sugar plantations.

In the grand era of the West Indian sugar trade of the eighteenth and nineteenth centuries, all levels of plantation society enjoyed and imbibed alcohol. Rum, a natural byproduct of the processing of sugarcane, was a very popular drink with all members of society and was standardly issued to slaves on or around holidays as a special treat. Additionally, during the reaping and harvesting of cane, and the brutally long work days in the sugar mills and boiler houses that followed, slaves were given grog and rum as a way of keeping them going and making the work more palatable.

Always on the lookout for ways to exploit the yield from their cane, sugar planters soon realized that they could profit greatly from the processing and exportation of a more refined rum product. It's no surprise, then, that Caribbean history and rum are inextricably combined. Although there is darkness in this legacy, there is also light because we use rum to be joyful. Rum appears in our desserts and our cuisine, and is most assuredly the favorite drink to celebrate island life's beautiful moments. From sorrel mimosas and ponche de crème at Christmastime, to rum and coconut water at a "soca fete," to a beach day made sweeter with a delicious coconut-rum punch or ti ponche in hand, rum in all its divine glory is the ultimate Caribbean liquor.

The wine in general use in the West Indies is of the very best quality; and malt liquor, acquires a degree of mildness and flavor which it ever attains in Britain. Beer, porter, and cider, are all drank at West India dinners....The most general beverage...is either brandy or rum and water:—this beverage is often rendered more agreeable to the palate by being milled, or beat in a large jug or glass rummer with a long three-fingered stick; this being done quickly, the liquor froths up, and forms at once the most cooling and safe beverage.

—Mrs. A. C. Carmichael, 1834

# COCONUT-RUM PUNCH

We had our first taste of coconut-rum punch in a quaint country café overlooking the hills of Dominica. Lightly refreshing, slightly sweet, and not too strong, it was the perfect accompaniment to a daytime meal. Every Dominican has their own special version of this punch—some are lighter and more watery, like the one we had at lunch, while others are stronger, sweeter, thicker, and richer, more like Baileys Irish Cream. This version rests somewhere in between. Each version, however, is a sinfully delicious treat that should be savored and sipped slowly. Once you get your first taste, you'll realize that's a lot harder to do than it sounds.

*Serves 6*

3 cups coconut milk
(preferably fresh)

1 12-ounce can evaporated milk

1 8-ounce can sweetened
condensed milk

2 cups white or dark rum

1 drop almond extract

2 drops vanilla extract

1 pinch ground nutmeg

2 sticks cinnamon

Combine all ingredients in a large jug or pitcher, and stir well. Bottle and seal, or store in a jug in the refrigerator. Sealed and chilled, it can keep for up to three weeks. Serve over ice.

# BELLEFIELD JAMAICAN GINGER BEER

When we ran Bellefield Great House, an eighteenth-century sugar estate in Montego Bay that has been converted to a wedding and event venue and a cultural and historical site, one of the first signature drinks we created was this homemade ginger beer. It was a favorite among both locals and tourists. The thing about ginger beer is the longer it sits, the stronger it gets; the problem is that it doesn't usually last that long. Jamaican ginger is potent, so this drink tends to be sweet and concentrated with a strong kick at the back of the throat. Feel free to adjust the quantities of sugar and water to suit your tastes. Traditional Jamaican ginger beer is not fizzy, so if you are accustomed to bubbles in your ginger beer, you can mix it with seltzer or soda water to serve.

*Makes 1 quart*

1½ **pounds fresh ginger**

2½ **cups brown sugar**

¼ **cup lime juice**

Wash and peel the ginger, and cut it into chunks. Place the ginger in a blender with 4 cups of water, and puree. Extract the ginger juice by straining the mixture through a fine sieve or cheesecloth; discard the pulp. Pour the juice into a large bowl or jug; add the brown sugar, and stir well to dissolve. Stir in the lime juice. Strain the ginger beer a final time through a sieve or cheesecloth. Serve over plenty of ice.

# HAITIAN RUM SOUR

Rum is the passion of every Caribbean national; we love experimenting with new ways to make rum drinks. Because the two of us are not overly fond of sugary-sweet cocktails, this has quickly become one of our favorite go-to cocktails for entertaining. It's fresh, easy to make, and truly delicious. Be sure to use a good-quality Caribbean rum, like Appleton or El Dorado.

*Serves 2*

2 tablespoons brown sugar

½ cup dark rum

pulp of 2 passionfruit

juice of 2 grapefruit

juice of 2 limes

zest of ½ lime

splash of Angostura bitters

lime slices, for garnish

Stir 1 tablespoon hot water into the brown sugar to make a syrup. Place all the ingredients in a shaker. Shake thoroughly until well combined; add ice and give another shake. Serve chilled or serve over ice, garnished with a lime slice.

# TAMARIND TI PONCHE

I n the French islands and St. Lucia, they make a delicious rum punch called, simply, *ti ponche* that combines lime, sugar, and rum over ice. For an extra flavorful twist, we incorporated a homemade tamarind simple syrup. Garnished with blossoms, it makes a great welcome drink at a cocktail party. If you can't find bougainvillea, you could use another mild-flavored edible flower such as pansy, violet, or rose.

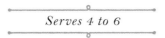

*Serves 4 to 6*

**1½ pounds fresh tamarind (or 1½ to 2 cups tamarind puree)**

**1½ cups brown sugar**

**2 tablespoons grated fresh ginger**

**3 fluid ounces dark rum**

**3 limes**

**bougainvillea petals, for garnish (optional)**

To extract the tamarind juice, remove the shell from the tamarinds, cleaning the fruit of any worms or dirt. Soak the tamarind fruit in about 5 cups water for 1 to 2 hours. Using gloved hands or a large spoon, squeeze the seeds together to remove the pulp into the water. Strain the tamarind juice through a sieve two or three times to ensure that all debris is removed. (If you can't find fresh tamarind, use a store-bought tamarind puree. Mix 1½ to 2 cups tamarind puree with 3 to 4 cups water, and proceed with the recipe.)

To make tamarind-ginger syrup, combine brown sugar, ginger, and tamarind liquid in a medium saucepan, and bring to a boil over medium heat. Simmer for 20 to 30 minutes until reduced to about 3 cups. (You will have leftover syrup—enough to make a second round of drinks!) Let cool to room temperature.

To make each cocktail, pour ½ ounce dark rum into a double old-fashioned rocks glass. Add 2 ounces tamarind-ginger syrup and juice of ½ lime, and serve over ice garnished with a wedge of lime and a bougainvillea flower.

**NOTE:** A traditional-style tamarind rum punch is also supremely delicious, so if you are short on time, you can skip making the tamarind-ginger simple syrup. After you have strained the tamarind juice, transfer it to a jug or pitcher, add rum, lime, grated fresh ginger, and brown sugar to taste, and stir until dissolved. Hold in the refrigerator until ready to serve.

# SORREL MIMOSAS
## *(Holiday Hibiscus)*

Christmas morning in our family has traditions of its own. One that we have created is Christmas brunch. Every year, the menu changes, but one thing always remains the same: sorrel mimosas. Delicious sorrel is chased with prosecco as a lovely alternative to the typical brunch mimosa or Bellini.

*Serves 4*

**8 fluid ounces strong and sweet Christmas Sorrel (page 218), chilled**

**16 fluid ounces prosecco or other good sparkling wine, chilled**

**4 pieces star anise, for garnish**

**4 Candied Sorrel Buds (page 187), for garnish**

Pour 2 fluid ounces Christmas Sorrel into each of four 6-ounce champagne flutes. Top with 4 ounces chilled sparkling wine. Garnish each glass with star anise and a candied sorrel bud.

# CHRISTMAS SORREL

The festive season in Jamaica is heralded by the appearance of a profusion of gorgeous sorrel blossoms at markets, vendors, and groceries across the island. *Sorrel* is our name for hibiscus or roselle, and is also the name of a drink made by blending the plant's beautiful crimson flowers with generous amounts of white rum, wine, ginger, and sugar. A notoriously sweet, strong, almost thick beverage, it is the drink of choice for many during Christmastime, when most households are busy steeping the flowers to make this divine concoction. Sorrel can be made without alcohol if desired; simply eliminate the wine and rum. Feel free to adjust the alcohol and sugar quantities to suit your own tastes; that said, the best way to enjoy sorrel is in the traditional way as the flavors improve over time, much like a good bottle of wine. Sorrel can be stored in the refrigerator in a sealed bottle or container for a long time, or it can be stored at room temperature in a sealed container by adding cloves to the blend, which prevents fermentation.

## Makes 8 cups

½ pound ginger, peeled and mashed or beaten

3 to 5 cinnamon leaves or ½ teaspoon ground cinnamon

3 to 5 whole allspice berries

2 pounds fresh sorrel flowers/ buds (see note)

1½ to 2 pounds brown sugar

1½ cups red wine

1½ cups white or dark rum

Combine 2 quarts water with the ginger, cinnamon leaf or ground cinnamon, and allspice berries in a large saucepan; boil for a few minutes. Add the sorrel buds and turn off the heat. Cover, refrigerate, and let the sorrel steep for two to three days (the longer the sorrel steeps, the richer the flavor). If time does not allow for multiple days, prepare the sorrel in the morning and let it steep for at least 6 hours.

Once the sorrel has steeped, strain the mixture and discard the solids. Sweeten the mixture to taste with sugar, mixing well to dissolve, and then add the wine and rum.

**NOTE:** See "Local Produce," in the back of the book, for more information about sourcing fresh sorrel buds.

# PONCHE DE CRÈME

Christmas in the Caribbean is a glorious, one-of-a-kind celebration of life. In Trinidad, the traditions include pastelles (cornmeal tamales filled with seasoned ground beef), parang (a style of folk music played at Christmastime), and of course ponche de crème. We suspect this is Trinidad's version of eggnog, but it blows eggnog out of the water; the addition of rum and delectable island spices make this beverage not only decadent and rich but ridiculously delicious.

*Serves 6*

½ 8-ounce can sweetened condensed milk

1 12-ounce can (1½ cups) evaporated milk or 1 cup heavy cream

3 egg yolks (optional)

¼ cup dark rum

¼ cup brandy

¼ teaspoon cinnamon

¼ teaspoon nutmeg

pinch of salt

1 teaspoon vanilla

In a blender, combine the condensed milk, evaporated milk, egg yolks (if using), and 1 cup water. Blend well. Pour the mixture into a large bowl or pitcher. Add the rum, brandy, spices, and vanilla, and mix by hand using a whisk or wooden spoon. Taste and adjust for sweetness, spices, and alcohol—add more condensed milk, alcohol, or water as desired, allowing your palate to be your guide.

# JAMAICAN JULEP

The delightful subtlety and sophisticated flavor of a traditional mint julep speaks to hot, languid, and lazy summer days spent idly on a porch—think Elizabeth Taylor as Maggie in the movie version of Tennessee Williams's *Cat on a Hot Tin Roof*. Since this cocktail would be just as refreshing on hot days in the islands, we feel that the julep is a drink worth reimagining and making at home. You never know, maybe Paul Newman will show up on our doorstep! So, here it is: our version of the traditional refreshing Southern cocktail incorporating rum and a few unique island flavors. If you can, use Jamaican rum—we love Appleton Estate V/X or Reserve.

*Serves 1*

1½ teaspoons brown sugar

2 pieces lime rind

2 pieces orange rind

few splashes Angostura bitters

2½ ounces dark rum

crushed ice

sprig of mint

1 orange slice

1 lime slice

Muddle the brown sugar with the lime rind and orange rind in a double old-fashioned glass or julep cup to release the oils from the rind and slightly dissolve the sugar. Add a few splashes of Angostura bitters, and continue to muddle. Add the rum, and stir until the sugar is completely dissolved. Fill the glass with crushed ice. Garnish with a sprig of mint, and float an orange slice and a lime slice on top.

# LIME SQUASH

It was summer 1985; the days were long, hot, and lazy, and we spent them at the Liguanea Club in Kingston, where we swam in the pool, played billiards, and pretended that we knew how to play squash. The highlights of those days, outside of the frolic and abandon with which we played, were the daily snacks of French fries and deliciously tart Jamaican lime squash. All Jamaican bartenders know how to make this drink: fresh-squeezed lime juice is sweetened with a simple syrup, chased with sparkling club soda, and garnished with a maraschino cherry. Drinking lime squash was a daily ritual that forever marks this beverage as one of our favorites of all time.

*Serves 4*

1 to 1¼ cups fresh lime juice
(juice of 6 to 8 limes)

⅓ cup simple syrup

2 12-ounce bottles club soda

ice cubes

4 maraschino cherries

Divide the lime juice between four glasses. Add simple syrup; stir to combine. Pour the club soda over the blend, fill the glass with ice, and garnish it with a cherry.

You can transform this classic drink into a delicious homemade "soda" by adding other flavors: try mango puree, passionfruit, orange-blossom syrup, or pomegranate syrup. Or make a simple syrup with lemongrass to transform the beverage into a light and refreshing lemongrass-lime squash.

# MODERN-DAY SANGAREE

**E**ighteenth- and nineteenth-century journals often reference a punch called sangaree. Despite its similarities to the word *sangria,* it did not contain any fruit, has the addition of nutmeg, and is said to originate in England, not Spain. One thing is for sure, it was a definite favorite in West Indian planter society. This modern-day version is inspired by a recipe we found in Caroline Sullivan's 1893 book, *The Jamaica Cookery Book.* Ours includes Cointreau, citrus peel, and bitters for good measure. If you buy your nutmeg whole and grate it yourself, so much the better—the strong, aromatic flavor of freshly grated nutmeg outshines the preground spice by far.

*Serves 2*

1 to 2 tablespoons granulated sugar

pinch of grated nutmeg

peel and juice of 1 lime

peel of 1 orange

6 ounces sherry

2 ounces Cointreau

splash Angostura bitters

2 pieces orange peel, for garnish

2 slices orange, for garnish

Combine 1 cup water with the sugar in a shaker. Add the nutmeg and stir. Add the lime juice and lime peel and the orange peel, and stir well until the sugar is dissolved. Add the sherry and Cointreau. Shake well to combine, and strain over crushed ice into two glasses. Finish each with a splash of bitters, a piece of orange peel, and a slice of orange.

# PASSION MARTINI

The intense flavor of passionfruit makes this martini singular for its unforgettably exotic mix of tart and sweet. With its unique tropical twist, it is the perfect shaken cocktail for easy summer evenings or predinner drinks.

*Serves 4*

**4 fresh passionfruit,
halved and pulped**

**4 fluid ounces coconut rum**

**2 fluid ounces
good-quality vodka**

**2 fluid ounces simple syrup**

**1 fluid ounce lime juice**

**rose petals or flowers
for garnish**

Combine all the ingredients in a shaker. Add ice. Shake, pour into martini glasses, and garnish with rose petals.

CHAPTER 10

# SEA SALT, SUGAR & SPICE

*Pickles, Preserves & Sauces*

THE TRADITION OF UTILIZING A LARGE VARIETY OF PICKLES, PRESERVES, SAUCES, AND CHUTNEYS TO FLAVOR AND complement a meal is still enthusiastically observed at most Caribbean tables. Lack of refrigeration and the need to preserve foods in the heat introduced the age-old techniques of pickling, salting, and preserving. Cooks in the region have always made use of three of the most essential ingredients in the eighteenth- and nineteenth-century kitchen: salt, sugar, and spices, which, in various forms and interpretations, were easily incorporated into the daily diet across all walks of life.

Sea salt was used to cure meats, and sugar from the processing of cane was used to preserve fruits and to create delightful treats, such as conserves, jams, jellies, and chutneys. All three components (sugar, salt, and spices) were combined with locally available fruits, vegetables, and even meats to create a delightful array of pickles: sweet, spicy, and savory. These little "relishes," esteemed by all who resided in the islands, added a wallop of gourmet flavor and balance to an otherwise simple and potentially repetitive diet.

Many meals in the Caribbean diet are enhanced with the addition of sweet and savory pepper sauces, pickles, and preserves that add heat, flavor, and texture to our dishes. (Trinidad, in particular, is home to an outstanding array of pepper sauces, chokas, chows, and chutneys that are added to every kind of dish—a defining characteristic of the island's cuisine. No other island does it quite like the Trinis do!) Any meal becomes more blissful with the addition of one or a few of these spectacular sweet and savory condiments.

> Just as I was meditating upon green limes and preserved ginger, (I was) offered some preserved raspberries, just come from England; the emphasis…on the word raspberries, at once shewed me that English preserves were quite as much esteemed in that country, as West India preserves are in England. I ventured to tell him how astonished I was to find that they relished our preserves, when theirs were so much superior.
>
> —Mrs. A. C. Carmichael, 1834

# PICKLED PEPPERS, FRUITS, AND VEGETABLES

Pickles of every kind have been staples in the Caribbean diet for centuries. In our family, pickling is a tradition that holds firm. Each of our grandparents on both sides always had jars of pickles in the fridge. Manga, our paternal grandmother, kept cucumber pickle, while Gampi, our maternal grandfather, favored killer spicy pickled shallots and Scotch bonnet pepper. When it was mealtime, that jar would appear on the table; you could use any component—either the pickled vegetables or the spicy vinegar they soaked in—to add flavor, heat, or sweetness to the meal. The gorgeous selection of pickles that appears here represents the best the Caribbean has to offer. They take virtually no time to make and can stay in your refrigerator for months. Whether you choose to make one or all, your pantry won't be disappointed.

## HAITIAN PIKLIZ

*Makes 6 cups*

1½ cups thinly sliced white cabbage (about ¼ large head)

1 cup thinly sliced red cabbage (about ¼ medium head)

1 cup julienned carrots (about 1 medium carrot)

½ cup thinly sliced red onion

½ cup thinly sliced red bell pepper

6 Scotch bonnet peppers, stemmed, quartered

5 sprigs thyme

3 cloves garlic

8 whole cloves

1 tablespoon whole red peppercorns

1 teaspoon fine sea salt

4 cups cane vinegar

4 tablespoons fresh lime juice

Layer the white cabbage, red cabbage, carrots, red onion, red bell pepper, Scotch bonnet pepper, thyme, garlic, cloves, red peppercorns, and sea salt in a 1½-quart resealable jar. Add the vinegar and lime juice, seal the jar, and shake until the ingredients are distributed and the salt is dissolved. Add more vinegar if needed to cover the vegetables. Chill for at least 24 hours before serving.

# CHUNKY LIME, JUNE PLUM, AND PEPPER RELISH

*Makes 4 cups*

10 habanero peppers, chopped

½ cup chopped carrot

½ cup chopped radish
or cho cho

2 cups diced June plum
or green mango

1 tablespoon chopped
culantro or cilantro

1 lemon or sour orange,
sliced thinly

1 teaspoon granulated sugar

salt to taste

juice of 3 limes

1 cup white cane vinegar

Combine all ingredients except the lime juice and vinegar in a glass bowl. Stir well. Add the lime juice and the vinegar, transfer to a sanitized jar, and cover. Place the jar in sunlight, and allow it to rest for 24 hours. Store in the refrigerator.

# PICKLED CUCUMBER

*Makes 2 cups*

1 to 2 cucumbers

1 red onion

3 to 5 slices
Scotch bonnet pepper

1 teaspoon chopped dill

¼ cup cane vinegar

2 tablespoons granulated sugar

salt and freshly cracked
black pepper to taste

Wash and partly peel the cucumbers, leaving alternating strips of green skin. Slice the cucumbers into thin rounds with a sharp knife or mandolin. Slice the onions into thin rounds. Place the cucumbers, onions, Scotch bonnet pepper, and dill in a bowl. Add 3 tablespoons water, the vinegar, and the sugar, and stir well until the sugar dissolves. Season with salt and pepper. Allow the mixture to sit at room temperature for about 20 minutes before eating. Transfer to a sanitized storage container. Store in the refrigerator.

# PICKLED SHALLOTS AND SCOTCH BONNET

*Makes 2 cups*

12 shallots

6 Scotch bonnet peppers

2 slices peeled ginger

1 tablespoon whole allspice
berries

2 cloves

2 bay leaves

2 cups white wine vinegar

1 teaspoon brown sugar

½ teaspoon salt

Peel the shallots and cut off the ends. Place the shallots, Scotch bonnet pepper, ginger, and spices in a sanitized jar. In a small saucepan, combine the vinegar, brown sugar, and salt, and bring to a boil. Boil just until the sugar dissolves. Pour the warm vinegar mixture over the vegetables and spices. Allow to cool; seal. Store in the refrigerator.

# PINEAPPLE CHOW

*Makes 4 cups*

4 cups cubed pineapple

¼ cup chopped culantro

1 Scotch bonnet pepper, seeds
and membrane removed, minced

juice of 1 lime

salt and freshly cracked
black pepper

Combine the pineapple, culantro, and Scotch bonnet pepper in a bowl. Squeeze the lime juice over the mixture, and season with salt and pepper to taste. This is best consumed fresh, so serve immediately. May be stored in the refrigerator for up to 24 hours.

# TRINI CHOW CHOW

*Makes 6 cups*

1 cup diced carrot

1 cup diced cauliflower

1 cup diced green beans

1 cup diced red bell pepper

1 cup diced green bell pepper

1 cup diced yellow onion

2 tablespoons sea salt

3½ cups white vinegar

6 pimiento (cherry) peppers or jalapeño peppers

10 cloves

6 tablespoons sugar

3 tablespoons mustard powder

2 tablespoons turmeric

2 tablespoons grated fresh ginger

2 tablespoons cornstarch

In a large nonreactive bowl, cover the vegetables (except the pimiento or jalapeño peppers) with 6 cups water; add the sea salt. Allow to sit, covered, overnight at room temperature. Drain the vegetables.

Combine the vinegar, pimiento or jalapeño peppers, cloves, sugar, mustard powder, turmeric, and ginger in a large saucepan over medium heat. Make a cornstarch slurry with 2 tablespoons cornstarch and 2 tablespoons water; stir into the vinegar mixture. Bring to a boil for about 3 minutes, whisking to remove any lumps. When the sauce is slightly thickened, stir in the drained vegetables. Bring to a boil, reduce heat, and simmer until the sauce is thickened and the texture resembles that of a relish, about 10 to 15 minutes. Remove from the heat and transfer to a sanitized container. Leave uncovered until cooled. Seal and store in the refrigerator.

# AUNT SHIRLEY'S GUAVA JAM

Having owned a home high up in the Blue Mountains of Jamaica for over forty-five years, our family friend Shirley Williams and her husband boasted a well-fruited garden with many exotic trees and shrubs that bear best in cooler climes: peaches, berries, guava. They discovered that most of the fruits ripened at the same time, resulting in an overabundance of guavas, which forced Aunt Shirley to become inventive and find a way to preserve them. One of her favored methods was to make jam. This delicious jam has become a family favorite and is always in stock in her pantry.

*Makes four to six 8-ounce jars*

**6 to 8 ripe fresh guavas (should yield approximately 2 cups of pulp)**

**4 cups (more or less) brown sugar**

Wash the guavas thoroughly, and cut them into halves. Place the fruit in a large pot over medium heat, and cook until tender.

Remove the cooked fruit from the heat, and blend into a puree. You can use an immersion blender or, working in batches, a stand blender or food processor. Strain the puree through a sieve, and measure the volume (should be about 2 cups). Return the puree to the pot, and add twice that amount of brown sugar (about 4 cups). Boil vigorously. Stir frequently with a wooden spoon, skimming the froth, until the mixture clears.

Once the mixture darkens and starts to thicken, after about 20 minutes, pour some room-temperature water in a small cup, and drop a little of the boiling mixture into it. If the drop turns into a ball, it is time to pour the liquid into sanitized bottles or jars (page 208). Cover the jars with a towel until the liquid gels. Once the jam cools, pour melted paraffin wax over it to seal it, ensuring a long shelf life. Store at room temperature until opened; then store in the refrigerator.

# DOVER SEVILLE ORANGE MARMALADE

This marmalade recipe is an heirloom, handed down through three generations of the women of our good friends the Donaldson family. Having stood the test of time, it represents the legacy of a line of wonderful cooks and homemakers who nourished all who showed up to eat at their abundant tables. Graciously shared for this book by Gwen Donaldson ("Mrs. D") and her daughter Janie, the recipe was passed to Mrs. D from her mother, Lexie Smith, and her mother-in-law, Helen Donaldson, when Mrs. D was a young woman. Dover, a former rectory, is a home the family owns in the hills of St. Mary, Jamaica, where Seville oranges grow and are turned into marmalade. A notable feature of this recipe is that no pectin is used; instead, the seeds are tied in muslin and boiled with the fruit, providing a natural thickening effect. Be sure to have muslin or cheesecloth and pure cotton kitchen string on hand.

*Makes four 8- to 12-ounce jars*

**6 Seville oranges**

**juice of 1 lime or lemon**

**about 6 pounds granulated sugar**

Peel the oranges. Cut each orange into four sections, and remove the thick white pith. Thinly slice the peel of three oranges. Remove the pulp and seeds from all six oranges, place in a cheesecloth or muslin bag, and tie tightly closed with kitchen twine.

Measure the volume of sliced orange peel, and place the peel in a large saucepan. Add 3 cups water for each cup of peel. Place the bag of pulp and seeds into the saucepan, and boil over medium heat for 1½ to 2 hours, until the peel is tender. Remove from the heat and, once the bag is cool enough to handle, squeeze the liquid from it into the saucepan, making sure the bag does not burst open into the saucepan. Discard the bag and its contents.

Add the juice of 1 lime or lemon. Measure the quantity of peel and liquid and add 1 cup sugar for each cup of liquid. Return the saucepan to medium heat and simmer, stirring to dissolve the sugar thoroughly. Continue to boil until the liquid is set. Test by dropping some liquid from a spoon into a saucer of water; the liquid should gel. Allow the marmalade to cool slightly, pour into sanitized jars, and seal (page 208). Once opened, store in the refrigerator.

# GINGER PEPPER JELLY

This spicy jelly is a revelation. The peppers are so flavorful that they make anything taste better. We love to eat pepper jelly with gourmet cheeses, with sandwiches and burgers, on the side of savory meals, or even as an accompaniment to curries. Give it a try with tart goat cheese or aged cheddar, and you will never think of cheese in the same way again! This versatile condiment can enhance just about anything you eat.

*Makes 4 cups*

1 cup whole Scotch bonnet or habanero peppers (red and orange only)

1 red bell pepper (about 1 cup chopped)

1 orange bell pepper (about 1 cup chopped)

¼ cup sliced peeled ginger

1 cup apple cider vinegar

1 package (1.75 ounces) pectin

2 cups granulated sugar

Wearing gloves, slice the hot peppers in half, and remove the seeds. Core the bell peppers and roughly chop. Place the hot peppers, bell peppers, and ginger in the bowl of a food processor, and pulse to a fine dice.

Scrape the pepper mix into a medium saucepan; add the vinegar and pectin. Bring the mixture to a rolling boil, stirring continuously. Add the sugar and return to a rolling boil, stirring continuously, for 1 full minute. Remove from the heat. Pour into a sanitized jar, seal, and let cool completely before moving. Refrigerate for up to two weeks.

# QUICK SORREL MARMALADE

**W**est Indian sorrel (known elsewhere as hibiscus), beautifully blood red in hue, makes delicious preserves, incredible syrups and drinks, and a wonderful glaze for roasted or barbequed meats. When soaked, the flower produces a liquid that is a the color of a deep and rich red wine. Many chefs and home cooks use the sorrel flower to make chutney or jam; here we add a twist by combining marmalade, rum, and cinnamon leaves. We often use this as the topping for our Baked Brie en Croute (page 170).

*Makes 1 12-ounce jar*

**2 pounds fresh sorrel buds (see note)**

**4-inch stalk fresh ginger, peeled and diced**

**handful whole allspice berries**

**2 bay leaves**

**3 cinnamon leaves**

**¾ cup granulated sugar**

**½ cup fresh cranberries**

**½ cup orange marmalade**

**¼ cup dark rum**

**¼ cup orange juice**

**1 teaspoon orange zest**

Deseed and wash the sorrel. Place in a saucepan with the ginger. Pour enough boiling water over to cover, about 4 cups. Add the allspice berries, bay leaves, and cinnamon leaves. Bring to a simmer, cover, turn off the heat, and allow to steep for about 1 hour.

Strain the sorrel from the liquid. Return the liquid to the pot. Roughly chop the sorrel. Return the sorrel to the cooking liquid, and add the remaining ingredients. Bring the mixture to a boil, whisking constantly. Reduce the heat to low, and cook, stirring frequently, until the liquid is reduced by half.

Cool and transfer to sanitized containers or jars. Store in the refrigerator.

**NOTE:** See "Local Produce," in the back of the book, for more information about sourcing fresh sorrel buds.

# PAPAYA-CHRISTOPHENE CHUTNEY

This outstanding chutney perfectly balances sweet, tart, and spice, and the christophene (or cho cho) adds some texture, permitting the papaya to hold up after long hours of cooking. It makes a fabulous accompaniment to any good-quality cheese.

*Makes 2 cups*

2 cups chopped ripe papaya (pawpaw), peeled and seeded

1 christophene, peeled and chopped

½ red bell pepper, chopped

1¼ cups granulated sugar

1 cup white vinegar

¼ to ½ whole lime, diced fine

3 teaspoons coarse salt

2 teaspoons minced fresh ginger

Mix all ingredients in a bowl to combine; transfer to a medium saucepan. Add ¾ cup water. Bring to a gentle simmer and cook, uncovered, for 2 hours over low heat, stirring occasionally to avoid burning. Transfer to a sanitized jar or container. Store in the refrigerator.

# WATERMELON-LEMONGRASS CHUTNEY

The inspiration for this recipe comes from our friend and fellow chef Bill Moore. The chutney is a beautiful light pink, yet it is sufficiently bold to act as the perfect accompaniment to any cheese. It always has a place at our table. We also love to use it as a dip for fritters or other fried foods. We added lemongrass for exotic flavor, and replaced bay leaves with fresh cinnamon leaves. The result is delicate, pretty to look at, and delicious to eat.

*Makes 1½ cups*

5 pounds watermelon

1 cup cane vinegar

1½ cups granulated sugar

3-inch piece fresh ginger, peeled and diced

4 cloves garlic, diced

1 whole Scotch bonnet pepper

6 whole cloves

2 fresh cinnamon leaves

2 whole lemongrass leaves, bruised or crushed (to release the oils)

salt and freshly cracked black pepper

3 teaspoons cornstarch

Cut the melon into manageable pieces, remove the pink flesh, and set aside. Peel the green outer rind from the white inner rind (the thicker the rind, the better), leaving a little of the red flesh clinging to the white inner rind to give the chutney an attractive appearance. Discard the green outer rind. Cut the flesh into ½-inch dice.

Bring the vinegar and 2 cups water to a boil in a large, heavy saucepan. Add the sugar, and stir to dissolve. Add the watermelon, ginger, garlic, whole Scotch bonnet, cloves, cinnamon leaves, and lemongrass leaves. Return to a boil, cover, reduce the heat, and simmer until the watermelon becomes translucent, about 1 hour. Add salt and pepper to taste. Combine the cornstarch with 3 teaspoons of water to make a slurry. Stir the slurry into the saucepan, and simmer for a few more minutes, until the mixture is thickened. Remove and discard the Scotch bonnet pepper.

Make at least 24 hours ahead of use. Store in an airtight jar in the refrigerator for up to four weeks.

# SEVENS MANGO CHUTNEY

Here we share another legacy recipe from the Donaldson family collection. Mrs. D served this mango chutney as a complement to meals of all kinds at her home known as Sevens, in the parish of Clarendon, Jamaica. Sevens was a sugar estate owned and operated by the family for many years. During mango season, chutneys were prepared and then stored for use, to make frequent appearances throughout the year when family and friends gathered to dine. This version is very much in keeping with the style of a traditional British chutney; it balances sweet and savory but isn't spicy. It is most often served as an accompaniment to cheeses, roasted meats, or curries. Mrs. D's soirees were legendary; she entertained up to a hundred guests, doing the cooking herself in her own kitchen. Lucky visitors were often sent home with a bottle of one of her famous preserves.

*Makes four 6-ounce jars*

1 pound green mangoe flesh

1 pound seedless raisins

¼ pound peeled garlic (or less)

1 pound brown sugar

2 cups good-quality cider
or cane vinegar

1 cup lime juice

Mince the solid ingredients; combine them in a large saucepan. Add the sugar, vinegar, and lime juice, stir to combine, and boil until well cooked, 30 to 40 minutes.

# RED ONION, TOMATO, AND HABANERO RELISH

This recipe is our take on an old-world Jamaican tomato preserve, traditionally prepared by simmering peeled tomatoes in sugar and spices such as cloves and cinnamon. We jazz up the classic by adding red onion, garlic, thyme, bay leaves, ginger, habanero, and allspice berries. The quintessentially Caribbean blend of flavors is further enhanced by the inclusion of red wine vinegar, resulting in a relish that perfectly balances texture with tart, spice, and sweet.

*Makes 2 cups*

3 medium red onions, peeled and finely sliced

8 ripe plum tomatoes, peeled, seeded, and chopped

4 cloves garlic, sliced

1 habanero pepper, seeded and chopped

1 cup brown sugar

⅔ cup red wine vinegar

2-inch piece ginger, peeled and minced

1 bunch thyme

2 bay leaves

15 whole allspice berries

1 tablespoon coarse sea salt

freshly cracked black pepper to taste

Combine all ingredients in a saucepan over medium heat and bring to a simmer, stirring to combine. Simmer over low heat for about 1 hour. Use the back of a wooden spoon to break up the onions; stir to combine with the other ingredients. Increase the heat, and bring the mixture to a gentle boil, allowing it to darken and thicken to the texture of a jam or chutney. Remove and discard the thyme stems and bay leaves. Spoon into sanitized jars and allow to cool before sealing or covering. Will keep, refrigerated, for up to four weeks.

# CILANTRO-COCONUT PISTOU

This creamy pistou is the sauce for our Oven-Roasted Pumpkin Flatbreads (page 71); it's also excellent with grilled vegetables or used as a spread. The pistou can be made up to one day ahead. Keep it covered in the refrigerator until ready to use, and bring to room temperature before serving.

*Makes 2 cups*

1 cup cream cheese, softened

¼ cup sour cream

¼ cup coconut cream

¼ cup unsweetened coconut flakes

2 cloves garlic, minced

½ cup fresh cilantro leaves

2 scallion stalks, coarsely chopped

juice of 2 limes (about 2 tablespoons)

1 green chili, sliced

salt and freshly cracked black pepper to taste

Combine the cream cheese, sour cream, coconut cream, coconut flakes, garlic, cilantro, scallion, lime juice, and green chili in a food processor. Pulse until combined. Season to taste with salt and pepper.

# GARLIC-LIME SAUCE

This is a quick and easy dipping sauce that can be served with any number of fried treats. It also makes the perfect spread or base for a sandwich.

*Makes ¾ cup*

½ cup mayonnaise

7 cloves garlic

1½ tablespoons lime juice

2 teaspoons sugar

3 leaves culantro

2 sprigs chive

In a food processor, blend all ingredients until smooth. Store in the refrigerator.

# TAMARIND-RAISIN KETCHUP

The bold, tart flavor of tamarind is balanced by raisins, brown sugar, and ginger. This sauce pairs perfectly with Cassava Fries (page 22) or Curried Eggplant and Potato with Roti (page 34).

*Makes 2 cups*

1½ cups raisins

1 tablespoon brown sugar

¼ cup Pickapeppa sauce or A1 sauce

¼ cup tamarind concentrate

1½ teaspoons grated ginger

¼ teaspoon minced Scotch bonnet pepper

salt and freshly cracked black pepper to taste

Place the raisins and brown sugar in a bowl; pour 1 cup boiling water over the raisins to soften them. Stir, cover, and allow to rest for up to 2 hours.

In a food processor puree the raisins with their soaking liquid. Add the remaining ingredients, and continue processing until the mixture is pureed. Scrape the puree into a storage container, cover, and refrigerate at least 2 hours before use.

# COCONUT-LIME
# DIPPING SAUCE

Cool, creamy, buttery, and bright, this dipping sauce is the perfect accompaniment to any hors d'oeuvres platter. Or try drizzling it on a veggie burger.

*Makes 1½ cups*

1 tablespoon coconut oil

1 tablespoon minced garlic

½ cup coconut milk

2 tablespoons dried
unsweetened coconut flakes

½ cup sour cream

½ cup mayonnaise

2 tablespoons chopped cilantro

1 tablespoon lime juice

2 tablespoons chopped scallion

salt and freshly cracked
black pepper to taste

Heat the coconut oil in a medium saucepan over medium heat. Sauté the garlic for 1 to 2 minutes until fragrant. Add the coconut milk and coconut flakes; bring to a boil, reduce the heat, and simmer for 5 to 10 minutes until reduced. Remove from the heat and allow to cool. In a small bowl, whisk together the sour cream, mayonnaise, cilantro, lime juice, and scallion. Add the cooled coconut milk, and season with salt and pepper. Hold in the refrigerator until ready for use.

# CREAMY SCOTCH BONNET DIPPING SAUCE

W e use this creamy, spicy sauce much as one would use a ranch or tartar sauce. It provides the perfect balance to anything fried or grilled.

*Makes 1½ cups*

1 cup mayonnaise

½ cup sour cream

2 tablespoons lime juice

1 tablespoon orange juice

2 tablespoons chopped cilantro

1 tablespoon sliced scallion

1 teaspoon minced Scotch bonnet pepper

1 teaspoon hot pepper sauce

1 teaspoon Dijon mustard

½ teaspoon honey

salt and freshly cracked black pepper to taste

Place all ingredients in a bowl, and stir to combine. Adjust seasonings as needed. Store in the refrigerator.

# PEPPER SAUCES

Variety, as they say, is the spice of life, and this amazing selection of pepper sauces will give you the exact kind of heat you crave. Each Caribbean island features its own style of pepper sauce, and we love them all. Some are simple and pure, some are complex and layered with flavor—but all are delicious. This perfect range of pepper sauces will add diversity to your spice pantry.

*Makes one 12-ounce jar*

## CLASSIC PEPPER SAUCE

12 Scotch bonnet peppers, cleaned and stems removed

¼ cup white vinegar

4 cloves garlic, peeled

1 tablespoon yellow mustard

1 tablespoon salt

Puree all ingredients in a blender until smooth. Store in a glass jar in the refrigerator.

## LEMON-LIME PEPPER SAUCE

1 lemon, cut into quarters, seeds removed

½ cup white vinegar

10 Scotch bonnet or habanero peppers, cleaned and stems removed

¼ cup chopped carrots

4 cloves garlic, sliced

1 tablespoon chopped culantro

juice of 1 lime

salt to taste

Bring 2 cups water to boil over high heat in a medium saucepan. Add the lemon quarters. Boil for about 15 minutes, until the rind is soft. Strain; discard the cooking liquid. Transfer the lemons to a blender with the remaining ingredients. Blend on low to a consistency you like. Store in the refrigerator in an airtight sanitized container.

# MUSTARD PEPPER SAUCE

16 Scotch bonnet peppers,
cleaned and stems removed

¾ cup white vinegar

2 cloves garlic

2 tablespoons chopped cilantro

1 tablespoon chopped turmeric

¾ teaspoon
yellow mustard powder

Combine all ingredients in a food processor; blend until smooth. Transfer to a sanitized bottle or jar for storage in the refrigerator.

# PINEAPPLE PEPPER SAUCE

*Makes 2 cups*

2 cups chopped pineapple flesh
(from 1 large pineapple)

1 cup whole green habanero
peppers, cleaned and stems
removed

¼ cup white vinegar

2 tablespoons chopped garlic

1 tablespoon grated fresh ginger

1 tablespoon salt

Combine all ingredients in a blender, and puree. Transfer to a sanitized container and store in the refrigerator.

# MANGO PEPPER SAUCE

*Makes 2 cups*

2 cups ripe mango flesh

1 cup whole yellow habanero or
Scotch bonnet peppers,
cleaned and stems removed

¼ cup white vinegar

2 tablespoons cilantro

juice of 2 limes

salt to taste

Combine all ingredients in a blender, and puree. Transfer to a sanitized container and store in the refrigerator.

# AFRICAN PEPPER COMPOTE

W e often pair this spicy compote with Roasted Ripe Plantain (see page 68). It also makes a wonderful sandwich spread.

*Serves 6*

5 Scotch bonnet peppers (a mixture of red, green, and orange), washed and hulled

3 plum tomatoes, cut into quarters

2 cloves garlic, peeled and crushed

1 medium onion, peeled and cut into quarters

1 scallion, washed, trimmed, and cut into 1-inch lengths

1 tablespoon Dijon mustard

salt and freshly cracked black pepper

Place the peppers, tomatoes, garlic, onion, scallion, and Dijon mustard in the bowl of a food processor fitted with the steel chopping blade. Pulse several times until the mixture is well-combined but chunky. Scrape the mixture into a small saucepan. Cook over medium heat for 3 to 4 minutes, until the mixture thickens. Add salt and pepper to taste. When the sauce resembles chunky salsa, it is ready. Transfer to a sanitized container and store in the refrigerator.

# GREEN SEASONING

This spicy seasoning blend, used in our Coconut Choka (page 40), is a versatile all-purpose flavor enhancer.

*Makes 1½ cups*

1 large onion

1 head garlic
(about 12 cloves), peeled

2 to 3 wiri wiri, pimiento (cherry),
or Scotch bonnet peppers

1 bunch thyme, leaves removed
and stems discarded

2 bunches scallion,
roughly chopped

½ cup culantro (chadon beni),
roughly chopped

2 tablespoons white vinegar

2 tablespoons vegetable oil

salt and freshly cracked
black pepper to taste

Combine all ingredients in a blender. Puree until combined. Store in the refrigerator.

# HOT PEPPER OILS

These spicy oils can be used to add flavor to many dishes; select one of them any time you're looking for a little extra kick.

## CULANTRO PEPPER OIL

*Makes 1 cup*

1 cup olive oil

4 green Scotch bonnet peppers, stems and seeds removed

½ cup fresh culantro or cilantro leaves

2 cloves garlic

2 tablespoons fresh lime juice

2 teaspoons sea salt

Blend all ingredients in a blender until smooth. Store in the refrigerator in a sealed, sanitized container.

## SCOTCH BONNET OIL

*Makes 1 cup*

1 cup olive oil

4 Scotch bonnet peppers, seeds removed

2 teaspoons salt

Blend all ingredients in a blender until smooth. Refrigerate in a sealed, sanitized container.

A. Brunias pinx.t et sculp.t

THE BARBADOES MULATTO GIRL

This Plate is Dedicated to John Geo. Felton Esq.r
by his most Obliged and devoted Serv.t A. Brunias.

London. Pub.d as the Act directs July 1.t 1779 by the Proprietor, N.o 9 Broad Street, Soho.

# AFTERWORD

OUR GOAL IN WRITING *PROVISIONS* HAS BEEN TO revisit eighteenth-, nineteenth- and twentieth-century West Indian life, especially from the female perspective; the quotes and images we've included are intended to be like snapshots or historical vignettes that showcase the way our history connects us to who we are today. These glimpses into the gardens, farmlands, kitchens, lives, and minds of the women of our past reveal the ingenuity of the female cooks and affirm their ability to make strange ingredients palatable. As these mysterious eras spring to life, we receive insight about the cooking techniques of each century.

In creating a modern book that will help today's cooks reimagine the traditional ingredients and flavors of the West Indies, we thought these snapshots might intrigue you, but they do not tell the whole story. To put the historical vignettes and our evolving cuisine into context, we share this afterword so that we can honor the roots of Caribbean cooking and help it continue to grow and evolve.

## WOMEN IN SUGAR–PLANTATION SOCIETY

The global sugar boom of the seventeenth and eighteenth centuries created a new "moneyed" class of West Indian planters who made sure to live well and enjoy the many benefits derived from the spoils of their trade. A sugar plantation was a self-contained world, a self-sustaining little kingdom run with absolute power by one individual: the planter. But the women on the plantation also played significant roles.

Although the circumstances and roles of slave women varied from island to island, typically they were of great value in the planter's home, as well as in multiple other facets of plantation life and society. Their presence was felt from the fields, provision grounds, and slaves' quarters to the markets and planters' houses. Laborers, wet nurses, housekeepers, nannies, and cooks—slave women were present even in the intimate spaces of a plantation, particularly on islands where the owners were absentee landlords and the estates largely populated with European males. On some islands, however, planters' wives helped to define the social manners and rules of society; when their husbands put on events and gatherings, it was the wives who hosted.

## THE PLANTER BANQUET
## AND THE "NEGRO POT"

West Indian planters were notorious for the
opulence and excess they observed when dining
and entertaining. The writings of Lady Maria
Nugent, wife of the governor of Jamaica from
1801 to 1805, give us an idea of the level of
gourmandizing that took place in the day-to-day
life of planter society:

> I don't wonder now at the fever the
> people suffer from here—such eating
> and drinking I never saw! Such loads

of rich and highly seasoned things, and
really gallons of wine and mixed liquors
that they drink!!! I observed some of our
party today eat at breakfast as if they had
never eaten before. A dish of tea, another
of coffee, a bumper of claret, another
large one of hock-negus; then Madeira,
sangaree, hot and cold meats, stews
and pies, hot and cold fish pickled and
plain, peppers, ginger sweetmeats, acid
fruit, sweet jellies—in short it was all as
astonishing as it was disgusting.[7]

---

7. Nugent, 78.

The plantation's kitchen must have been bustling with activity. These elaborate meals were always prepared by the house cook, usually a woman, whose skill was such that she could produce an incredible gourmet feast from a simple brick oven and open-flame hearth. Extravagant banquets with a copious variety of dishes were the norm, and they all had to be produced in rudimentary cooking facilities. Accordingly, a West Indian banquet featured a balance of both room-temperature and hot items, a tradition that lives on at the Caribbean table.

By contrast, slaves' meals were meager and modest, prepared by the matriarch. (Despite her many hours of work on the plantation, a woman slave was also responsible for the preparation of meals in her own home, as well as for the maintenance of her home and the simple but necessary chores like laundry, sewing, and cleaning.) Spare kitchen facilities, rustic cooking utensils, and lack of time made meal preparation for the slaves a relatively simple, efficient task that centered around a single pot over an open flame. This style of cooking produced two main types of nourishment: well-seasoned, hearty one-pot dishes like soups, stews, porridges, and pap, and simple flame-roasted starches served with salted fish. These dishes were often called the "negro pot."

Ironically, the white population also relished the negro pot. Partly this was out of necessity—the islands' hot climes did not bode well for typical European dishes and ingredients. The ingredients and foods the slaves ate were easy to prepare, had a longer shelf life, were suited to the climate, and above all were fresh, readily available. As a result, the dining habits of slaves and their owners began to see some similarities. Mrs. A. C. Carmichael often references how the Europeans and slaves alike enjoyed the same fare:

> All the various soups, whether tanias, calialou, pigeon pea, or pumpkin, are to be found almost daily at the tables of the white population, whose children are almost fed upon those messes. I never met with a European who did not relish (the) "negro pot."[8]

These completely different culinary worlds, those of slave and master, of negro pot and planter banquet, began to merge in the kitchen. Through the language of food, a common gastronomic narrative was developed.

## PROVISIONING

For a sugar plantation to function, it required three essential features: a large tract of flat farmable land, slave labor, and low operating costs. Estate holders were determined to keep their operating costs down by spending as little as possible on feeding slaves. And on islands with a lot of uncultivated land, they could manage to feed the slaves at little or no cost to themselves— by placing the burden of providing food on the shoulders of the slaves themselves.

Under the Jamaica Consolidated Slave Act of 1792, if land was available, every slave, male and female, from the date they were born or bought had to be supplied with a tract of land called a provision ground on which they could farm their own produce:

> Every master, owner, or possessor, of any plantation or plantations, pens, or other lands whatsoever, shall allot and appoint a sufficient quantity of land for every slave he shall have in possession…as and for the proper ground of every such slave, and allow such slave sufficient time to work the same, in order to provide him, her, or themselves, with sufficient provisions for his, her, or their maintenance.[9]

This was actively practiced in the islands of Jamaica, Grenada, St. Vincent, St. Lucia, and Trinidad and Tobago, where slaves subsisted largely on the food they grew and harvested themselves. The provision ground was often as far as ten miles from the plantation. What's more, slaves were only allowed one day every two weeks to work on their grounds, so the system increased their workload. The much closer, though smaller, kitchen garden was invaluable; it was a piece of land near the slave village where they could cultivate garden plots and raise small livestock.

The ability to grow fruits and vegetables, and even raise chickens and pigs, close to home was essential to the slaves' survival. Because slaves were typically given a meager weekly allowance of cheap imported cured fish and a small amount of grain, without the ability to grow their own food,

---

8.  Carmichael, vol. 1, 181.

9.  Consolidated Slave Act.

they most likely would not have survived the brutal physical demands made on them. And the women most certainly would not have been able to feed their families. If she wanted her family to eat, a "negro" woman had to find the strength, energy, and means to ensure that, outside the seventy-two hours a week she already worked, she kept her grounds and kitchen gardens well maintained and thriving with produce. Furthermore, she had a second motivation beyond self-sustenance to cultivate bountiful grounds.

## SUNDAY MARKETS

In an ironic twist of fate, slaves owned whatever they could produce in their provision grounds and kitchen gardens, and they could sell or trade that food at weekly markets. The benefit of working in the "great house" was that the women were exposed to the kitchen and the dining habits of the planters. Savvy women knew exactly what produce would be in demand, and they grew those items in their own gardens. That way they could trade the desirable ingredients at the Sunday market and with the estates.

This is where women took the lead, ultimately helping to create a market economy. Eventually, ships, local merchants, and even plantation owners came to rely on the goods grown, traded, and bartered by female slaves. In her first-person account of life as a West Indian slave, published in 1831, Mary Prince describes how she earned money through barter and trade:

> I took in washing, and sold coffee and yams and other provisions to the captains of ships....Sometimes I bought a hog

cheap on board ship, and sold it for double the money on shore; I also earned a good deal by selling coffee.[10]

Although the law mandating provision grounds may have resulted from the planters' effort to avoid spending money to feed slaves, it also provided one of the first legitimate pathways to financial autonomy for a British West Indian slave. Despite being a huge burden to slaves, provision grounds also afforded them independence, a temporary respite from the plantation, social structure, and the ability to earn an income outside the labor they were forced to perform.

---

10. Prince, Kindle location 365.

## EMANCIPATION
## AND A NEW SOCIETY

The Slavery Abolition Act of 1833 put an end to
slavery in the British Empire (the slave trade itself
had already been outlawed in 1807)—eventually.
If slavery had been truly abolished right away,
planters wouldn't have been able to rely on
slave labor to make their businesses profitable;
to control the impact on sugar production,
the British Crown implemented a period of
"apprenticeship" for the newly freed slaves. The
law dictated that they had to continue to work for
their former masters in exchange for provisions
in a sort of replica of slavery. While the Crown
was paying out huge sums of money to the
"inconvenienced" planters for losing their slave
"assets," the former slaves were forced to fend for
themselves. They were given no remuneration
for the many years of toil, abuse, and servitude
they'd been forced to endure and were expected
to continue to work as bonded, unpaid employees
on the same estates over a period of four to six
years before they became "full free." In many
cases, the newly freed people were subjected to
even worse treatment than before by resentful
plantation owners; it was especially bad for
women, who were often abused, forced to work
while pregnant, and sent to workhouses to "walk
the treadmill," a vicious device designed as a
form of corporal punishment for insubordinate
workers. Apprenticeship was abandoned in 1838,
years before its scheduled end, due to social
pressure and fear of rebellion.

## EASTERN INFLUENCES

In the islands that had provision grounds,
including Trinidad and Jamaica, many freed
people refused to work under the apprenticeship
system. Planters imported indentured laborers
from China and India to replenish the labor
force.

Much as the "negro pot" had made its way
into the planter's banquet, Asian influences
began to make their way into West Indian
cooking, adding yet another delicate and subtly
sophisticated layer to the food of the region.
The main ingredients (ground provisions, salted
and cured meats, vegetables, fruits, legumes,
and grains) remained the same, but the cuisine
evolved as Eastern flavor profiles and culinary
techniques were introduced. It was during this
period that ingredients like geera (cumin seed),
curry, rice, and soy sauce—along with cooking
implements like the tawah (a flat roti griddle),
kalchul (a metal ladle used to make choka),
dhal gutni (wooden utensil used for making
dhal), and wok—became more common on
the islands. This was also when Eastern dishes
such as roti, curries, dhal, rice dishes, choka,
and chutney became a part of the daily diet,
particularly in Trinidad, Guyana, and Jamaica.
The combination of influences became firmly
entrenched as Indian and Chinese families
merged with Caribbean society. After the period
of indenture was complete, most of the Indian
and Chinese laborers chose to stay in the islands,
further blending in and solidifying their presence
in the budding island society.

# MAKING A NEW LIFE

With the arrival of new cultures, tastes, and opportunities, the recently freed men and women became wholly engaged in building new lives for themselves. Accordingly, after full emancipation was declared in 1838, in islands where there was available land, like Jamaica, many free people avoided wage labor and became independent cultivators, allowing them to grow food both to feed and to financially support their families. Many freed people fled the estates, abandoning slave villages and provision grounds. Their goal was to create lives for themselves in mountain communities; they procured small plots of land and set about establishing subsistence farms. As self-reliant slaves, they had built their homes themselves, and were quickly able to re-create the small-scale farming model that had existed with their provision grounds and kitchen gardens.

Free people were anxious to restructure their lives. No longer content to be under the dominion of others, they were intent on choosing their own working hours and building a home life. Afro-Caribbean women were determined to escape the brutal abuse of apprenticeship and slavery; whenever possible, they retreated from agricultural wage labor. Families had to survive, so they re-created the system that had worked well for them before, dividing the labor within the family: the men farmed family land or worked for wages while the women worked from the home to supplement the family income. They established small farms that grew a wide variety of produce, and the women headed to market to trade. And trade they did. Fruits, vegetables, jams, jellies, preserves, candies, coconut oil, coffee, cocoa, tobacco—all manner of provisions were farmed, produced, and sold by these budding female entrepreneurs.

> The Trinidad market is very attractive: there are numerous bottles of comfits, sweetmeats of all kinds, and coloured papers of comforts, under the name of dragee. There are no seats for the sellers of fruit, vegetables, or other wares—some bring a chair or a stool; but many are seated on the grass, in the open area where the market is held. The market of Port of Spain [is] a very animated scene…coloured handkerchiefs, on the heads of the coloured and negro women, the diversity of tongues spoken: English, Scotch, Irish, French, Spaniards, Dutch, Germans, Italians, Chinese, and Turks, [and] the coloured and negro population, free or slave, African, Indian, or creole.[11]

This newly self-sufficient culture shaped the archetype of the independent, powerful Afro-Caribbean matriarch, marked by ingenuity, dignity, pride, and the determination to avoid being subjected to the rule of another. Mary Williamson, a former slave, offers an early example of this resilience. In a letter penned to her former master, she asks for assistance in reestablishing her land and grounds after her personal residence and grounds were destroyed:

> [They came] early in the morning and pulled down both my houses, and took away the Timbers; Now Honoured Sir, as

---

11. Carmichael, vol. 2, 69.

I was sold [off] the property [and freed], having no property or, [like my sisters, no right] to a house on their Masters Estate. Their children are young and left without a shelter. I was a great help to them [when I had my own land and home] having a ground and garden with provisions which [I often] gave to them, but it pleased your Attorny and Overseer to destroy every thing plowing up the garden and turning the Stocks into the ground or provisions, so that I am not only a sufferer but your poor negroes, are deprived, of the means of subsistence....I must beg my Honoured Master, for to give me a little spot somewhere on the Estate, for I do not wish to go from my family, as they want every assistance I can give them.[12]

12. Williamson.

SOLD ONLY BY AGENTS OF THE UNIVERSAL PHOTO ART CO.

the women of polite British society, being "full free" brought them autonomy and the possibility of true financial independence. It also created another kind of freedom: the freedom to use their ingenuity to redefine the cuisine—and ultimately their role in society.

## FREEDOM, INGENUITY, AND AN ENTREPRENEURIAL SPIRIT

From the late 1800s to the first three decades of the 1900s, women began making a new kind of economic impact on West Indian social structure by entering into professional trades, procuring work as seamstresses, secretaries, teachers, and nurses. At the same time, growing numbers of female entrepreneurs engaged in commercial trade through the preparation of food. They made use of their culinary prowess and the raw materials available to them to earn extra income in support of the home and family. It is during this era that our great-grandmother, Martha Matilda Briggs, who pioneered the Jamaican patty, was born. Ma Briggs's business—and her cooking—were famous among folks from all walks of life in Jamaica in the early 1900s. Her patties were even immortalized by actor and playwright Charles Hyatt in his memoir, *When Me Was a Boy*:

The formerly enslaved women of the era were survivors. Unafraid to stake their claim, they represented a new branch of Caribbean society: the sophisticated, elegant Afro-Caribbean woman whose main concern was creating a comfortable home and fashioning a better life for herself and her family—something she was prevented from achieving under slavery.

Because women of color weren't subject to the boundaries, rules, and obligations borne by

> When me was a likkle bwoy—there was some things that if anybody did tell me that them wouldn' be around for us to enjoy today ah woulda tell them that them mad. A Brigg's patty? Now plenty people use to swear by Bruce's patty, but me did prefer Briggs. Bruces an Brigg's was two establishments situated in Cross Roads an

did face one another from either side of the beginning of Retirement Road. The two place use to sell patty…Briggs…patty was uptown story.…While every other patty…was sellin' fi fourpence, Briggs patty was sixpence. So when yuh buy them patty deh is spen' yuh a spen'.[13]

Ma Briggs's life was unusual for a woman of color. As the owner of numerous properties, she was successful, recognized, and financially independent; her story stands out in an era when there were very few "acknowledged" black female business owners. Still, despite her many honorable and pioneering traits, it is only through the stories of her food that we know her at all and can begin to understand how she touched people's lives. She lives on not because of who she was or what she accomplished, but simply because of what she cooked and how her food made people feel.

As atypical as Ma Briggs's story was, it is symbolic of the stories of many women throughout our region who never had the opportunity to record, document, or be recognized for their work, their sacrifice, and the way in which they nurtured, supported, and raised so many. Examples of female food entrepreneurs like Ma Briggs were common in all levels of society. There were the Jamaican candy ladies who sold homemade sweets throughout the streets of Kingston; the *dulce* sellers of Cuba who sold fruit "cheeses" and preserves of all kinds; and many commercial food producers, caterers, bakers, ice cream makers, and restaurant and tavern owners. One particularly well-known

example is Sybil la Grenade, a home economics teacher and the originator of the famous Grenadian nutmeg preserve and liqueur known as "la Grenade."

By introducing ingredients and dishes they had created in their home kitchens into the mainstream, women shifted consumers' perspectives and helped refine their fellow citizens' palates. Their sophisticated products, which held an appeal that crossed social boundaries, were craved and loved by people from all parts of the culture. They shaped market demand, set trends, and kicked off a movement in the region's cuisine to promote delicious foods that were easily available to all.

## REFINEMENT, RESILIENCE, AND REVIVAL

Many women took a more studied approach to the making of a refined home life. In 1935, the Jamaican newspaper *Daily Gleaner* began publication of a magazine titled *Our Women's Page: A Variety of Topics Presented from the Feminine Point of View*. A column penned by a writer under the byline "a Mother" expounds on ways that cooking good food can enhance life for the family and oneself. "Mother" advocated an "epicurean" experience and the use of local ingredients in creative and innovative ways:

In food as in interior decoration, knowing people make the fullest use of home products and only mix or vary them judiciously with exotics. So let us try our old friend Gros Michel [banana] first in some new dresses; Every woman with

13. Hyatt, Kindle locations 1691–1699.

anything of the Epicurean in her has already found out that banana fritters are greatly improved by the addition of a little brandy or Jamaica rum.[14]

The advent of World War II further wove the newly independent women of color into the fabric of Caribbean society. They supported the war effort both on the home front and abroad in whatever way they could; approximately one hundred West Indian women volunteered, and those who stayed behind tapped even deeper into the resilience and survival skills displayed by their ancestors to sustain their families.

It was a period of ingenuity. As ships stopped making the passage across the Atlantic and imported goods grew scarcer, reliance on local ingredients increased, and ancient cooking techniques were revived. Using the traditions of their ancestors—making flour from provisions; using cho cho for "apple" pie; producing homemade candies, sweets, and preserves—women became more creatively self-reliant. With this came a willingness to step outside the frame and carve out their own independence. This trait continues to define the lives of Caribbean women into the modern era, which is full of examples of successful, innovative, savvy, resilient, and creative female entrepreneurs.

## HERSTORY

Until the mid-twentieth century, except for a handful of journals and cookbooks written by women in the nineteenth century, the personal stories of the intimate lives of West Indian women, or what we term *herstory*, were rarely written down. Instead, they were passed down orally and manually, shared in the drawing rooms, birthing rooms, bedrooms, dining rooms, and, yes, "cooking" rooms of West Indian society. These stories, and by extension our story, were whispered into the ears of daughters as a near-silent truth. To speak about West Indian food—and by natural extension Caribbean food—without telling the stories of the women who created it results in a misappropriation or misunderstanding of the authentic cuisine. We intend to change that in this book with an expanded and nuanced perspective on the region's cuisine, the influences that shaped it, and the spirit in which it has been prepared, served, and shared.

---

14. *Daily Gleaner,* Feb. 23, 1935.

# A FURTHER NOTE
# ON OUR NINETEENTH-CENTURY
# HISTORICAL SOURCES

IN THIS COOKBOOK WE HAVE INCLUDED PRIMARY source quotations from nineteenth-century publications that we feel bring perspective to West Indian society, cuisine, and cultural norms. We chose these publications for specific reasons. First, all were written by women who resided in the British West Indies in the mid- to late nineteenth century, and thus they shed light on the domestic and social aspects of plantation life that were often ignored in the journals penned by males. Second, they help to re-create the culinary, domestic, and cultural landscape of the era by describing in great detail the local ingredients that were available to the cook and defining for the unfamiliar reader what those ingredients were, what they could be compared with, where they were found, and the most popular methods of preparation and consumption.

The earliest, by Lady Maria Nugent, wife of Sir George Nugent, governor of Jamaica from 1801 to 1806, was written between 1801 and 1815 and first published in 1839. One of the only works that addresses the day-to-day life of planter society, it is composed of a fascinating series of entries that track Lady Nugent's various social activities, feasts, balls, and breakfasts. One thing remains constant: the activities always involved food. She describes vast meals and gargantuan feasts. It appears that members of the local planter society were quite desperate to impress the governor and his young and beautiful wife. Lady Nugent was a petite, rather vain woman with curly brown hair and a strong constitution that belied her delicate looks; she possessed a great love of fashion and social engagements of all kinds. It is through her incredibly vivid descriptions of the social life of the Jamaican planter that we get a glimpse into the drawing rooms of the island's "power brokers."

Lady Nugent is often quite disgusted by the extreme levels of gourmandizing:

> At the Moro today our dinner at 6 was really so profuse it is worth describing. The first course was of fish with an entire jerked hog in the centre, and a blak crab pepper pot. The second course was of turtle, mutton, beef, turkey, goose, ducks, capons, chicken, ham, tongue and crab patties. The third course was of sweets and fruits of all kinds. I felt quite sick, what with the heat and such a profusion of eatables.[15]

---

15. Nugent, 95.

Her scorn carries over to women and children, who were known to indulge to excess in both food and drink, which she believed resulted in their ill health:

25th: I now found the reason that the ladies here do not eat at dinner. I could not help remarking Mrs. Cox, who sat next to me at the second breakfast. She began with fish, of which she eats plentifully, all swimming in oil. Then Cold veal, with the same sauce!! Then tarts, cakes, and fruit. All the other ladies did the same, changing their plates, drinking wine etc. as if it were dinner. I got away to my room as soon as possible

28th: I am not astonished at the general ill health of the men in this country, for they really eat like cormorants and drink like porpoises. All the men of our party got drunk tonight, even too a boy of 15, who was obliged to be carried home[16]

Another source we consulted, *Domestic Manners and Social Condition of the White, Coloured, and Negro Population of the West Indies* (early 1830s), is a controversial work by Mrs. A. C. Carmichael, a Scottish woman who evidently was a member of upper-class West Indian society. A resident of St. Vincent and Trinidad and Tobago, she wrote two volumes documenting in great detail the domestic, working, and social life of all spectrums of society in both these islands.

Three times a week, hucksters used to come, from St. Josephs to our estate, with great trays on their heads, loaded with bread, cakes, and pastry; and they seldom carried many of their dainties away. They went on the system of barter and exchange; and these huckster women might be seen, coming across the pasture from the negro houses, equally heavily laden as when they went; but with this difference, that they now carried fruit, vegetables, and eggs, to retail at St. Josephs.[17]

The highly class-conscious Mrs. Carmichael held a firmly entrenched belief that there was nothing wrong with the plantation system, and that "negroes" were well treated and better off than the European peasantry. Her work is laced with justifications for slavery and gross glamorization of plantation life. She spends a large amount of ink describing market life, daily routines, dining habits, the fruits, vegetables, fish, and meats available, and how island dishes were consumed and prepared.

There is a well-known root in Trinidad, common all over the West Indies I believe, known by the name of the eddoe. It abounds upon every estate. The leaves make excellent wholesome greens; and the negro, with the addition of a bit of salt fish, or salt pork, has an excellent pot of soup. He may add pigeon peas during the months they are in season; and as for capsicums—his seasoning for all dishes—

---

16. Nugent, 106, 108.

17. Carmichael, vol. 2, 166.

they are never wanting. This soup is excellent, wholesome, and palatable to all—creoles, white, free, coloured, or slave; and indeed is one of the great blessings of the West Indies. It is needless after this to say, that in point of food our people, new comers as they were, were not to be pitied.[18]

At the other end of the spectrum, Mary Prince, a woman born into slavery in Bermuda who also resided in Antigua and Turks and Caicos, reveals a different reality from the ease and abundance depicted by Lady Nugent and Mrs. Carmichael. *The History of Mary Prince, a West Indian Slave, Related by Herself* (1831) is a first-person account of the brutal treatment she received as she was bought, sold, and moved between slave "owners" during her time in the British West Indies. She went to London in 1827 with her then owners, Mr. and Mrs. John Wood. At that time, although slavery was still legal in the West Indies, it was illegal in Britain, so she ran away to the Anti-Slavery Society, where she met abolitionist sympathizers who helped her pen her story. *The History of Mary Prince* was the first published account of enslavement written by a woman and is considered a crucial part of the abolitionist movement.

> The next morning my mistress set about instructing me in my tasks. She taught me to do all sorts of household work; to wash and bake, pick cotton and wool, and wash floors, and cook. And she taught me (how can I ever forget it!) more things than

these; she caused me to know the exact difference between the smart of the rope, the cart-whip, and the cow-skin, when applied to my naked body by her own cruel hand. And there was scarcely any punishment more dreadful than the blows received on my face and head from her hard heavy fist. She was a fearful woman, and a savage mistress to her slaves.[19]

In complete contrast to Carmichael's description of the life of a slave, on the topic of working the salt mines in Turks and Caicos, Prince depicts arduous work and meager food and provisions:

> My new master was one of the owners or holders of the salt ponds, and he received a certain sum for every slave that worked upon his premises, whether they were young or old....I was immediately sent to work in the salt water with the rest of the slaves. This work was perfectly new to me. I was given half barrel and a shovel, and had to stand up to my knees in the water, from 4 o'clock in the morning until nine, when we were given some Indian corn boiled in water which we were obliged to swallow so fast as we could for fear the rain should come on and melt the salt. We were then called again to our tasks and worked through the heat of the day; the sun flaming up on our heads like fire, and raising salt blisters on those parts which were not completely covered. Our feet and legs, from standing in the saltwater for so

---

18. Carmichael, vol. 2, 165.

19. Prince, 6.

many hours, soon became full of dreadful boils, which eat down in some cases to the very bone, afflicting the sufferer with great torment. We came home at 12; ate our corn soup called "Blawly," as fast as we could, and went back to our appointment until dark at night. We then shoveled up the salt in large heaps, and went down to the sea, where we washed the pickle from our limbs, and clean the barrows and shovels from the salt. When we returned to the house, our master gave us each our allowance of raw Indian corn, which we pounded in a mortar and boiled in water for our suppers.[20]

She describes working the provision grounds of yet another owner in the island of Bermuda:

I was several years the slave of Mr. D—, after I returned to my native place. Here I worked in the grounds. My work was planting and hoeing sweet-potatoes, Indian corn, plantains, bananas, cabbages, pumpkins, onions, &c. I did all the household work, and attended upon a horse and cow besides,—going also upon all errands. I had to curry the horse—to clean and feed him—and sometimes to ride him a little. I had more than enough to do—but still it was not so very bad as Turk's Island.[21]

We also consulted the earliest known book on Jamaican cooking, penned by Caroline Sullivan. First published in 1893, *The Jamaica Cookery*

*Book: Three Hundred and Sixty-Four Simple Cookery Receipts and Household Hints* reveals interesting insights into the use of commonplace ingredients in both the plantation kitchen and the "native" kitchen. Recipes are included for some of our most popular island meals. But other foods are mentioned only in passing, implying that the more "rustic preparations" that were regularly consumed by the natives were unworthy of inclusion in a book whose purpose, as stated by its author, was to acquaint newcomers with the preparation of local dishes. Sullivan writes:

In this little work…my desire is merely to introduce to new comers to Jamaica our own native methods of cooking our own products, and to by no means attempt to cope with the many excellent works that at present exist on English or other cookery. It will be noticed, therefore that nothing will be mentioned here except a few hints that may be of service to those who are strangers to our native dishes, provided as they must already be with cookery books which will guide them in (the preparation of more classical dishes).[22]

Very little is known about Caroline Sullivan, but it can be surmised from her in-depth knowledge of island ingredients and methods of preparation that she was in charge of the kitchens of a well-established Jamaican estate home. The original book was advertised in the *Gall's* weekly newsletter of Saturday December 23, 1893, and a second edition in the *Daily Gleaner* of Monday January 10, 1898. Sullivan's work in particular

---

20. Prince, 10.

21. Prince, 13.

22. Sullivan, 15.

demonstrates the sensibility of a true gourmand, showcasing her profound understanding of island ingredients and how to manipulate them to produce simple but refined meals.

Despite the glaring prejudices and inaccuracies of many of the historical journals, the female authors' commentary on the era's culinary practices are as compellingly accurate, informative, and relevant today as they would have been in the nineteenth century. Through their voices, we are able to get a glimpse of a time gone by when women, in particular women of color, were invisible, inferior, and irrelevant. Theirs was a history rarely told; by connecting to this history—our history—we bring the stories of their past into our present. Many of the preparations and recipes they describe still appear on tables in very much the same way they would have two hundred years ago. There is no denying that the dining habits that began in the West Indies during the slavery and colonial periods still resonate throughout the region today.

# LOCAL PRODUCE, PREPARATION NOTES, AND INGREDIENT SUBSTITUTIONS

THIS SECTION IS A GUIDE TO WORKING WITH THE fruits and vegetables of the Caribbean. If you don't live in the West Indies and have trouble sourcing any of the ingredients called for in this book, look here for possible substitutions. Keep in mind that many of them can be ordered online in one form or another. If your usual grocery store doesn't carry a certain item, find out if there's a Caribbean market in your community.

**Ackee,** Jamaica's national fruit, is native to tropical West Africa. It came to Jamaica on a slave ship. It is said that slaves wore the seeds around their necks as talismans for good luck. Captain William Bligh carried the fruit from Jamaica to the Royal Botanic Gardens of England in 1793. Ackee and saltfish is one of Jamaica's best-known local dishes. Unfortunately, ackee has a bit of a reputation as the bad boy of

## How to Select and Boil Fresh Ackee

*1 dozen ackee pods yield about 1 cup cooked ackee*

**Step 1:** The red ackee skin must be open, as this indicates ripeness. Please note that consuming ackee when the skin is closed (indicating underripe fruit) can result in severe illness, as certain parts of the ackee are poisonous. Remove the ackee pods from the skin (each ackee has about three pods). You will be left with a firm, waxy, yellow pod with a large black seed on one end.

**Step 2:** Remove the seed from the flesh by twisting it to the right. Find the little split on one side of the ackee pod; use a small knife to remove the red thread-like substance from inside the pod. Clean the ackee well, as the

red threads are the poisonous part, but leave the pod whole.

**Step 3:** Bring salted water to a boil; add the whole, cleaned pods. We like to add thyme to the water, but this is optional.

**Step 4:** Boil for 15 to 20 minutes until the flesh turns a brighter yellow and is less waxy and is soft and buttery in texture but still firm. Avoid overcooking, as it will become very mushy and difficult to work with. Once cooked, the ackee is ready to go. (Canned ackee has been boiled.) The freshly cooked ackee may be frozen in a zip-top bag for up to one week.

Caribbean cuisine because it can be poisonous if incorrectly prepared. Be assured, however, that it is perfectly safe to eat. There is no substitute for ackee. Canned and frozen varieties are widely available online and in Caribbean grocers.

**Allspice (pimento)** is used in many dishes, the most well-known of which is the famously spicy jerk seasoning. Most of the world's supply of allspice is grown in Jamaica. The allspice or pimento berry has a unique taste—like a blend of nutmeg, cinnamon, black pepper, and clove.

**Blue Mountain coffee** gets its name from the mountain range where the coffee beans are grown. The coffee industry began in Jamaica in 1725, when Sir Nicholas Lawes, then the governor of the island, brought seedlings from Martinique and planted them on his estate. Over the last several decades, Blue Mountain coffee has developed a reputation that has made it one of the most expensive and sought-after coffees in the world.

**Breadfruit** is a species of flowering tree in the mulberry family. Its name is derived from the texture of the cooked fruit, similar to that of fresh-baked bread. In the late eighteenth century, the quest for cheap, high-energy food sources for British slaves prompted colonial administrators and plantation owners to call for the introduction of this plant to the Caribbean. William Bligh commanded an expedition to collect live

# How to Roast and Peel Breadfruit over an Open Flame

*1 medium roasted breadfruit serves about 10*

**Step 1:** Remove and discard the stalk. At the opposite end of the fruit, use a sharp knife to cut an X into the flesh.

**Step 2:** If you have a gas stove, place the breadfruit directly on the burner, bottom (stem) side down. Over a medium flame, roast the breadfruit for 30 minutes.

**Step 3:** After 30 minutes, use a potholder or cloth to turn the breadfruit upside down over the flame, and roast for another 30 minutes. Next, turn it on its sides for 10 minutes, rotating periodically as it roasts. The breadfruit is finished roasting when the exterior is black and charred and the interior is soft and cooked through. Remove from the heat.

**Step 4:** After about 30 minutes, while the breadfruit is still warm inside but has cooled enough to handle, hold the stem end in your open palm on a paper towel (this can get messy). Peel the breadfruit over a garbage can starting at the top (where you cut the incision) and using a circular motion as though you were peeling an orange. Allow the rind to fall away. Avoid getting the black char on the peeled breadfruit. Alternately, you can stand the breadfruit on its end on a cutting board and cut the rind away in a downward motion, from stem end to top. Remove the center or heart of the breadfruit. Slice and serve.

breadfruit plants from Tahiti and transport them to Jamaica.

**Callaloo (calilou),** a leafy, spinach-like vegetable, has a distinctively Caribbean origin. The *Amaranthus viridis* variety found in Jamaica, better known as Chinese spinach or Indian kale, should not be confused with the callaloo found in the eastern Caribbean, which refers to the leaves of the dasheen plant. In some countries (e.g., St. Vincent), the leaves and stem of the dasheen plant are cooked and pureed into a thick liquid, which is served as a side dish similar to creamed spinach. Callaloo is sometimes prepared with crab legs, coconut milk, pumpkin, and okra and served with rice or made into a soup. In Jamaica, callaloo is steamed with onions, garlic, and Scotch bonnet—usually for a hearty breakfast. Some like it soft while others prefer it crisp; either way it is delicious. Kale is the best substitute.

**Cassava (yucca, manioc),** a tuberous root vegetable six to twelve inches in length and two to three inches in diameter, has a tough brown skin and a very firm white flesh. Both kinds of cassava, sweet and bitter, can be made into flour (or meal), tapioca, and farina. Cassava or manioc meal is used to make bammy, a Jamaican flatbread. Cassava should never be eaten raw as it contains an acid that is potentially poisonous.

**Chadon beni (culantro, shado beni)** is one of the key herbs in the cuisine of Trinidad and Tobago. It is also used to make the intensely green Puerto Rican sauce known as recaito. Cilantro is similar in flavor to chadon beni but is much less dense and potent.

**Cho cho (chayote, christophene, mirleton),** like melons and squash, is a member of the gourd family. This rough-skinned, pear-shaped vegetable grows on vines in cool temperatures. Upon slicing it open, you'll find a very pale green and watery interior, with a soft white seed. Cho cho is probably the most widely used vegetable in the Caribbean, Latin America, and southern United States, each country featuring its favorite recipe. Zucchini makes a great substitute.

# How to Clean and Prep Fresh Callaloo

*1 large bunch of callaloo yields about 4 cups prepped*

**Step 1:** Cut off the stems, and strip the leaves from the stalks. (This step is optional; you can leave the leaves on the stalk if desired, but when making a quiche, filling, or dip it is best to strip them off.) Place the leaves in a medium-sized stainless steel bowl.

**Step 2:** Sprinkle a teaspoon of salt over the leaves, and rinse the leaves with cold water to remove any insects. Stack and cut the leaves into chiffonade. At this point the callaloo is ready to be sautéed or steamed.

**Step 3:** Cook until bright green in color; do not overcook as the leaves will turn brown. Note: callaloo yields a lot of water during cooking, so use very moderate amounts of fat to sauté and very little water if steaming or "shallow boiling."

# How to Prep Fresh Cassava Root

*1 pound of cassava serves 4 to 6*

**Step 1:** Select cassava roots that are firm and have no soft spots, which indicate rotting. They should smell clean and have a white center when cut open.

**Step 2:** Cut off the narrow, tapered end. Then cut the root crosswise into manageable lengths (about six inches long).

**Step 3:** Stand each piece on its end on a cutting board. Using a sharp knife, cut away the peel of the cassava root in a downward motion.

**Step 4:** Cut the peeled cassava root lengthwise into quarters to expose the woody core. Remove the core.

**Step 5:** Peeled, cored cassava can be stored in water in the refrigerator for two to three days. It may be boiled, roasted, or fried. Cook it completely before consumption.

# How to Peel and Prepare Cho Cho (Chayote)

*4 cho cho serve approximately 8*

**Step 1:** Peel under running water with a potato peeler. Slice in half lengthwise, and scoop or cut out the core. Raw, peeled cho cho can be diced, chopped, or julienned. Cho cho has a high water content and cooks quickly.

**Step 2:** Sauté in a little oil, or toss with olive oil and herbs and roast in the oven.

# How to Make Fresh Coconut Milk

*1 dry coconut yields 2½ to 3 cups coconut milk*

**Step 1:** Crack open the dried coconut with a hammer. Remove the hard coconut meat from the shell using a small knife. Clean away the thick brown skin.

**Step 2:** Chop or grate the coconut meat, and then blend it with 3 cups water in a blender until it is completely pureed.

**Step 3:** Strain the liquid through a fine-mesh sieve, and squeeze the remaining pulp with your hands until all the remaining liquid is removed and the pulp is dry and trashy. Coconut milk can be made ahead and frozen for up to four weeks.

**Coco (malanga, tannia, cocoyam),** a tuberous plant with large leaves, takes a year to mature. Coco is great in soups and for making bread. Because of its creamy texture, it is also good mashed, like potatoes, with a little butter.

**Coconut** is the edible seed of a tropical palm tree that yields fruit all year long. Coconuts, widely available throughout the world, are edible in both their green and mature forms. Both the water and the "jelly" of the green coconut find their way into many island drinks, and meat from the mature coconut adds to tasty desserts. Coconut milk (liquid and powdered) is widely sold in cans and packets. Although doing so is labor intensive, coconut milk and coconut oil are still made fresh from scratch in many West Indian kitchens.

**Dasheen (taro),** a root vegetable, is similar to a smaller variety of corms called "eddo" in the English-speaking countries of the West Indies.

It is cultivated and consumed as a staple crop in the region. Taro or dasheen is mostly blue when cooked, and eddoes are small and slimy. In the Spanish West Indies, dasheen is called *ñame.*

**Green banana** looks much like a yellow banana, but its flesh is firm and starchy rather than soft and sweet. A staple starch for many Caribbean populations, green bananas make great chips, salads, and porridge, or they can be enjoyed simply boiled.

**Guava** grows all over the islands, making it readily available for juice, jellies, and sauces. This small, pink-bellied fruit has a seed-filled flesh. It is naturally sweeter when ripe, but can be enjoyed greener and tarter, and can even be added to savory dishes like salads.

**Gungo peas (pigeon peas)** originated in eastern India. A dish of rice and gungo peas is common in the Caribbean, usually accompanied by a meat. They can be used in soups, and can

## How to Peel and Boil Green Bananas

*1 dozen banana fingers serves 6 to 8*

**Step 1:** Before beginning, rub about 1 teaspoon vegetable oil on your hands to help prevent the starchy bananas from staining your hands and making them sticky. Have a bowl of water nearby in which to immerse the bananas once peeled.

**Step 2:** Cut off the root end of the banana. With the tip of a sharp paring knife, score several cuts lengthwise along the ridges of the banana. The cuts should only go skin deep. Cut off the base of the banana.

**Step 3:** Peel the skin using your hands. Then use the edge of the knife to scrape away any excess strings of skin. Immediately submerge the peeled banana in a bowl of water if you're not cooking it right away.

**Step 4:** To cook green bananas in the traditional way, bring a pot of well-salted water to a boil and add the whole bananas. Boil for about 20 minutes or until the fruit is tender and can be speared with a fork.

# How to Cook Dried Peas for "Anytime Rice and Peas"

*Use 1 cup of peas to approximately 2 cups of rice.*

**Step 1:** Soak the gungo peas in a large bowl, covering them by 3 inches with cold water. Cover and set aside overnight. By the next day, the beans will have absorbed much of the water. Drain whatever liquid is left and pick through the beans, discarding any shriveled ones.

**Step 2:** Transfer the beans to a large pot, and cover by 2 inches with cold water. Season the water with ½ small yellow onion, sliced,

4 stalks scallion, 4 cloves garlic, and 1 tablespoon salt. Bring to a boil. Skim off and discard any foam that rises to the surface.

**Step 3:** Reduce the heat, cover the pot, and let simmer for about 1 hour. Add more water as needed to keep the beans submerged. Stir occasionally. Once the peas are cooked, drain them. The cooked beans may be frozen in an airtight bag for up to two weeks.

be split to make dhal. In Jamaica, we consume stews and soups made with fresh gungo peas at Christmastime, when they are in season; in Trinidad they are used to make Trinidadian Pelau, a delicious one-pot dish of rice, pigeon peas, and chicken.

**June plum (pomsiterre, pomme cythere, golden apple)** is a tropical tree with edible fruit containing a fibrous pit. It is known by many names in various regions, including pomme cythere in Trinidad and Tobago, Dominica, Guadeloupe, and Martinique; and June plum in Bermuda and Jamaica. This versatile fruit can be enjoyed whole or juiced when ripe. In its unripened state, it is good for making jellies, jams, pickles, and sauces. Delicious, too, when stewed with sugar and spices. Carambola (starfruit) is a good substitute.

**Melongene (eggplant, baingan)** grows readily in the islands of the Caribbean and is present in many local dishes, particularly in

Guyana and Trinidad and Tobago, where it stars in East Indian–inspired recipes.

**Okra,** a tall annual herb cultivated for its green pods, is avidly consumed throughout the West Indies. Its origins are claimed to be either West Africa or South Asia. Indisputable is its health benefits: it is high in fiber, vitamin C, and antioxidants. The long green pods are very slimy when cooked, but are still enjoyed in soups, in stews, or with steamed fish.

**Ortanique (tangor),** discovered in the Jamaican parish of Manchester in the early 1920s, is a cross between a Valencia orange and a tangerine. According to folklore, it developed with the help of a pair of lovebirds—one living in an orange tree, the other in a tangerine tree. Jamaican ortaniques are widely considered to be the best variety. Extremely sweet, but well balanced with acidity, they have a strong, rich aroma.

**Otaheite apple (otaheiti apple),** originally from the Pacific Islands, has a pear shape, a ruby-red color, and a refreshingly delicate, sweet floral flavor. It is usually eaten straight off the tree, but is also delicious juiced or poached in red wine. The fruit consists mostly of water, adding to its refreshing quality. If you can't find otaheite apples, substitute apples or pears.

**Papaya,** or pawpaw as Jamaicans call it, is native to the tropics of South America. It was first cultivated in Mexico several centuries before the emergence of the classical Mesoamerican civilizations. When ripe, it has an orange color and houses many small seeds. It is mildly sweet and usually enjoyed with a squeeze of lime. Green (unripened) papaya is better in chutneys and relishes.

**Passionfruit (granadilla),** pleasantly sweet and tart, is said to come from South America. Both types, purple and yellow, are widely cultivated in the Caribbean and other tropical locales. Inside the fruit are sacs containing light-orange, pulpy juice and many small seeds. The pulp and seeds can be eaten by themselves or as an ingredient in salads, sauces, or juices.

**Plantain** is technically part of the banana family but is generally treated as a starchy vegetable. Inedible raw, plantains in their cooked state are served as appetizers or side dishes. Sometimes referred to as cooking bananas, plantains can be used when green (unripe), "turned" (not quite ripe), or fully ripe. They become sweeter and less starchy as they ripen and turn yellow. Ripe plantains—fried, boiled, or roasted—are the most popular in the region.

**Scotch bonnet pepper,** fiery and ranging in color from yellow to orange to red, is considered the leading hot chili in Jamaica. A cousin to the habanero, the Scotch bonnet has a heat rating of 100,000 to 350,000 Scoville units. (For comparison, jalapeños have a rating

## How to Peel and Press Green Plantain for Tostones

*1 medium plantain (10 to 12 inches) yields about six 2-inch plantain rounds*

**Step 1:** Cut off both ends of the plantain, and score the skin lengthwise along the ridges with the tip of a paring knife. Peel away the skin.

**Step 2:** Cut the plantain into 2-inch pieces. Sprinkle with salt.

**Step 3:** Pour vegetable oil into a deep frying pan 1 inch deep; heat the oil over medium-high heat. Once the oil is very hot, fry the plantain pieces for 3 to 5 minutes, working in batches, until the fruit is soft.

**Step 4:** Remove the plantains from the oil, and drain on paper towels. Place the plantains between the folds of a dishcloth, and press hard with the heel of your hand to flatten the fruit. Press until the plantain is half its original thickness.

**Step 5:** In the still-hot oil, fry the plantains again, turning occasionally, until they are golden-brown and slightly crispy on both sides.

# How to Work with Scotch Bonnet and Other Hot Peppers

Avoid touching your eyes and face when handling Scotch bonnet peppers. You may wish to wear gloves.

If you primarily want the aroma, simply place the whole pepper into the dish while it is cooking. This approach is mostly suitable for soups and stews. Be careful to avoid bursting the pepper, and remove it before serving.

For mild spice, remove the seeds and pith, and use two to three slices of the flesh. Cut from the end opposite the stem.

To increase the spice, add more flesh, and throw in a few seeds as well.

---

of 2,500 to 8,000 units.) It is used worldwide in many different dishes, especially hot sauces and condiments. The seeds, which can be saved for cultivation, carry the sharp heat.

**Sorrel (hibiscus, roselle),** sometimes called flor de Jamaica or Florida cranberry, is an annual that originated in West Africa. It produces deep red flowers that are used in chutneys and are steeped to make tea and other beverages. Popular around the Christmas season, sorrel blends well with ginger, cloves, sugar, and other seasonings for a festive beverage. Outside the Caribbean, sorrel/hibiscus is most readily available dried or in a syrup; fresh buds may be found in specialty markets, especially around Christmastime. You can also shop online for fresh sorrel buds while they're in season (late fall to early winter). Check the website of the Florida Cranberry Alliance (www.floridacranberry.org). In most recipes that call for fresh sorrel buds, it's better to substitute fresh cranberries rather than dried sorrel.

**Sweet potato,** a large, starchy, tuberous root vegetable, is hard when reaped but softens when cooked. Sometimes referred to as "yam" in parts of North America, the sweet potato is botanically very distinct from a genuine yam, which is native to Central Africa and Asia. Its skin color ranges between yellow, orange, brown, and purple, and the flesh from light yellow to orange. Enjoy it boiled, roasted, fried (as chips or fries), or even as a pudding, studded with raisins and spices.

**Tamarind** produces a fruit that is used in many cuisines around the world. It is fleshy with a sweet and sour taste when eaten straight from the red-brown pod, and is used in many savory dishes, as a pickling agent, and to make sauces. Tamarind balls, coated in granulated sugar and a blend of spices, are a popular snack in the Caribbean.

**Tangerine,** an orange-colored citrus fruit, is closely related to the mandarin orange. It is smaller than the common orange and is usually easier to peel and to split into segments. The taste is considered less sour, but sweeter and stronger, than that of an orange. A "good" tangerine is firm or slightly soft, heavy, and has pebbly skin with no deep grooves or bruises. The fresh fruit can also feature in salads and desserts.

**Yam (yampi)** is one of the most popular starchy tubers in Africa, Asia, Latin America, and the Caribbean. Across the globe there are over 150 varieties of yam. Although the sweet potato is sometimes called a yam in parts of the United States and Canada, the two are from different families. The true yam—which comes in white, yellow, and purple varieties—is a versatile vegetable that is enjoyed barbequed, roasted, fried, boiled, and mashed. A staple crop of the Igbo people of Nigeria, yams are agriculturally and culturally important as a commodity in West Africa, where over 95 percent of the world's yams are said to be harvested.

# How to Peel and Prepare Yellow Yam or Other Ground Provisions for Boiling

*3 pounds of yam or ground provisions yields approximately 8 servings*

**Step 1:** Have nearby a bowl of fresh water with 1 tablespoon salt stirred in for submerging the freshly peeled yam. Yellow yam immediately turns black when peeled.

**Step 2:** Before peeling, rinse the yam well under running water to remove any dirt particles.

**Step 3:** Using a sharp knife, peel the yam under running water. It is quite slimy and oxidizes quickly. Alternately, rub 1 teaspoon of vegetable oil on your hands before peeling to prevent skin irritation. Immediately place the peeled yam in the bowl of salted water.

**Step 4:** Yam may be boiled and eaten whole (once peeled), or cut and prepared according to recipe instructions.

**Step 5:** To boil, bring salted water to a boil in a deep pot, and add the yam. Cook for about 30 minutes or until tender. Serve warm.

# ACKNOWLEDGEMENTS

To thank the women who have contributed their time, energy, talent, and memories to this wonderful collection of recipes and heritage is a precious task. To begin we are obliged to acknowledge the spirits and voices of our female ancestors, who kept gently nudging us from beyond the veil to tell their stories. Thus began our inquiry and research into the lives of our great-grandmothers and grandmothers and the many women from all walks of life who lived in Jamaica and in other islands across the West Indies. With gratitude, we thank the following women who shared family recipes and personal recollections of cooking and entertaining from a bygone era: Gwen Donaldson, Janie Trench, Shirley Williams, Marjorie Henriques, Martiza Warwar, Tammy Hart in Jamaica; Jamila Liddie in St. Kitts; Danielle Duenas-Ernandes in Curacao. Nadine Burie for recipe ideas from her homeland, the Ivory Coast, along with her impeccable baking skills that were so helpful in testing the pastry and dessert sections of this book. Denese Grey, Hyacinth Haynes, and Anita Watson for their joyful assistance in the kitchen and at home during the long, crazy days of the photo shoot. Our aunt, Hester Rousseau, for allowing us to wander through her beautiful home on a daily basis in search of props, and for allowing us to use plates, platters, silverware, china, and crystal from her exquisite collection. Wayne Nasralla for allowing us access to his vast collection of antiques for the photo shoot. Professor Barry Higman for his editorial insight, advice, and knowledge of the culinary history of the region. Dr. Verle Poupeye and O'Neil Lawrence at the National Gallery of Jamaica, and Mrs. Valerie Facey for help with accessing the historically relevant artwork featured herein. Sincere gratitude to our friend Odette Dixon Neath, who was instrumental in the processes of writing, testing, and editing this work; her sense of our mission, her understanding of our emerging West Indian identity, and her keen editorial eye have been invaluable. We were blessed to have a magnificent and gifted team of women who worked with us to bring our manuscript to life: foremost, our treasured agent, Joy Tutela, who always gets it right and has been our cheerleader from day one; Claire Schulz of DaCapo Lifelong Books, big thanks for your vision and guidance, and for allowing us to create the book we imagined and wanted to create; Ellen Silverman, thank you for another exciting and rewarding adventure, and for capturing the simple beauty of our local cuisine; Frances Boswell, your zany inspired work was flawless and so joyful, we are lucky to have found our way to you. We are eternally grateful to and for our parents, Peter and Beverly Rousseau, who have championed all our causes and supported all our efforts over many years and through many manifestations. It is because of them that we understand what it means to celebrate our life and our heritage in a truly West Indian way.

# BIBLIOGRAPHY

Anonymous. "A Speech Made by a Black of Guadeloupe, 1709." In *Caribbeana: An Anthology of English Literature of the West Indies, 1657–1777.* Chicago: University of Chicago Press, 1999.

Beckford, W. E. *A Descriptive Account of the Island of Jamaica*, vol. 1. London: T & J Eggerton, 1790.

Carmichael, A. C. *Domestic Manners and Social Condition of the White, Coloured, and Negro Population of the West Indies.* 2nd ed., vol. 1. London: Whittaker and Co., 1834.

———. *Domestic Manners and Social Condition of the White, Coloured, and Negro Population of the West Indies.* Vol. 2. London: Whittaker, Treacher, and Co., 1833.

Carney, J. A., and R. N. Rosomoff. *In the Shadow of Slavery: Africa's Botanical Legacy in the Atlantic World.* Berkeley: University of California Press, 2011.

Cassidy, F. G., and R. B. Le Page. *Dictionary of Jamaican English.* Mona, Jamaica: University of the West Indies Press, 2002.

Consolidated Slave Act, 1792 (Jamaica W. I.). Section II.

Cooper, T. *Facts Illustrative Condition of the State of the Negro Slaves in Jamaica.* London: J. Hatchard and Son, 1824.

Covey, H., and D. Eisnach. *What the Slaves Ate: Recollections of African American Foods and Foodways from the Slave Narratives.* Santa Barbara, CA: Greenwood Press, 2009.

*Daily Gleaner.* "Make Food a Gift For Mother's Day," May 4, 1966.

———. *Our Women's Page.* "For a Sweet Tooth," February 23, 1935.

———. *Our Women's Page.* "Bake Me a Cake as Fast as You Can," March 23, 1935.

———. *Our Women's Page.* "Lady, Look at Your Husband!," March 23, 1935.

Equiano, O. B. *The Interesting Narrative of the Life of Olaudah Equiano, or Gustavus Vassa, the African: Written by Himself.* Vol. I and II. Chapel Hill: University of North Carolina Press, 2001. First published 1745 and 1789 in London.

Fay, P. J. "Coalpot and Canawi: Traditional Creole Pottery in the Contemporary Commonwealth Caribbean." *Interpreting Ceramics* 10 (2008). Available at www.interpretingceramics.com/issue010/articles/05.htm (accessed March, 2018).

Goucher, C. *Congotay! Congotay! A Global History of Caribbean Food.* Hoboken, NJ: Taylor and Francis, 2014.

Hannah, F. S. L., and P. Toussaint. *Memoir of Pierre Toussaint, Born a Slave in St. Domingo.*

Boston: Crosby, Nichols, and Company, 1854.

Higman, B. W. *Jamaican Food: History, Biology, Culture.* Kingston: University of the West Indies Press, 2008.

———. *Slave Populations of the British Caribbean, 1807–1834.* Kingston: University of the West Indies Press, 1995.

Houston, L. M. *Food Culture in the Caribbean.* Westport, CT: Greenwood Press, 2005.

Hyatt, C. *When Me Was a Boy.* E-Book. Kingston: University of the West Indies Press, 2007.

Kingsley, C. *At Last a Christmas in the West Indies.* Leipzig: Bernhard Tauchnitz, 1871.

Kiple, K. *The Caribbean Slave: A Biological History.* Cambridge, UK: Cambridge University Press, 1984.

Lewis, M. G. *Journal of a West India Proprietor: Kept During a Residence in the Island of Jamaica.* London: John Murray, 1834.

Nugent, M. *Lady Nugent's Journal: Jamaica One Hundred Years Ago.* C. Frank, ed. New York: Cambridge University Press, 2010. First published 1907 by Institute of Jamaica.

Prince, M. *History of Mary Prince, A West Indian Slave Narrative, Related by Herself.* E-Book. T. Pringle, ed. London: F. Westley and A. H. Davis, 1831.

Smith, A. *Food and Drink in American History: A "Full Course" Encyclopedia.* Santa Barbara, CA: ABC-CLIO, 2013.

Sullivan, C. S. *Classic Jamaican Cooking: A Collection of 19th Century Cookery and Herbal Recipes.* Kingston: Mill Press, 1990. First published as *The Jamaica Cookery Book: Three Hundred and Sixty-Four Simple Cookery Receipts and Household Hints* in 1893 by Aston W. Gardner and Co.

Thornton, J. K. *A Cultural History of the Atlantic World, 1250–1820.* New York: Cambridge University Press, 2012.

Verdin, G. "Coffee Houses in the Eighteenth Century." In *Proceedings of the Oxford Symposium on Food and Cookery.* Oxford, UK: Prospect Books, 2001

Warner, A. *Negro Slavery Described by a Negro: Being the Narrative of Ashton Warner a Native of St. Vincent.* London: Samuel Maunder, 1831.

Williams, J. *A Narrative of Events Since the First August 1834 by James Williams, an Apprenticed Labourer in Jamaica.* London: W. Ball, 1837.

Williamson, M. Mary Williamson to Haughton James, October 26, 1809. "'I Was a Few Years Back a Slave on Your Property': A Letter from Mary Williamson to Her Former Owner," edited by Diana Paton. Available at www.historyworkshop.org.uk/i-was-a-few-years-back-a-slave-on-your-property-a-letter-from-mary-williamson-to-her-former-owner (accessed March 2018).

# PHOTO CREDITS

# INDEX

Note: Page references in *italics* indicate photographs.

# S

Whipped cream. *See* Chantilly
White Sauce, 110
Williamson, Mary, 259–260
Wine
    Christmas Sorrel, 218
    Sorrel Mimosas (Holiday
        Hibiscus), *216,* 217
Women, Caribbean
    as food entrepreneurs,
        261–263
    life after emancipation,
        259–263
    role in plantation life, 253–255
    self-sufficient culture among,
        259–260
    sharing of stories among, 263
    story of, 1–6
    during World War II, 263

# Y

Yams
    about, 279
    peeling and preparing, 279
    Roast Provisions with Haitian
        Pikliz, 14
Yogurt
    Berry-Coconut Overnight
        Oats, *184,* 185–186
    Cucumber, Tomato, and Onion
        Raita, 38
    Frozen, Ginger-Lime, *174,* 175
    Frozen, Guava, Mango, or
        Passionfruit, *174,* 175
    Spiced Cilantro, *46,* 47–48

# Z

Zaboca Toast with Coconut and
    Pumpkin Seeds, 49
Zucchini
    Pinda (Peanut) Stew,
        137–139, *138*
    Sweet Pot Herbs, Plantain,
        and Roasted Channa,
        Couscous with, *142,*
        143–144

# ABOUT THE AUTHORS

JAMAICAN-BORN SISTERS MICHELLE AND SUZANNE Rousseau established their culinary reputation with the debut in 1996 of Ciao Bella, a groundbreaking Kingston restaurant that created a paradigm shift with its artful use of Jamaican ingredients and classic cooking techniques. The restaurant was a manifestation of many years of travelling and living in the Caribbean and Europe, and a curiosity for playing with a medley of cultures and influences.

They share an avid love of history, the arts, languages, and culture. Suzanne holds a BA in English Literature with a minor in Art History and has taught English Language and Literature at the local high school level. Michelle holds a BA in Spanish Language and Literature and a MA in Latin American Studies, and has worked with the Jamaican Foreign Service. Their combined backgrounds, extensive knowledge and avid curiosity informs their unique perspective on West Indian cuisine.

The success of Ciao Bella led to the women being called on to create premium culinary events, including several state dinners and an official dinner for His Royal Highness, the Prince of Wales. Their expertise has since evolved into creating food and beverage concepts for global clients.

At home, Michelle and Suzanne used their culinary knowledge and effervescent personalities to inspire appreciation for Jamaican traditions with their hugely popular food and travel show, "Two Sisters and a Meal." They also produced and starred in the web series, Island Potluck, a joint production with the Jamaica Tourist Board.

Their first cookbook, *Caribbean Potluck* received critical acclaim and was named among NPR's Best Books of 2014.

They have now come full circle as restauranteurs, with the recent opening of Summerhouse at The Liguanea Club in Kingston Jamaica, a Caribbean gastro-pub with the mission to celebrate the soul, heritage and lifestyle of the islands.

They can be found at:

www.summerhouseja.com   www.2sistersandameal.com
@summerhouseja             @2sistersandameal